MW01632431

THE PERSISTENCE OF ORDER

VOL. I

THE PERSISTENCE OF ORDER

VOL. I

Essays on Religion and Culture

Edited *by* Christopher Dawson and T. F. Burns

CONTENTS

CLUNY MEDIA

Cluny Media edition, 2019

This Cluny edition is a republication of *Essays in Order*, Volumes I, II, III, and X.
Volumes I–III published by The Macmillan Company, 1931.
Volume X published by Sheed & Ward, 1933.

Religion and Culture translated by J. F. Scanlon
Crisis in the West translated by E. I. Watkin
The Nature of Sanctity translated by Ruth Bonsall and E. I. Watkin

For more information regarding this title
or any other Cluny Media publication,
please write to info@clunymedia.com, or to
Cluny Media, P.O. Box 1664, Providence, RI 02901

VISIT US ONLINE AT WWW.CLUNYMEDIA.COM

ISBN: 978-1950970278

Cover design by Clarke & Clarke
Cover image: August Macke, *St. Mary's with Houses and Chimney (Bonn)*, 1911, oil on canvas
Courtesy of Wikimedia Commons

CONTENTS

General Introduction

Western civilization today is passing through one of the most critical moments in its history. In every department of life traditional principles have been shaken and discredited, and we do not yet know what is going to take their place. There are those who hold that Europe has had her day and that our culture has entered the first stage of an inevitable process of decay, while others believe that we are only beginning to realize the possibilities of modern science and that we are about to see the rise of a new social order which will far transcend anything that the world has known. One thing is certain—the old order is dead; and with the old order there has passed away that traditional acceptance of the truth of Christianity and that general recognition of Christian moral principles, which even in the nineteenth century still retained so strong a hold on the minds of men.

It is the aim of the present series to attempt to face the problems which arise from this new situation and to examine the possibilities of cooperation and of conflict that exist between the Catholic order and the new world. It will not confine itself to any single aspect of the question, but will deal with general principles and with the concrete problems of contemporary life. Indeed, it is impossible to limit the inquiry to any one field, since the present disorder and confusion of ideas shows itself in every department of thought—in literature and philosophy, no less than in sociology and ethics. Hence, it is clear that this series must be tentative and unsystematic in character. It cannot attempt to propound a definite solution or to embody a formal program. For Catholicism has no *policy* nor can the Catholic compete with the Marxian Socialist in offering the modern world a panacea for its material ills. Yet it would be equally impossible to dismiss the problems of the modern world as though they had no meaning for those whose lives were based on the supernatural certitude of the Christian faith. The Puritan or the sectarian Christian can isolate himself from the age in which he lives and construct a private world in harmony with his religious convictions. But for the Catholic this should be impossible. Catholicism stands essentially for a universal order in which every good and every truth of the natural or the social order can find a place.

The disorder of the modern world is due either to the denial of the existence of spiritual reality or to the attempt to treat the spiritual order and the business of everyday life as two independent worlds which have no mutual relations. But while Catholicism recognizes the distinction and the autonomy of the natural and the supernatural orders, it can never acquiesce in their segregation. The spiritual and the eternal insert themselves into the world of sensible and temporal things, and there is not the smallest event in human life and social history but possesses an eternal and spiritual significance.

It is the Catholic ideal to order the whole of life towards unity, not by the denial and destruction of the natural human values, but by bringing them into living relation with spiritual truth and spiritual reality. But this can only be achieved if Catholics are prepared to make the necessary effort of moral sympathy and intellectual comprehension. If they remain passively content with their own possession of the truth, they do not, it is true, compromise the divine and indefectible life of the Church, but they prove false to their own temporal mission, since they leave the world and the society of which they form a part to perish.

As Maritain writes in the following essay: "It is certain that some good and some truth are immanent in the new temporal forms which are emerging from the obscure chrysalis of history, and that they manifest in some way the will of God, which is absent from nothing that exists. They may in the same way serve eternal interests on this earth." It is our business to understand all this, and in order to do so it is necessary to be equally on our guard against the weak acquiescence in current fashions of thought which would cause us to lose our grasp of the eternal principles and from that "narrowness of heart which prevents us from knowing the work of man" and doing justice to the work of God in time and history.

Difficult as this task may be, there is, we believe, a greater opportunity for carrying it out than at any time during the last hundred years. The old barriers are falling, and though the destructive and negative tendencies in modern culture have destroyed much that was valuable in the traditions of the past, they have also swept away many of the inherited prejudices and fixed forms of thought which isolated the Catholic tradition from vital contact with the realities of modern life.

The present generation is intensely sensitive to the existence of a religious problem. It is true that the ordinary Englishman no longer goes to church and that his theological beliefs are so vague as to be practically non-existent. He does not take religion for granted, as he did in the last century, when church-going was a mark of social respectability and religion occupied a distinct and strictly limited place in the national life. But this is very largely due to a recognition of the unreality and narrowness of the old sectarian ideals. There is a justifiable reaction against a type of religion which imposed rigid restrictions on any kind of rational enjoyment, while it left men free to exploit one another and to make life hideous in the race for wealth. Today men demand of religion that it should be in touch with realities, that it should offer some solution to the social and intellectual problems of the modern world and that it should be at the service of human needs, though at the same time they often fail to realize the absolute and transcendent element which is inseparable from any true religious ideal. Consequently, if the interest in religion is weaker today than in the last century, it is wider and more diffused. It has come out of the pulpit and the meeting-house into the columns of the daily press and the programs of the BBC. Both in England and America there is a constant stream of literature dealing with religion and the modern age and with the problems of Christianity in the light of modern knowledge.

Unfortunately, the greater part of this literature is of little positive value. It witnesses to a real need, but it provides no adequate solution. It is vitiated by a complete absence of philosophical principles and by a vague optimism which slurs over the real difficulties of the situation and offers good will as a substitute for clear thinking. In order to come to terms with the modern world it has jettisoned the theological traditions of Protestant orthodoxy, and it is left with nothing but moral ideals and social aspirations unsupported by any solid intellectual foundation. The writers of such literature can have neither sympathy nor understanding for Catholic thought. To them Catholicism seems entirely out of touch with the needs of the modern world. They regard it as a refuge for those shrinking souls who are unable to face reality, and its philosophy as a relic of medieval obscurantism. But in reality it is they themselves who are living in the past and who do not realize that a new age has begun. Just as the schoolmen of the seventeenth century went on discussing the problem of the fifth essence and the theories of Aristotelian cosmology when Galileo and Newton were creating their new physical synthesis, so today the representatives of modern religious thought continue to murmur their platitudes about the liberation of religion from dogma and the ethical genius of Christianity, when the world is turning away from subjectivism and idealism and once more seeks absolute standards and spiritual realities. In the eighteenth and nineteenth centuries, it is true, the whole trend of Western civilization was hostile to Catholicism. The absolutism and realism of Catholic philosophy was incomprehensible to an age which followed Rousseau and Kant, or Bentham and Herbert Spencer. When Pius IX denied that it was the duty of the Church to come to terms with Liberalism and Progress and Modern Civilization, his pronouncement was greeted with a chorus of execration from every country in Europe. It seemed as though the Papacy was pronouncing its own sentence of death, for the triumph of material progress seemed inevitable and no one could conceive the possibility of its failure.[1]

Today all this is changed—Liberalism and Progress and Modern Civilization appear in a very different light from that of seventy years ago. We no longer believe that progress is a necessary and automatic process, and that if men are left free to follow their own devices they will inevitably grow wiser and happier and more prosperous. We admit the reality of modern progress as a vast material achievement, but it means something very different from what our predecessors believed. Human life, like animal life, depends on a balance of forces, and if the balance is upset by the removal of restrictive factors, the process of readjustment is full of danger and difficulty.

Thus the rapid growth of wealth and population which followed the Industrial Revolution does not continue indefinitely; it creates its own limits by calling into existence new restrictive forces. Machinery makes possible a vast expansion of industry, but it also leads to over-production and unemployment. Science increases man's control over disease, but it also adds to the destructiveness of war. Colonial and economic expansion gives Europe the hegemony of the world, but it also awakens the hostility and rivalry of the oriental peoples. Capitalism creates new sources of wealth, but it also involves exploitation and social unrest.

It is now generally realized that we cannot progress indefinitely by drifting with the current, for the same current which has brought us to prosperity and power may equally drag us to destruction. Order and guidance are necessary if disaster is to be avoided, for civilization is not the result of a natural process of evolution, it is essentially due to the mastering of Nature by the human mind. It is an artificial order, governed and created by man's intelligence and will. There is no question today of the necessity of order; the only question at issue is whether the order we create shall be exclusively a material one, or whether it must be also spiritual.

This is the vital issue of the modern world. On the one hand we have the Communist solution which is the only thorough-going and consistent attempt to create an order on exclusively material foundations. But there is also the American solution which is less uncompromising, and also less inhuman. It is based on a combination of the political tradition of Liberalism and democracy with the material order of a standardized mass civilization. As a working system it is infinitely more successful than the Russian experiment, but there is a latent contradiction between its political ideals and its economic practice, which produces intellectual dissatisfaction and moral unrest. There is no organic connection between the mechanism and materialism of the new mass civilization and the old ideals of political liberty and social democracy which have their origin in the simpler conditions of an earlier period. Consequently, the American solution is not an absolute one. It is bound up with local and temporary conditions, and its evolution is still incomplete.

On the other side we have the historical tradition of European culture. That tradition has never been a purely material one, for in the past it was bound up with the Christian religion, and during the last century it has been largely identified with the ideals of liberal humanitarian-ism and liberal nationalism. The French Revolution and English Liberalism, the Italian Risorgimento and German Nationalism, Parliamentarianism and Socialism—all these movements have contributed to the making of modern Europe and all of them possess a spiritual element. Yet they are not of themselves capable of producing a spiritual order. They are essentially *impure* phenomena, mingling idealism with selfishness and spiritual aspirations with materialistic aims. During the last half century, however, they have all been undergoing a kind of negative purification. The nationalism of Mazzini and Young Italy has become transformed into the nationalism of Mussolini and the Fascists. English Liberalism has passed from the hands of Lord John Russell and Gladstone to those of Lloyd George. Socialism has descended from the visions of Utopia to the realities of Westminster. The making of a world safe for democracy has involved four years of intensive slaughter and a peace that is in danger of ending peace.

In every case it has been the ideal element that has suffered, and today all the ideals that inspired the nineteenth century are shattered and discredited. Liberalism is everywhere in decline, and Parliamentarianism and democracy have suffered a general loss of prestige. Nationalism alone is still powerful, but in a grim and menacing shape which bodes little good to the cause of civilization.

This decline in the forces of idealism does not, however, necessarily prove that Europe is ready to accept a purely material order. On the contrary, our confidence in material order is diminishing in proportion to our loss of faith in nineteenth-century ideals. We feel the need for spiritual order far more acutely than did the prosperous and self-confident nineteenth century, but we no longer believe that it will be the inevitable result of the political and economic evolution of the modern world. For behind all these various disappointments and disillusionments there is something still more profound—we have lost our faith in humanity, and that faith was the central dogma and inspiration of the whole modern development. This is somewhat surprising when we consider that the modern world is supposed to have begun with a revolt against the anthropocentric *Weltanschauung* of the Christian world, but as T. E. Hulme trenchantly says: "The change which Copernicus is supposed to have brought about is the exact contrary of the fact. Before Copernicus man was not the center of the universe; after Copernicus he was. You get a change from a certain profundity and intensity to that flat and insipid optimism which, passing through its first stage of decay in Rousseau, has finally culminated in that state of slush in which we have the misfortune to live."[2]

But during the present century there has been a general reaction against this idealization of man. The psychologists have sounded the depths of the human soul and have found nothing there but a little mud. The men of letters have blasted the romantic view of life with ridicule and scorn. The artists have substituted abstract for naturalistic ideals. The physicists have abandoned the naive empiricism of the old scientific materialism for the mathematical abstractions of Relativity. Even the philosophers have begun to desert the tradition of subjectivity and idealism and are returning to realism and ontology.

This philosophical reaction is particularly marked in Germany, so long the stronghold of the opposite tradition. Even the neo-Kantians are retracing their steps and reinterpreting their master in the light of the older traditions of European thought. The philosophy of Aristotle and St. Thomas is no longer relegated to the limbo of dead systems, and there is a distinct tendency in German thought towards metaphysical and epistemological realism.

It is obvious that these changes have a profound effect in the attitude of the European mind towards religion. The exaltation of man and the idealization of Nature led to the depreciation and the denial of spiritual reality. Protestantism succeeded in accommodating itself to the modern environment by the abandonment of metaphysics and dogma and a concentration on ethical ideals. But Catholicism could not live in an atmosphere of subjective idealism and moral pragmatism. It was forced to go into the desert. Today we are witnessing what Wust has called "the return of Catholicism from exile." Once more Catholic thought can find a place in European culture and can give its message to the modern world. For Catholicism is not compromised by the bankruptcy of nineteenth-century idealism. It has never denied—as sectarian Christianity tends to deny—the existence and the good of the natural order, but it recognizes the limitations of human nature and maintains that spiritual order is only attainable in the light of absolute spiritual principles.

Hence the remarkable revival of Catholic intellectual life that has taken place during the last twenty-five years. Half a century ago it was taken as a matter of course in France and Germany that the intellectual should be an unbeliever, and that the practicing Catholic should be an exile from the living thought of the age. Today this is no longer the case, and it is among the intellectuals and the men of letters that the influence of Catholicism is most marked. This is most strikingly exemplified in respect to philosophy, where the Thomist revival inaugurated by Pope Leo XIII has been justified by results. In France we have Père Sertillanges and Jacques Maritain, both of them brilliant interpreters of St. Thomas to the modern world; Etienne Gilson, the historian of medieval thought; and the late Père Rousselot, S.J., the author of that remarkable book, *L'Intellectualisme de St. Thomas.* In Belgium there is the School of Louvain, which has been for forty years a pioneer of the Catholic revival of philosophical studies, and which has recently produced a work of the first importance in Père Maréchal's *Point de Départ de la Métaphysique*. In Germany the revival of Catholic thought first showed itself in the historical work of scholars like Denifle, Ehrle, Baümker, von Herlting, and Grabmann, who have done so much to restore our knowledge of medieval thought in all its branches; but the influence of Newman, as well as that of modern German thinkers like Max Scheler also contributed to the renewed activity of Catholic thought. It is true that Scheler's personal adhesion to Catholicism was incomplete and temporary, but his criticism of Kantian ethics and his return to objective spiritual values in his treatment of ethical and sociological problems made the intellectual world conscious of the spiritual riches of the Catholic tradition and aroused Catholics themselves to a new consciousness of their intellectual mission. Consequently, the last few years have seen a remarkable development of religious thought; and today it is in Germany that Catholic philosophy is most in contact with the tendencies of modern thought and most alive to the needs of the present age, as we shall see in the work of such writers as Przywara, Wust, Carl Schmitt, Theodor Haecker, and von Hildebrand.

At the same time there has been an equally striking revival of Catholic activity in the field of pure literature. This is most obvious in France, where so large a number of the younger writers have devoted themselves to the service of Catholic ideals. The movement had begun before the war with Péguy and Claudel and Psichari, and it owed much to the influence of Maurice Barrès, although he was not himself a Christian. Today it is represented by poets and dramatists like Claudel and Henri Gheon, critics such as Henri Bremond, Charles du Bos, Gabriel Marcel and Henri Massis, and novelists such as François Mauriac and Julian Green—these, with many others, contributing to such series as the *Roseau d'or*, the *Cahiers de la Nouvelle Journée*, the *Questions Disputées* and *Virgile*.

In Germany this movement is more recent and is far less known in this country. This is regrettable, since the German situation has many points of similarity to our own. The central tradition in German literature is derived from a Protestant culture, and Catholic writers in the past have suffered from the restricted atmosphere of an opposition minority culture. Today, however, these disadvantages are being overcome by a new spirit of confidence and intellectual energy, and one has only to look at modern Catholic reviews, such as *Hochland* or *Der Gral* to realize the vitality and activity of the new movement.

In England, Catholics suffer in an even greater degree from the same unfavorable conditions that exist in Germany, yet here also there is a noticeable revival of literary activity among English Catholics; indeed, their achievement is greater than we should expect from the social and numerical weakness of the Catholic element.

Nevertheless, the Catholic intellectual revival, as a whole, is predominantly a Continental movement, and its significance is not yet realized in this country. The existence of Catholic philosophy is hardly recognized except in academic circles, and it is still possible for writers like Dr. Coulton and Bishop Barnes, whose own mental outlook is entirely that of the past, to treat Catholicism as an exploded superstition which is completely out of touch with the mind of the present age.

It is one of the chief aims of the present series to make the contemporary movement of Catholic thought on the Continent better known in this country. In an age when England is ceasing to be an island, and when the external forms of civilization are becoming everywhere more uniform and more cosmopolitan, it is necessary for all of us to do what is in our power to restore the intellectual community of European culture—and for Catholics before all, since they stand almost alone today as the representatives of a universal spiritual order in the midst of the material and external uniformity of a cosmopolitan machine-made civilization.

We must not, of course, exaggerate the importance of the intellectual element in the Catholic revival. It would be a great mistake on the part of Catholics to claim for themselves a monopoly of intelligence. Catholicism makes its appeal, not to those who demand the latest intellectual novelty nor to those who always want to be on the winning side, but to those who seek spiritual reality. Our advantage lies not in the excellence of our brains, but in the strength of our principles. Like the proverbial conies, we may be a feeble folk but we make our dwelling in the rocks. Our thought is not "free" in the sense that it is at liberty to create its own principles and to make gods in its own image. But it is just this "freedom" which is the cause of the discredit and anarchy into which modern thought has fallen.

The attempt of the nineteenth century to prescribe spiritual ideals in literature and ethics, while refusing to admit the objective existence of a spiritual order, has ended in failure, and today we have to choose between the complete expulsion of the spiritual element from human life or its recognition as the very foundation of reality. In so far as the modern world accepts the latter alternative, it can no longer disregard the existence of the Catholic solution, for Catholicism is the great historic representative of the principle of the spiritual order—an order which is not the creation of the human mind, but its ruler and creator.

The following essay of Maritain's deals with this problem in its most fundamental aspect—it is concerned with the essential relations between religion and culture. It carries the discussion of the inter-relation of the spiritual and the temporal, which was the subject of the same author's *The Things That Are Not Caesar's*, out of the political sphere to its ultimate spiritual and metaphysical basis. It is an old subject and one that has been buried under the accumulated *débris* of dead controversies and extinct heresies, but none the less it remains a living issue for the world today, not only to the Catholic, to whom this essay is primarily addressed, but to all those who believe in the social realization of Christian principles.

Jacques Maritain is one of the most representative figures in that Catholic intellectual revival which has already been referred to. The idea of spiritual order has been the guiding principle of all his literary activity and he has been one of the leaders in that reorientation of thought which he has himself defined as "a return to the real and the absolute, by the way of intelligence, for the primacy of the spirit." If his allegiance to the pure Thomist tradition seems at times to lead him to an excessive depreciation of modern philosophy and modern scientific method, it must be remembered that this is not due to any lack of familiarity with them. He was a pupil of Bergson and came to St. Thomas fresh from the study of the moderns. Indeed, it was his very familiarity with modern thought which led him to appreciate the objectivity and intellectual strength of the *philosophia perennis*.

The author of the second essay, Peter Wust, is a thinker of a very different type.[3] His philosophy is not the result of the acceptance of a classical tradition but the fruit of an intense personal struggle, the goal of a long spiritual odyssey. The motive of his speculation was not an intellectual curiosity, but a spiritual need. As Fichte says, in a sentence which Wust takes as the motto of his work, "We begin to philosophize out of wantonness and thereby we destroy our innocence: and then we realize our nakedness and thenceforth we philosophize from the need for deliverance."

Nevertheless, Wust, no less than Maritain, represents the same movement of return from subjectivity to realism and to the primacy of the spiritual which is characteristic of the new tendency of European thought. He has described the state of spiritual isolation and exile which was the portion of a Catholic in the intellectual world of Berlin twenty years ago, and the gradual change of thought in the years which followed the war that has liberated German Catholicism from the spiritual Ghetto in which it had been confined for so long. That state of things has passed away, let us hope for ever, and the way is open for a renaissance of Catholic action, both in intellectual and social life, but for that very reason a new responsibility rests on us all today.

Christopher Dawson
England, 1931

Notes for General Introduction

1. Cf. Maritain, *The Things That Are Not Cæsar's*, Appendix V, "Liberalism."
2. T. E. Hulme, *Speculations*, p. 80.
3. *Crisis in the West*.

RELIGION AND CULTURE

by JACQUES MARITAIN

I. *Nature and Culture*

Cultivating a field means inciting nature by some human labor to produce fruits which nature left to itself would have been incapable of producing, for what nature left to itself alone produces is "wild" vegetation. Such a figure gives us an idea of what that culture means in the vocabulary of philosophy, the culture not of an expanse of soil, but of humanity itself. Man being a spirit animating a body of flesh, his nature in itself is a progressive nature. The labor of reason and the virtues is natural in the sense that it is in conformity with the essential inclinations of human nature; it brings into play the essential springs of human nature. It is not natural in the sense that it is supplied ready-made by nature; it is an addition to what nature produces by itself and by itself alone. Nature, no doubt, can also be considered without this labor of reason, and as reduced therefore to energies of a sensitive order and mere instincts, or considered before this labor of reason, that is to say, in a state of, as it were, embryonic involution and absolute primitiveness.

Culture so appears to be natural to man in the same sense as the labor of reason and the virtues of which it is the fruit and earthly fulfillment: it answers the fundamental aspiration of human nature, but it is the word of the spirit and liberty adding their efforts to the effort of nature. Instead of the word culture, which relates to the rational development of the human being considered in all its generality, I might equally well have used the word *civilization*, which relates to that same development considered in an eminent case—I mean to say in the production of the state and civil life of which civilization is, as it were, the prolongation and enlargement. The state and civilization are, at one and the same time, works natural to man and works of reason and virtue.

Many German and Russian philosophers draw a distinction between civilization and culture and employ the former, conceived in a pejorative sense, to denote a development of social life which is above all material, mechanical and extrinsic (a decrepit and sclerosed culture). We are free to define the terms we use as we like. In the sense in which I understand it, a civilization is deserving of the name only if it is a culture, a truly human and therefore mainly intellectual, moral, and spiritual development (taking the word *spiritual* in its widest acceptation).

Three observations may be related to the foregoing remarks. My first observation is that culture or civilization, presupposing both nature and the labor of reason, ought to keep within the line of nature, but may deviate from that line, allow itself to be sponged upon by an *artificialism* contrary to nature and by perversions of varying degrees of gravity (even in animal "communities" we see communities of ants ruined by a passion for the intoxicating sugar they derive from certain domesticated insects, which devour the eggs of these drug-addicted ants[1]). If the *per accidens* is confused with the *per se*, it must be admitted with Rousseau, at the sight of such perverted and therefore execrable societies, that culture and civilization, left to themselves, corrupt man.

But as *perseities* are unavoidable and as civilization of its very nature derives from reason, it is impossible, and this is my second observation, impossible, I say, to execrate civilization without, at the same time, execrating the *form of reason*, the formation vitally achieved by reason in human things, for that would be to assert the pre-eminence of potentiality and the formless, on the pretense that they are more productive.

My third observation is that, if we do so, we tend to the destruction of man. Man, unlike the other animals, has not a solid rock bottom, as it were, of instinctive life constituting a definite structure of behavior sufficiently determined to make the exercise of life possible. Any erosion or excavation or elimination of rational life in an attempt to discover that solid rock bottom is a deadly error. There will be no end to the excavation, there is no solid and perfect structure, no natural regulation of the instinctive human life. The whole play of the instincts, be they as numerous and powerful as you like, is, in the case of man, open and exposed to view, involves a relative indetermination which finds its normal perfection and normal regulation in reason alone. If Freud absurdly calls the child a *polymorphous pervert*, it is because he fails to take account of this indetermination. A general philosophy of a very inferior kind prevents this very remarkable observer (who is also goaded by a violent metaphysical hatred of the form of reason) from distinguishing between potentiality and act; he substitutes for potentiality a sum of conflicting actualities, for indetermination orientated towards normal actuation (but susceptible of manifold abnormal actuations) a constellation of opposite actuations, in which what we describe as normal ceases to be normal and becomes merely a particular instance of the abnormal. Nevertheless, the kind of infinitude peculiar to the mind in the case of the human being gives a sort of infinity, a sort of indetermination, to the very life of the senses and instincts, which is incapable of finding its natural point of fixation—I mean in conformity, with the peculiar requirements and destinies of human nature—elsewhere than in reason and the formations which reason produces. Otherwise it will be fixed awry, as any chance dominating passion determines, and deviate from nature. The truly and fully natural man is not nature's man, the uncultivated soil, but the virtuous man, the human soil cultivated by undeviating reason, man formed by the inner culture of the intellectual and moral virtues. He alone has a consistency, a personality.

If nature by itself alone were formed in us, had a countenance, there would be reason to fear that every virtue might be like the false virtues, like the pharisaical virtues, and distort that countenance or cover it with a plaster.

But nature acquires a countenance in our case only when it is perfected by the mind, man acquires his truth only when he is fashioned from within by reason and virtue (I mean undeviating reason whose supremacy in our life is guaranteed only by the supernatural gifts; I mean true virtue which is entirely deserving of the name only if it is vivified by charity). Genuine *sincerity* presents a mirror which is clear as crystal to the larvae dwelling in us and contemplates them with courage, in order to give them a human countenance by a work of freedom; it does not refuse to bear a countenance. There is no more mendacious influence than sincerity as conceived by André Gide, the resolution of the human being in the vain postulates, discordant and simultaneous, of the formless, the *materia prima*.

I will not continue the parenthesis. Let our conclusion be that culture or civilization is the expansion of the peculiarly human life, including not only whatever material development may be necessary and sufficient to enable us to lead an upright life on this earth, but also and above all the moral development, the development of the speculative and practical activities (artistic and ethical) peculiarly worthy of being called a human development.

It is important in the next place to realize fully that culture or civilization by its very nature belongs to the *temporal* sphere, in other words has a specifying object—the terrestrial and perishable good of our life on this earth—the subject matter of which is of the natural order. It must doubtless be subordinated to eternal life, as an intermediate end is subordinated to the ultimate end. And such subordination to a superior end gives it an intrinsic super-elevation in its own peculiar order: a Christian civilization has higher standards, a more perfect earthly propriety than a pagan civilization; if we reflect that the friendship of charity itself constitutes the essential bond of peace in Christian civilization, that the infused moral virtues inform social life in Christian society, we see that the supreme moral regulations, by virtue of which it performs its work on earth, fall within the province of the supernatural order. Even a Christian civilization, however, a civilization superelevated in its peculiar order, because it is Christian, by virtues proceeding from above, becomes so superelevated through realizing (rather than through the unaided forces of nature) the very postulates of nature. It applies the rules of the Christian reason to a subject matter in the natural order, *versatur circa materiam naturalis ordinis*,[2] and the sphere in which it develops so considered may be said to be the sphere of the natural activities. In itself and by its specific object, it is involved in time and the vicissitudes of time, is perishable, essentially human. And it incorporates the benefits it derives from the supernatural order, from the virtues of the saints, for example, or the intercession of the contemplatives, in its own peculiar substance, draws them towards its own peculiar end, which still remains, even superelevated, a certain common good of man on this earth, in his terrestrial life.

Because this human development is not only material, but also and mainly moral, it goes without saying that the part played in it by the *religious* element is consequently a *principal* part. In truth the religion which the concept of culture or civilization, *in abstracto*, of itself requires is only natural religion. But human civilizations have in fact received a better, and more onerous, burden. We know "that a *state of pure nature*, one in which God *ex hypothesi* had abandoned man to the sole resources of the activities of his mind and will, has never existed. From the earliest times God willed to bring to the knowledge of men things far in excess of the requirements of any nature that ever was or ever could be created. He revealed to them the depths of His divine life, the secret of His eternity. And to guide their footsteps to such heights, to prepare them, on this earth already, for the vision of such splendors, He spread over the world, like a tablecloth, grace which was capable of divinizing our knowledge and our love. God makes such divine advances to all men at all times; for He is the light 'which enlighteneth every man' (John 1:9). He will have all men to be saved, and to come to the knowledge of the truth (1 Tim. 2:4). His advances are accepted or rejected."[3]

This is the reason why none of the religions recorded in history is the simple natural religion contemplated in the abstract by philosophers. There are, no doubt, many features to be found in such religions answering the natural religious aspirations of the human being, but all in fact derive from a more remote origin, all retain some vestige of the primordial revelations and ordinations, and have all, with the exception of the religion of Christ, declined from the supernatural order and more or less deviated consecutively from the natural order.

And these religions, let it be observed, by the very fact of becoming naturalized, of shrinking to the dimensions of fallen nature, became particularized to some definite culture hostile to other cultures, became differentiated like languages and social groups. The piety of pagan antiquity admirably perceived the vital need the state has of religion; its great misfortune was that it absorbed religion into civilization, into a particular local civilization, by confusing the state and religion, by deifying the state, or—it comes to the same thing—by nationalizing the gods who were turned into the first citizens in the state. In this *sociological* collapse of religion is doubtless to be found the deep-set cause or at all events the most significant characteristic of polytheism, which was nevertheless powerless to efface completely the fundamental "henotheist" feeling. The marvel of Israel, a supernatural marvel, forcibly imposed on stiff rebellious necks is that the God of Israel is also the one, transcendent, ineffable God, the God of Heaven and earth, of the whole earth. Exclusivism and universalism, observed Père Clérissac—"the Decalogue appeals not to a local conscience but to the conscience of all mankind; and the Jerusalem of Messianic times is the vision of a country which is chiefly spiritual, the country of souls. The Prophets speak and strive with the sole object of securing the predominance of the Kingdom of God which is in men's hearts in the first place and embraces all nations."[4] Everywhere else in the ancient world nationalism sponged upon and corrupted religion; it absorbed religion in culture, made it an element of a civilization, of a culture. I mean to say that the ancient world, while riveting social life to, and occasionally crushing it under, religion, while honoring religion with a terrifying power of veneration, while enslaving man to the gods, nevertheless enfeoffed religion to civilization—not in the least after the manner of the modern profane world, which makes religion the mere servant of civilization considered as something superior, but on the contrary by making religion the governing principle of the state, yet individuated by the state, living with the same unique and indistinct life, ruling like a despot over the state, but inconceivable without the state, and bound substantially to it, enclosed within the state, determined and circumscribed by the state and, finally, in an absolutely metaphysical sense, existing *for* the state, as the soul of a plant exists for that plant. The *caritas humani generis* appears but as a wan, sublime, and ineffective prefiguration of authentic charity, a mere philosopher's ideal, a sigh heaved by reason, alien, if not hostile, to religion.

True religion, however, is supernatural, come down from Heaven with Him Who is the Author of grace and truth. It is not of man or of the world or a civilization or a culture or of civilization or culture: it is of God. It transcends every civilization and every culture. It is the supreme beneficent and animating principle of all civilizations and cultures, while in itself independent of them all, free, universal, strictly universal, Catholic. It is with reference to those two aspects of things, the necessary immanence of the religion of Christ in culture, as of God in the creature—and the absolute transcendence of that same religion—that I would offer the following observations.

II. *The Catholic Religion and Culture*

The modern world is no more a creation of polemics than modern philosophy: it is a certain historical type of civilization, spiritually dominated from the very beginning by the humanism of the Renaissance, the Protestant Reformation and the Cartesian Reform. What are its characteristics from our present point of view? Like every other civilization it contains a positive element of ontological tension and vitality which in this case seems to be constituted by a courageous, untiring effort to make human nature yield its maximum earthly output. But this positive element, good in itself, praiseworthy and deserving of affection, is accompanied by a privation. Let me say—it has become a commonplace, but is none the less eternally true—that culture, while continuing its natural growth, has become separated in the modern world from the sacred and turned back on man himself. The Middle Ages had fashioned human nature according to a "sacral" type of civilization, based on the conviction that earthly institutions, with all their vigor and strength, are at the service of God and divine things to realize His Kingdom on this earth. The Middle Ages doggedly strove to realize that Kingdom on earth, dreaming—yet without any rigor of austerity and without preventing life from pursuing the normal course of its activity—of a hierarchically unified world, in which the Emperor on the summit of the temporal should maintain the body politic of Christendom in unity, as the Pope on the summit of the spiritual maintained the Church in unity. Such was the dream of the Holy Roman Empire, a dream which constituted an ideal, a "myth" strictly appropriate to the cultural conditions of the period; it was a dream which has been dissolved forever: it presupposed, along with a magnificently bold appreciation of principles, a vast ignorance of the universe and an imperious optimism: its corpse has long encumbered modern history. It required Napoleon and the whole nineteenth century to bury it once and for all.

To return, however, to the modern world. The object of culture, as that world conceives it, is purely terrestrial ends which are henceforth self-sufficient, no longer super-elevated in their peculiar order by their ordination to the Kingdom of God; to use a word which latterly has enjoyed considerable vogue, it is a type of *anthropocentric* culture. We should not forget that in virtue of a natural law of growth and as a consequence of the leaven of the Gospel deposited in humanity, a certain progress takes its course in the heart of that civilization, a progress which may be described as *material* if the word *material* be understood in its widest philosophical extent, for the equipment of culture has progressed not only in the order of the scientific and industrial means of exploiting nature, but also in the order of intellectual, artistic and spiritual means and technique. There has even been a rise in the level, I do not say of moral life or moral ideals, but of the ideas and feelings which constitute the static conditions as it were of moral life. That the structure is a fragile one, I am well aware; be that as it may, the idea of slavery or torture or the use of military methods to impose constraint upon consciences and a certain number of similar ideas are, it would appear, spontaneously repugnant at the present day to more people than formerly; disapproval of such ideas, at any rate, has attained the dignity of an official commonplace, and that is always something.

In short, it appears that in retiring within himself man has undergone as it were in spite of himself the introvertive movement peculiar to the mind; he went inside his own self—and his object was not to seek God. A general progress in the *assumption of self-consciousness* has thus been the characteristic of modern times. While the world turned away from spirituality *par excellence* and that love which is our true end to proceed towards exterior advantages and the exploitation of sensible nature, the universe of immanence was opening its doors—and sometimes they were very low—a subjective intensity of scrutiny was revealing their own peculiar spirituality to science, art, poetry, to the very passions of man and his vices, and the exigency of liberty became all the more clamorous as men moved farther and farther away from the true conditions and the true notion of liberty. In a word, in virtue of the law of compensation that governs history, the *reflex age*, with all the diminutions and losses which the word connotes, involved in other respects an undeniable enrichment, which must be considered a positive gain, in the knowledge of the creature and human affairs, even though such knowledge was destined to find its outlet in the inner hell of man gnawing his own vitals. That murky way is not a blind alley and the fruit gathered in passing has been incorporated into our substance.

I had in mind everything that I have just summarily indicated when I referred to the *material* progress taking place in modern civilization and the effort being made therein to make human nature produce its maximum earthly output.

Need I add—it explains certain aspects of the modern world—that many things which ought to have been done (and at all costs, because the will of the Master of history brooks no let or hindrance), many things which Catholics should have done, were done by others and against them, when Catholics failed? Heresies, also, and schisms, wars and catastrophes, the Devil himself, are under the universal dominion of the divine government and work against their will in weaving a woof which God sees, stimulate history and procure the advancement of His work. Their empire defines precisely the extent of our bankruptcy.

Joseph de Maistre considered that the French Revolution was of Satanic origin. He was too profound a philosopher to draw the conclusion that one should strive purely and simply to erase the French Revolution from the great book of history. That would be folly indeed! That book is written under God's will, and by His leave Satan may hold the pen: it is then an act of cowardice not to see and not to call by its name the evil which is done forever; but it is an act of stupidity not to realize also that the line of being continues amid all possible deviations, that the divine text may still be read by the angels, that some good, great or little, has been achieved (however little it be, it does not matter; God has willed it). We know that wheat and cockle grow up together and will be separated only at the last day. We have even been advised not to gather up the cockle lest we root up the wheat also together with it: which shows that the distinction is beyond our capacity; I mean the distinction of the *utility* value of events or men for the divine barns and in relation to the common good of creation, that is to say, in relation to an ultimate goal beyond our ken. The bishops of the Restoration period thought they were working for the Lord when they sought to prop the altar against a worm-eaten throne; they were unwittingly sowing the seeds of misunderstandings which came near to proving the undoing of Europe. It is another kind of distinction which the mind requires from us, the distinction of the *truth or falsity, good or evil value* things on this earth have in relation to intemporal laws which are well within our knowledge; and we must make an effort to perceive clearly, from this point of view, the significance of the spiritual dominants of our history.

This was not an idle digression. I was saying that the spiritual dominant of modern culture, whatever may be its positive historic vocation, whatever progress may be taking place in it, is, as I have attempted to show, that it is an anthropocentric culture: humanism *dissociated* from the Incarnation. We are now in a position to distinguish three degrees or moments in the conception which modern times have formed and continue to form of culture. There is a first moment when civilization lavishly produces the most magnificent fruits, forgetful of the roots from which the sap ascends, and it is thought that it must establish by the sole virtue of reason a certain human order, still conceived according to the Christian pattern inherited from preceding ages, a pattern which becomes a constraint and begins to be spoiled. That moment may be described as the *classical* moment of our culture, the moment of Christian naturalism.

There is a second moment when it is perceived that a culture which keeps itself dissociated from the supreme supernatural standards must necessarily take sides against them: it is then required to establish an order which shall be considered to be based upon nature, and is expected to emancipate man and guarantee the spirit of riches undisturbed possession of the earth; that is the moment of rationalist optimism, the *bourgeois* moment of our culture. We are just about to emerge from it. A third moment is the moment of materialist pessimism, the *revolutionary* moment, when man, irrevocably considering himself to be his own last end and unable any longer to endure the machinery of this world, engages, as we see in Russia at the present day, in a deliberate battle against natural law and its Author and undertakes to produce out of a radical atheism an entirely new humanity. These three moments are related in continuity in spite of strong secondary oppositions; making a violent schematization of things, we may say that they have succeeded one another chronologically; but they are also co-existent, mingled with one another in varying degrees. All these conceptions misunderstand human nature and ultimately conduce to claiming for human nature the conditions of pure spirit, yet in the flesh itself and by the exasperation of an absolutely material power. It is a fictitious emancipation, the waste and dispersal of the human substance in the endless multiplication of needs and sadness; the control of procreation not by chastity, but by doing violence to natural finalities; the control of the race by the eugenic sterilization of defectives[5]; the control of the self by the abolition of family ties and unconcern for descendants; the control of life by liberty to commit suicide and euthanasia. It is remarkable that a certain conception of the control of nature by man is compensated in the balance sheet, with startling uniformity, by one same single consequence: the cessation of life.

To such a conception of culture the Christian conception is opposed as a truly human and *humanist* conception, and, in using the word *humanist,* I have in mind the only humanism which does not belie its etymology, the humanism of which a Thomas Aquinas gives us the example: humanism purified by the blood of Christ, the humanism of the Incarnation.

Such a humanism, respecting essential hierarchies, sets the contemplative above the active life; it knows that the contemplative life tends more directly to the love of the first Principle in which perfection consists. It is not a question of sacrificing the active life, but of making it tend to the type it realizes in the perfect, that is to say, to an activity all overflowing from the superabundance of contemplation.

But if the contemplation of the saints be placed upon the summit of human life, must *it* not then be said that all the activities of man, and civilization itself, are ordered thereto as to their end? It would appear to be so, says St. Thomas Aquinas (with a note of irony, perhaps). For what is the object of servile work and trade unless to provide the body with the necessaries of life so that it may be in a fit state for contemplation? What end do the moral virtues and prudence serve, if not to appease the turbulence of the passions and secure the interior tranquility which contemplation needs? What end does the whole government of civil life serve but to assure the exterior tranquility necessary to contemplation? "So that, properly considered, all the activities of human life seem to be in the service of such as contemplate the truth."[6]

There is an idea of the hierarchy of values far different from the industrialist conception, wholly concentrated on production, which the modern world forms of civilization. We see to what an extent the supremacy of the economic, itself derived from a system based on the fecundity of money—a fecundity which, like everything that transgresses the conditions laid down by nature, knows no limits—to what an extent the materialist or capitalist or Marxian conception of culture is at variance with the mind of the common Doctor of the Church.

Are we then to understand that the relation between the Christian conception of culture and the contemporary world is merely one of incompatibility, and that the only ideal the Christian conception has to set before us is the outworn ideal, now definitely engulfed in history, of medieval times? How often must I repeat that I am well aware that the course of time is irreversible? Christian wisdom does not suggest that we return to the Middle Ages: it would have us move further forward. Besides, the civilization of the Middle Ages, however magnificent and splendid it may have been, more splendid still, no doubt, in the refined memories of history than in the reality of experience, was very far removed from the full realization of the Christian idea of civilization.

The Christian idea is opposed to the modern world, I agree, to the extent that the modern world is *inhuman*.

But to the extent that the modern world, in spite of all its defects in quality, involves a real growth of history—no, the Christian conception of culture is not opposed to it. Rather the reverse: it would endeavor to preserve in the modern world and bring back to the order of the spirit all the riches of life the modern world contains.

The anguish, the great anguish, which rends the modern world, whence does it proceed if not from all the inhumanity it involves? That is to say that it aspires unwittingly to a civilization of a Christian type, a civilization like that of which the principles of St. Thomas give us an idea.

I cannot refrain from indicting in the present controversy one genius at all events among the many responsible for the evils which afflict us: need I mention the name of my dear enemy, René Descartes? It would be interesting to point out the repercussions on culture—in the context, I mean, of politics and economics in the first place—of Cartesian dualism. Descartes, as everybody knows, conceived the human being as a composite of two substances, each complete in itself: pure spirit and geometrical extension. An angel driving a machine.

Transpose such a conception into the order of political and economic relations. Such a transposition, I hasten to say, was never made by Descartes himself; but I blame the *Cartesian spirit.*

We shall then have the conception of a political and economic machinery similar to the machine of the body in the Cartesian philosophy and governed solely by natural laws of the same sort as the laws governing mechanics and chemistry. To this machinery, existing with a value of its own and with its peculiar and purely material, inhuman requirements, you may, if you are an idealist and have a regard for moral values, add a moral superstructure, the requirements of justice and virtue, which will there take the place of the spiritual soul in the Cartesian machine. If you are inclined to realism or cynicism, you will consider such a superstructure as a perfectly useless epiphenomenon, just as La Mettrie, in the eighteenth century, considered the Cartesian soul to be useless and invented the theory of the Man-Machine, as Descartes had invented the theory of the animal-machine.

Be that as it may, what is important is that in such a conception politics and economics have each their own peculiar and specific ends, which are not human ends, but purely material ends. The end of politics is the material prosperity, the power and success of the state, and everything that may procure such an end—even an act of treachery or an act of injustice—is *politically* good. The end of economics is the acquisition and limitless increase of riches, material riches as such. And everything that may procure such an end—even an act of injustice, even oppressive and inhuman conditions of life—is *economically* good. Justice, friendship, and every truly human value thenceforth become alien to the structure of political and economic life as such, and if morality intervenes with its peculiar exigencies, it will be to engage in conflict with political and economic reality, with political and economic science. A *homo economicus* will be invented whose sole function is to accumulate material goods. If you attempt to duplicate him with a man subject to the control of morality, a truly human man, the duplication will be ineffective; the economic man, whose appetite is insatiable, will in reality eat up the moral duplication and everything else and exert himself to pound, like an ogreish machine, the wretched true humanity toiling in the basements of history.

This kind of political and economic physicism has really poisoned modern culture. In opposition to it the traditions of the *philosophia perennis* may once more teach us a specifically human conception. Such a conception—it is certainly not the invention of St. Thomas; all the superior minds of antiquity, even pagan antiquity, shared it, but St. Thomas, following Aristotle, clearly formulated the principles of it—considers politics and economics not as physical sciences, but as branches of ethics, the science of human actions. However immense the part played therein by conditions determined by the nature of material things and their automatic action, such a science is, nevertheless, defined by reference to the use which our freedom makes and ought to make of such conditions. Its end is the upright life, the good *human* life on this earth: a system of life worthy of man and of what is of most importance in man, that is to say, the spirit. Political and economic laws are not purely physical laws, like the laws of mechanics, or chemistry, they are laws of human action, investing in themselves moral values. Justice, humanity, unswerving love of one's neighbor, are essentially part of the very structure of politics and economics. An act of treachery is not merely a thing forbidden by individual morality, but a thing *politically* bad, tending to ruin the political health of the social body. Oppression of the poor and the acquisition of riches, considered as an end in itself, are not merely things forbidden by individual morality, but things *economically* bad, tending to thwart the very end of economics, because the end of economics is a *human* end.

St. Thomas teaches that to lead a moral life, to develop in the life of the virtues, man needs a certain minimum of comfort and material security. Such a doctrine signifies that extreme poverty is socially, as Léon Bloy and Péguy so clearly perceived, a kind of Hell; it also signifies that social conditions which expose the majority of men to the close risk of committing sin, by requiring a kind of heroism from those who desire to fulfill the law of God, are conditions which it is a duty in strict justice unceasingly to denounce and to strive to *change.*

The world at the moment seems to be in the grip of two opposite forms of barbarism. I have not the least idea whether it will escape. In any event it must not be forgotten that if the Christian conception has not been the spiritual dominant of civilization for some centuries past, it has still remained alive, dammed up, not abolished. That such a conception may succeed in dominating culture is still a *possibility* today: whether such a possibility will be realized or not is God's secret. We must therefore work with our whole hearts to bring such a realization about, no longer, certainly, according to the ideal of the Holy Roman Empire but according to a new ideal, a much less unitary ideal, in which an entirely moral and spiritual activity of the Church shall preside over the temporal order of a multitude of politically and culturally heterogeneous nations, whose religious differences are still not likely soon to disappear. If facts are fated to fall short of such an expectation, if the work of Christendom must henceforth develop in the bosom of what Scripture calls the mystery of iniquity, as that mystery formerly developed in the bosom of the work of Christendom, we may, at any rate, indulge the hope that, in the new world, an authentical Christian culture will arise, "a culture no longer gathered and assembled, as in the Middle Ages, in a homogeneous body of civilization occupying a tiny privileged portion of the inhabited earth, but scattered over the whole surface of the globe—a living network of hearths of the Christian life disseminated among the nations within the great supra-cultural unity of the Church. Instead of a fortress towering amidst the lands, let us think rather of the host of stars strewn across the sky."[7]

The foregoing observations make it clearly apparent what a prime, fundamental necessity it is to the life of the world that Catholicism penetrate to the very depths of and vivify culture, and that Catholics form sound cultural, philosophical, historical, social, political, economic, and artistic conceptions, and endeavor to transmit them into the reality of history.

The supreme detachment which is the boast of the separated churches of the East, the refusal to lend a helping hand to the sorry labors of this earth, the all too human vertigo of spiritual humility and liberty which impelled Dostoyevsky to revolt against the wisdom of Rome, dissemble an abandonment of the vocation imposed upon baptized souls by the supreme laws of the redeeming Incarnation. They go down the road from Jerusalem to Jericho with their eyes raised to Heaven and weep for compassion over wounded nature; they dare not lay the unctions of justice on its ailing body; they have such regard for its infirmity that they consider the attempt to cure it by endeavoring to subject terrestrial and social things to the order of the Gospel and of reason as a seduction of the spirit of the world.

As far as we Catholics are concerned, it is incumbent on us to recover much time lamentably lost. How many things would be different if, some sixty years ago,[8] it had been a disciple of St. Thomas who had written a book on capital as decisive as that of Marx, but based on true principles! Our principles, alas, are asleep and error is ever on the watch, active and enterprising. I have referred elsewhere to the terrifying lack of attention shown by the Catholic world to the warnings issued by Leo XIII with reference to social affairs. On the whole, and in spite of the effort of a few who kept honor safe, the bankruptcy of this world in the last century in face of problems directly involving the dignity of human personality and Christian justice is one of the most distressing phenomena of modern history.

That the religion of Christ should penetrate culture to its very depths is not required merely from the point of view of the salvation of souls and in relation to their last end: in this respect a Christian civilization appears as something truly maternal and sanctified, procuring the terrestrial good and the development of the various natural activities by sedulous attention to the imperishable interests and most profound aspirations of the human heart. It ought from the point of view also of the specific ends of civilization itself to be Christian. For human reason, considered without any relation whatever to God, is insufficient by its unaided natural resources to procure the good of men and nations.[9] As a matter of fact, and in the conditions governing life at present, it is not possible for man to expand his nature in a fundamentally and permanently upright manner unless under the shy of grace. Left to himself, he cannot but fail to achieve the difficult harmonies of the virtues, the difficult rational regulations, the pure consonances of justice and friendship without which culture deviates from its most exalted ends. St. Augustine's words with reference to the state apply equally to civilization: "The state does not derive its felicity from another source than man, for the state is merely a multitude of men living in harmony."[10] And one Name only has been given to men in which they may be saved. However great civilizations may be which ignore that Name, they inevitably decline, in one respect or another, from the complete notion of civilization and culture; order and liberty become equally cruel therein. Even an authentically Christian civilization does not escape many accidental blemishes. Only a Christian civilization can be exempt from essential deviations.

The relations between culture and the Catholic religion involve, however, as I have said, yet another aspect. If Catholicism is to penetrate culture for the good of the world and the salvation of souls, it is not so that it shall be itself bound to one culture or another, or even to culture in general and its various forms, otherwise than as a transcendent and independent and vivifying force—rather in the manner (but no comparison is adequate) of a spiritual soul subsisting apart, like the "separate intellect" of the Averroists, and imparting its own life to various living things. It *forms* civilization, it is not formed by it. It feeds on the fruits of the earth, because it dwells on the earth, but it is not of the earth, and it has an essential food which is not a fruit of the earth. All the elements it borrows from human civilizations, the languages of its liturgies, the languages of its preaching, the architecture and ornamentation of its shrines, the common or precious things assumed by its religious worship, the human wisdom assumed by its theology, the flower of the liberal arts and human poetry assumed by the very sanctity of a Gertrude or a John of the Cross, are each and every one adopted out of compassion, the same compassion which decreed the Incarnation. Jesus ate and drank in the houses of His friends in Bethania; He was received in Bethania; but it was Bethania which received from Jesus. The Roman peace and Roman order were not a condition imposed from below on the divine Incarnation and the propagation of the Church, but a means chosen from above, freely chosen. Not in itself necessary or indispensable, but, rather, on the contrary, deriving its merits only from that free choice. And the Church is indebted to it in the first place for the persecutions and the martyrs. And when that order believed itself to be indispensable to the world, it was shattered.

I have already observed but it is proper to insist upon it:

> All religions other than the Catholic religion are in more or less narrow and servile fashion, according as their metaphysical level is more or less elevated, integral parts of certain definite cultures, particularized to certain ethnic climates and certain historical formations. The Catholic religion alone is absolutely and strictly transcendental, supra-cultural, supra-racial and supra-national—because it is supernatural....
>
> This is one sign of its divine origin. It is also one of the signs of contradiction which until the end of time will be a cause of the passion of the Church, raised like her Master between earth and sky. It is conceivable from this point of view that the world is entering a phase of particularly stern conflicts which may perhaps be compared to the conflicts

of apostolic times in the Rome of the Caesars. On the one hand the non-Christian nations are incapable of distinguishing between their autochthonous culture, with all its human values in themselves deserving of respect and filial piety, and the errors and superstitions of their religions. And Christian universalism will have to show them how such a distinction can be made and how the Gospel respects and superelevates, and by slow degrees transforms, such particular values. The demonstration is, as a rule, not unattended with bloodshed. And the imbecile dogma of positivist sociology, taught in all countries in the name of European science, and according to which every religion is merely the specific product of the social clan (and Christianity therefore a specific product of the European races), will not make it any the easier.

On the other hand, when faith and charity diminish among the majority in the Christian nations many come to think that, because Christianity was the vivifying principle of their historic culture it is essentially bound, enfeoffed to it. Certain apostles of Latinity (I bear it no grudge, let me assure them) are convinced—the remark was made to me one day—that *our religion is a Graeco-Latin religion*. Such an enormity is full of significance. Not realizing from what spirit they derive, and oblivious of the divine transcendence of what constitutes the life of their life, they end in practice by worshiping the true God in the same fashion as the Ephesians worshiped Diana and primitive man worshiped the idols of his tribe. Christian universalism will have to remind them that the Gospel and the Church, without injuring any particular culture or the state or the nation, yet dominate them all in a pure unsullied independence and subordinate them to the eternal interests of the

> human being, to the law of God and the charity of Christ. Nor is that demonstration made without opposition.[11]

The Church knows that no civilization, no nation, has clean hands: *omnes quidem peccaverunt et egent gloria Dei.* But she also knows that all the civilizations and cultures on earth, though born far away from her and in spiritual climates overcast by error, whatever erroneous forms they may involve, endure only in virtue of the good which they contain and are pregnant with human and divine truths, and that the common Providence of God watches over all nations. That is the reason why grace can maintain them all in their particular types, correcting and superelevating each.

III. *Practical Considerations*

Certain practical consequences affecting our conduct emerge from these considerations. Culture or civilization, as I observed in the beginning of this essay, is rooted in the soil of natural life, whereas the Church has her roots in the sky of the supernatural life. But a Christian civilization, even supernaturally superelevated in its order by the Christian virtues and its subordination to the last supernatural end, is still something temporal, essentially terrestrial and therefore deficient, continues to belong to the sphere of nature. We must therefore be careful not only not to confuse the Church with any civilization whatsoever, but we should also be careful not to confuse the Church in any particular whatsoever with Christian civilization or the Christian world, Catholicism with the Catholic world. The Church and Catholicism are essentially *supernatural*, supra-cultural things whose end is eternal life. Christian civilization and the Catholic cultural world remain a civilization and a world whose specific end, although ordered to eternal life, is in itself of the temporal order.

The Church, the mystical Body of Christ—a supernatural society—has a bond, a supernatural social spirit, which is the Holy Spirit.

By a natural, too natural phenomenon, a return of the *natural social* spirit, let me say, if you like, in memory of Durkheim, a return of spontaneous *sociologism*, may come and sponge upon our consciousness to the extent that we conceive ourselves, in the Catholic community, as in a natural or temporal community—to the point of identifying the interests of Catholicism itself, the cause of the heavenly Father, with "our cause" and the interests of our human group of a Catholic denomination. So far as we do so, we allow our religion to sink, in practice, into naturalism, for the Holy Spirit is not the spirit of any clan or party. And, so far as we do so, we run the risk of shutting the gates of the Kingdom of God against souls and, because of our pride and our own miserable deficiency, making the nations blaspheme the name of the true God. It is immediately apparent how, such an error, which consists after all in considering Catholicism *as though it were itself a terrestrial state or a terrestrial civilization*, and therefore requiring for it and divine truth the same sort of triumphs as for a state or civilization on earth, is a kind of IMPERIALISM *in spiritualibus* and so related to the error we referred to above, which consists in enfeoffing Catholicism to a terrestrial civilization and is a kind of NATIONALISM *in spiritualibus*. These two errors derive from one same source, and I am inclined to believe that they have weighed very heavily upon the history of Christian nations and that it has become a pressing necessity to denounce both alike. Each is a blind delusion under the new law like the blind delusion of the carnal Jews under the old law. Such delusions are expensive.

Catholics are not Catholicism. The errors, apathies, shortcomings and slumbers of Catholics do not involve Catholicism. Catholicism is not obliged to provide an alibi for the failures of Catholics. The best apologetic does not consist in justifying Catholics or making excuses for them when they are in the wrong, but on the contrary in emphasizing their errors and pointing out that, far from affecting the substance of Catholicism, they serve only the better to display the virtue of a religion which is still a living force in spite of them. The Church is a mystery, her head is hidden in the sky, her visibility does not adequately manifest her nature; if you seek to know what represents, without betraying, her, consider the Pope and the episcopate teaching the faith and morals, consider the saints in Heaven and on earth, avert your eyes from us poor sinners. Or, rather, consider how the Church heals our wounds and leads us hobbling to eternal life. Leibniz pretended to justify God by showing that the work which proceeded from the hands of that perfect Workman was itself perfect, whereas in reality it is the radical imperfection of every creature which best attests the glory of the Uncreated. The great glory of the Church is to be holy with sinful members.

It would be impossible to be too careful and tactful in paying practical homage to such truths. It is proper to admire so many *Catholic* newspapers, *Catholic* cinemas, *Catholic* novels which profess with candor and undeniable good-will to be the recognized purveyors of good. Is it not the professed object of every Catholic magazine, especially if it is a young people's paper, to be *the organ of the Catholic revival*, or if it is a review of doctrine, eager also to inform opinion, *to give a complete idea of contemporary Catholic thought and Catholic activity*? That will be apparent when the world comes to an end, and the subscribers run the risk of being somewhat startled.

We should also admire so many Catholic men of letters who are convinced that their works constitute Catholic literature, one might as well say God's literature. Far be it from me to suggest that the operation of grace is incapable of being treated as a theme for fiction or romance; grace is more intimately associated with human life than life itself, and it is impossible for a novelist to consider it as non-existent. What is requisite, however, is that his work shall not diminish the operation of grace, shall respect its transcendence, the profound secret which is characteristic of the divine mysteries. It ill becomes us to judge the divine ways by our standards, even for the purpose of justifying them after the fashion of Leibniz, Malebranche, and the friends of Job, or of certain works of the imagination which seem to plead the cause of God, as though God needed to be acquitted. His works bear their own justification, are *justificata in semetipsa*; the novel which He has been writing since the world began is terribly free of every apologetic contrivance and every prejudice of spiritual politics. He wrote the Bible as He governs the universe, Himself giving us in those two works the supreme exemplar of all inspired creation.

The truth is, a Catholic writer is tortured and terrified by the thought that Catholicism may perhaps be judged by the standard of his own insufficiency. He would rather be taken for a Muslim and, as such, pay a tribute of homage to truth and the Church which would run no risk of compromising either; fortunately, his fellow writers are on the alert and take it upon themselves to secure as far as he is concerned an almost equivalent result.

To speak of more momentous matters. The result of such a temporalization of religion as that to which I referred a moment ago is mendaciously to transform Catholicism in the minds of those affected by it into a party and Catholics into partisans. Such a transformation appears with most manifest characteristics in the state of mind of anti-Semites, who proclaim the Gospel by a series of pogroms, and people who attribute all the worries of life to a permanent world-wide conspiracy of the wicked against the good. Another indication of it is to be found in those who seem to consider the conversion of souls as in the first place bringing a strategic reinforcement to an army or as a series of successes to be entered in a score-book. A conversion, however, is not a political or military operation. Operations of that sort, if they lose the ground at first won, are operations which have failed. But the return of a soul to God, even if it should afterwards not visibly persevere, is an event inscribed in Heaven, a testimony valid by itself, a promise whose ultimate fulfillment is beyond our ken. Catholicism is not a religious party; it is religion, the only true religion, and it rejoices, without envy, in *every* good, even though it be achieved outside its boundaries—for that good is only apparently outside the boundaries of Catholicism, in reality it belongs to it invisibly. *Are not all things*, indeed, *ours, we who are Christ's*? The expansion of the Kingdom of God has no common standard with any temporal conquest or any temporal victory. If the dragoons of Louis XIV harass and martyrize the Huguenots, nothing is thereby gained for the Kingdom of God. If, in a country oppressed by schismatics, the Catholics gain the upper hand and plunder the schismatics as the schismatics plundered the Catholics, nothing is gained for the Kingdom of God. If the integrity of doctrine or virtue serves only to cement the pride of a faction or a caste, if the object of a certain beneficence is rather to recruit adherents than to serve poverty, nothing is gained for the Kingdom of God.

An entirely different course of action has been enjoined upon us and the Church herself acts differently. The only proper attitude to adopt in regard to souls is one of service. The example was given once and for all time. As far as non-Christian cultures and civilizations are concerned, those of us who are engaged in studying them find ourselves faced with a delicate problem. We have been content only too often merely to depreciate them; complaisance is no better, it is truth which is necessary, but with love to vivify knowledge. Our ardent desire should be not to destroy such cultures, but to serve them loyally; I mean to say, to help them rediscover whatever authentic elements they may contain of everything that is venerable, wise and true, to purge themselves of their impurities, to disencumber the toothing which invites the building on of more exalted truths. If we do so, they will make ready to receive at the appointed time the visit of the Son of Man. The peculiarly Catholic task is to foster and stimulate the truth everywhere.

The controversy with which we are now concerned is the controversy between what Péguy called mysticism and politics—let us say, in a more precise terminology, between the spiritual and the temporal. As an illustration of this controversy and of what we have said of the transcendence of the spiritual, consider for a moment the story of the Invincible Armada. A most Catholic King, all Spain in prayer, the defense and promotion of God's cause in the world, the extirpation of heresy in a hotbed: was not another Lepanto a certainty? A puff of wind upon the water and the entire fleet was at the bottom. God took it upon himself to give the answer. If we believe as we are bound to in the divine government, we must conclude that God, Who in the conduct of history sets before Himself in the first place His Kingdom and His Saints, in this instance most strikingly dissevered the interests of His glory and the interests of the banners which thought to serve it. The merits of the martyrs of Tyburn—and future recoveries of which we have no idea—were doubtless more important to the divine plans than the triumph of the Catholic King. Philip II, the artificial and tormented replica of St. Louis, looks like one of those giant saurians in which some Paleozoic phylum finally exhausted itself. All his work seems to me to have a definitely characteristic significance. It puts before our eyes, carried to the extreme at which virtue becomes vice and to a degree of austerity and extravagance which the Middle Ages for all their excesses never erected into a system, the mediaeval conception of the temporal as the instrument of the spiritual—but the instrument in this case was so welded to the hand that the hand lost its freedom; is it any wonder that it came to disaster?

The true and living Middle Ages find their most authentic representative in St. Louis. In him the temporal is truly, with all the dignity and humility which such a title involves—supple, free, really ordered and subordinate—the means of incarnation of the spiritual. We have the problem of Christian royalty then rising before us in all its dimensions and proper proportions; and the problem of Christian royalty, considered in the most eminent and purest particular case, is the common problem of *Christian temporal activity*, as it presents itself to each one of us who strive to be faithful while working in the profane world. Considered from the point of view of worldly successes, such work is rather a thankless task. It is the case of a lamb trying to impress its views on wolves. Let us not forget that St. Louis was not a great conqueror, that he failed in his crusades, that he was defeated—but yet not in the same way as Philip II! His repulses, no less than his victories, merely extended still further his power and influence. Because the virtue of *the* energies of the spirit was really transmitted into the instrument wielded by that king. The temporal then participated in a way in the law of the spiritual, entered into the calculations of that divine arithmetic in which everything is done contrary to common sense, in which the first are the last and the laborers who have done nothing during eleven hours out of twelve receive the same wages as those who have toiled all day.

Here we may usefully find room for a scholastic distinction. There are two functions to be considered in an instrument, its own peculiar causality and its instrumental causality. In the case of the temporal the very subtle relation between these two functions imposes a varying degree upon the endless intertwinements of gains and losses. In the peculiar order of the temporal, so far as the temporal is worth anything by itself, while being ordered to more exalted ends to the extent that it has its own peculiar goods to safeguard, its peculiar virtue to exercise, what counts for the decisive issue is victory or defeat. In this case we ought—yet without ever exalting it above the law of God—terribly to wish for victory;

it has a biological importance: as well to die as fail to gain it. So far as the temporal acts precisely as the instrument of the spiritual and is useful to the peculiar order of the spiritual, what counts for the decisive issue is not victory in the battle, but the way in which the battle is fought and the weapons employed. Weapons of light! Of truth, loyalty, justice, innocence, let our weapons be unsullied! We shall be beaten, that goes without saying, historians and politicians are right in warning us. But it is impossible to be beaten; when the stake is not biological but spiritual, defeat or victory with unsullied weapons is always a victory.

It is not enough to realize that the things of time must be, on the double ground just mentioned, the means of the intemporal—not a temporal means imposing on the intemporal, to ensure its success on this earth, the law of the flesh and sin, for that would be an outrageous prevarication, but a temporal means itself subject to the supreme law of the spirit. It must also be realized that there are an order and hierarchy of such temporal means, I mean, of temporal means good in themselves, legitimate and normal. There is the labor of the soldier and the labor of the ploughman, the labor of the politician, the poet, the philosopher, there are the works of us Christians of the common herd, the works of the saints; there are the works of saints with a mission to discharge, such as the duty of state imposed upon St. Louis or the temporal mission of Joan of Arc, and the works of saints exempt from any such mission.

Well, then, the richer such works and temporal means are in matter, the more they have their own peculiar exigencies, their own peculiar conditions, the more heavily weighted they are. The more also, in accordance with the law just mentioned, do they regularly postulate a certain degree of temporal success. "Whoever loses his soul for my sake," our Lord said, "shall find it again." He did not say: "Whoever loses his kingdom shall save it." St. Louis was an excellent administrator of his kingdom; he increased its power and prosperity. Controlled by the strong hand of the eternal decrees, the Roman soldier was bound to subject the world to his arms and so unconsciously prepared the arena in which the Church had to fight her first battles. Ever so much more profoundly, what a weight of glory for the temporal was the history of the patriarchs and the long carnal preparation for the Incarnation! A work of time, but of eternal importance, in the least mesh of which God took a personal interest, the paradigm of the natural sanctity, if I may say so, of every successful and well-made work.

We may describe as *rich temporal means* those which, so implicated in the density of matter of their own nature, postulate a certain degree of tangible success. By that very fact the evangelical law of the reversal of values and immolation, which is the supreme law of the spiritual, affects them only imperfectly, and it is the shadow of the Cross which passes over them. Such means are the peculiar means of the world; the spirit, as it were, ravishes them, they do not belong to the spirit; in truth, and in fact, ever since the sin of Adam, they fall within the dominion of the Prince of this world. Our duty is to wrest them from him by the virtue of the blood of Christ. It would be absurd to despise or reject them: they are necessary, part of the natural stuff of life. Religion must consent to receive their assistance. But it is proper for the health of the world that the hierarchy of means be safeguarded and their proper relative proportions.

And there are other temporal means, which are the peculiar means of the spirit. They are *poor temporal means.* The Cross is in them. The less burdened they are by matter, the more destitute, the less visible—the more efficacious they are. Because they are pure means for the virtue of the spirit. They are the peculiar means of wisdom, for wisdom is not dumb, it cries in the market-place, it is the peculiarity of wisdom so to cry, it must therefore have means of making itself heard. The mistake is to think that the best means for wisdom will be the most powerful means, the most voluminous.

The pure essence of the spiritual is to be found in wholly immanent activity, is contemplation, whose peculiar efficacy disturbs no single atom on earth in order to touch the heart of God. The closer one gets to the pure essence of the spiritual, the more spontaneously tapering become the temporal means employed in its service. That is the condition of their efficacy. Too tenuous to be stopped by any obstacle, they pierce where the most powerful equipments are powerless to pierce. *Propter suam munditiam.* Because of their purity they traverse the world from end to end. Not being ordered for tangible success, involving in their essence no internal exigency of temporal success, they participate, for the spiritual results to be secured, in the efficacy of the spirit.

When Rembrandt painted, when Mozart and Satie composed their works, when St. Thomas wrote his *Summa* and Dante his *Divina Commedia,* when the author of the *Imitation* wrote his book and St. Paul his epistles, when Plato and Aristotle spoke to their disciples, when Homer sang, when David sang, when the prophets prophesied, these were all poor temporal means.

In the last resort, let us consider the spiritual man *par excellence.* What were the temporal means of Wisdom incarnate? He preached in villages. He wrote no books—that again was a means of action too heavily weighted with matter—He founded no newspapers or reviews. His sole weapon was the poverty of preaching. He prepared no speeches, gave no addresses; He opened his lips and the clamor of wisdom, the freshness of Heaven, passed over men's hearts. What liberty! If He had wanted to convert the world by the great means of power, by *rich temporal means,* by American methods, what could have been easier? Did not somebody offer Him all the kingdoms of the earth? *Haec omnia tibi dabo.* What an opportunity for an apostolate! The like will never be seen again. He refused it.

The world is perishing of dead weight. It will recover its youth only through poverty of the spirit. To seek to save the things of the spirit by going in the first place to try and discover, in order to serve it, the most powerful means in the order of matter, is an illusion which is all too common. You might as well tie the wings of a dove to a steam-hammer. In the last resort, it is the great modern Minotaur himself, all the gear and strategy of big financial business, which will be entrusted with the task of saving souls; banks will be founded and world-wide trust corporations organized for the worldly success of the Gospel with founders' shares. It would be hypocrisy to deny that the work of evangelization and every spiritual undertaking need money, as a man needs food. Much money is required for missions, schools, and charitable enterprises. But money may be used as a poor temporal means (it is then spent in order to procure things) or as a rich temporal means (it is then used to invent machinery for acquiring more money). With the divine *sans-gêne* of sanctity, the Blessed Cottolengo and his fellows testify to the face of the modern world to what an extent money, even though it pour in in abundance, can yet remain a means of poverty. What makes the modern world so terribly tempting is that it puts forward, it vulgarizes so, rich temporal means which are so crushing and oppressive; it uses them with such ostentation and such power as to induce the belief that they are the principal means. They are a principal means for matter, not a principal means for the spirit.

When David resolved to face Goliath, he first tried on the armor of King Saul. It was too heavy for him; he preferred a poor weapon. David was the spirit. Poor Saul, a pitiable figure of the temporal power royally equipped to serve the divine order and fight the Devil! And when David became king, he in his turn sinned. David, however, repented. "Jesus therefore when he knew that they would come to take him by force and make him king, fled again into the mountain himself alone" (John 6:15).

IV. *Of Catholic Thought and Its Mission*

The intellectual task confronting the Catholic is a difficult task, as difficult as it is important. As a man, he is in time, and subject to all the vicissitudes of becoming; as a member of the mystical Body of Christ, he is joined to eternity; his most fundamental life has its roots where there is no change nor shadow of alteration, his mind is fixed in primal Truth, loyalty to which is the foundation of the whole edifice of grace in him and the primary benefit which every creature expects from him. This sort of mediation between time and the eternal is for the Christian mind at once a sort of painful cross and a sort of redemptive mission. It must at every moment think of the passing, changing world in the light of eternity.

Our problem today is so to think the modern world; not only to think the eternal outside the world, which is the first precept of contemplative thought, but also by a second precept similar to the first, to think the world and the present moment in the eternal and by the eternal. And this problem is all the more pressing in that all around us we see the temporal forms in which the world of culture had for centuries received, however haphazardly, the imprint of eternal truths for the most part in a state of collapse and dissolution; this is undoubtedly a grave misfortune, for man is thereby deprived of a multitude of supports which helped him to maintain within himself the life of the spirit; but it is also, in certain respects, an incalculable advantage, for, at the same time, that life—and the very life of the Church of Christ—is disencumbered of the terrible human deadweight with which so many abuses and prevarications had burdened the old once Christian world. A new world is emerging from the obscure chrysalis of history with new temporal forms; it may be, all things considered, less habitable than the old; but it is certain that some good and some truth are immanent in those new forms, and that they manifest in some way the will of God, which is absent from nothing that exists. They may to the same extent serve eternal interests on this earth. The question is to understand this state of the world; and to regulate accordingly our loves and hatreds and our activity.

A double danger, a double error, must here be avoided. We might be tempted to abandon, if not theoretically, at any rate in practice, to lose sight more or less completely of the eternal, to the advantage of time, and allow ourselves to be carried away by the flux of becoming instead of mastering it by the spirit; the truth is that those who do so rather suffer the world than think it; they are acted upon by the world and do not act upon it otherwise than as instruments of the very forces of the world; they glide like fluttering leaves or sodden tree trunks on the water down the stream of history. They are often generous and forewarned of the exigencies of the moment by the intuitions of the heart, but in their hurry to pursue practical realizations they forget the very first conditions of practical efficacy itself, which are of the spiritual order and presuppose the intellectual courage to strip appearances bare, to grapple with principles and to keep thought centered at all costs upon the immutable.

Upon the plea of fidelity to the eternal, the other error, quite the opposite, consists in remaining attached not to the eternal, but to fragments of the past, to moments of history immovably fixed and as it were embalmed in memory, moments upon which we rest our heads to go to sleep; those who do so do not despise the world like the saints, they despise it like the ignorant and the arrogant; they do not think the world, they refuse it; they compromise divine truths with dying forms; and should they happen to possess a higher intelligence than the former of principles which are unchanging and the most acute perception of the errors, aberrations and deficiencies of the present moment, their learning remains barren, incomplete, and negativist, because a certain narrowness of heart prevents them from "knowing the work of men" and doing justice to the work of God in time and history.

The former error is as it were a misconception of the Word by Whom all things are made, and by Whose Cross the world is conquered; it would reduce Christian thought to impotence and mere versatility in the eyes of the world. The latter is as it were a misconception of the Spirit Who hovers above the waters and renews the face of the earth; it would make Christian thought repugnant and hostile in the eyes of the world.

It is difficult to remain absolutely unaffected by one or other of these two errors, not to decline more or less to one side or the other. For it is not a question of an eclectic dosage or finding an equilibrium to balance two weights; exact proportion in this sphere, as in general in the sphere of the virtues, is to be obtained only by eminence, by rising far above opposite excesses. Man achieves it only with the utmost difficulty. The Church, however, goes her way in divine fashion amid the too human thoughts and opposite errors of some of her children; the exact measure of virtue is realized in her in full perfection and the superior unity of diverse extremes, more particularly of absolute fidelity to eternal things and sedulous attention to the things of time. However difficult the attainment of such an eminent harmony may be for each of us, we must yet strive to achieve it and there, in our time, for the reasons urged above, is a task of manifest urgency. Every delay opposed to the accomplishment thereof is liable to involve irreparable catastrophes, if not for the Church, who has the promises of eternal life, at any rate for the world and culture. To guide us in our task we have the teachings of the Popes and the wisdom of the common Doctor of the Church.

By recovering its spirit of conquest and advancing boldly to grapple with fresh problems and to occupy new positions, the philosophy of St. Thomas will help us to transcend an apparent antinomy which presents itself today in its regard. On the one hand, we realize that the Church, in recommending that philosophy with insistence, proposes in the first place to recommend her common Doctor precisely as common Doctor, rather than to revive quarrels dividing the schools. On the other hand, we also realize that the doctrine of the Angelic Doctor is so lofty, and so solidly coherent that it cannot suffer the slightest diminution of its specific determinants without losing its efficacy to penetrate reality. The common Doctor is not the commonplace Doctor in whom there is to be found merely what all the others are agreed upon; he teaches us to assume in the principles of a superior unity every truth uttered by the others, and often manifests a peculiar grace in enhancing the value of particular aspects of things.

The schools will continue to dispute until the end of time; but let us shift our positions and move forward, let us grapple with fresh difficulties, and by those very aspects in which reality is most starkly apparent: then we shall best realize the necessity—under pain of lapsing into an impotent mediocrity—of maintaining in all their rigor the principles of the greatest assembler of truth the world has ever known and have the opportunity of seeing spontaneously united in the radiance of his pure doctrine finds hailing from the four corners of the earth. Let there be no mistake. It is the most arduous and serious problems, problems most closely affecting the heart and flesh of humanity, which now press for solution on the Christian mind, as though they had long been kept in reserve for a general assault; what that mind has to face and conquer or assimilate is philosophies, scientific or artistic researches, fashions of thought and culture of a rare technical nature and a precious human quality. It will succeed in its task only if it equips itself with the most formed wisdom, the most exacting science, the most perfect and reliable intellectual harness, the most vigorous and comprehensive doctrine and method. So furnished, it will be able to fulfill its mission, which, as I suggested a moment ago, by the very fact of being a Christian mission is in some sort a crucifying mission. *Quis scandalizatur, et ego non uror?* Catholic thought must be raised with Christ between Heaven and earth, and it is by living the painful paradox of an absolute fidelity to the eternal closely united to the most sedulous comprehension of the anguish of the time that it is invited to work for the reconciliation of the world and truth.

Post Scripta

I. The Fecundity of Money (Note to pp. 16–18)

I will endeavor to define in some further pages which I hope to write in completion of the present essay the sense in which these words are here used. The most summary explanation must for the time being suffice.

Nobody certainly has ever maintained that money is productive *by itself alone*. It is no less certain, on the other hand, that it is not an evil that money should not remain unproductive. What I mean is something quite different.

In theory and in the abstract, a system of association between money and productive labor may easily be conceived in which the money invested in an undertaking represented an owner's share in the means of production, and was used to feed the undertaking, enabling it to procure the needful material, equipment and resources in such a way that, the undertaking being productive and producing profits, a share in such profits should be returned to the capital. No fault can be found in such a scheme.

In reality and in the concrete, this same faultless scheme works in an absolutely different fashion and does harm. In the human judgments which mold the economic system values have in fact been reversed, while the fundamental mechanism has retained the same configuration, instead of being considered as a mere feeder enabling a living organism, which the productive undertaking is, to procure the necessary material, equipment and replenishing, money has come to be considered *the living organism*, and the undertaking with its human activities as the feeder and instrument of money; so that the profits cease to be the normal fruit of the undertaking fed with money, and become the normal fruit of the money fed by the undertaking. That is what I call the fecundity of money. Values have been revised, and the immediate consequence is to give the rights of dividend precedence over those of salary, and to establish the whole economy under the supreme regulation of the laws and the fluidity of the *sign* money, predominating over the *thing*, commodities useful to mankind.

II. Theatrum Mundi (Note to pp. 13–15, 22–23, 28)

The Church alone on this earth plays with absolute exactitude and propriety the part of her character, because her part and her character are both divine. As for the world, it is a theatre in which parts and characters rarely correspond.

The secret of history is concealed from us like the secret of hearts. From the point of view of the appearances amid which we move, it may be said—without attaching to the words the slightest suggestion of hypocrisy or dissimulation, but intending rather to designate the reality we conceive to be apparent—that all we know approximately of men is the mask or the character—and the part they play. One sign of the disorder in which life on this earth runs its course, especially in disturbed moments of history, is what may be described as the *confusion of parts* or the discord between the part and the mask or the character. It is Oedipus who buries Polyneices, Antigone who confronts the Sphinx, Phèdre who falls in love with Romeo, and the Moor of Venice who laughs at the sonnet of Oronte. It is useless to add that such parts are badly played and develop all wrong. An astonishing hybridization blends the part which his nature in spite of everything insists that he shall play, with the part which the character merely borrows.

At the dawn of modern times, Descartes mounts on to the stage of this world and comes forward masked. "Hoc mundi theatrum conscensurus, in quo hactenus spectator exstiti, larvatus prodeo." And I would willingly agree that such a "mask" is his very self, his own believer's face. His philosophy does not correspond with it. The part of the seducer played by the noble father, of the denier by the dogmatist, of the dissolver of the mind by the spiritualist and Christian apologist—three centuries of intellectual history will not exhaust the consequences of the event. In the time of Luther, it was the opposite spectacle which had been witnessed, the part of the reformer was then played by the heretic.

The Church doubtless intervenes when the issue at stake becomes too serious, and discovers to us something of the real character of Luther, of the real part played by Descartes. Reason also can divine what is concealed under the appearance. Nevertheless, the full meaning of the drama invented throughout the course of time by the will of the Creator and that of the creature remains concealed. Who can estimate the number of historical necessities drained by the part assumed by Luther or the authentically Christian remnants in the character of Descartes?

We must wait for the day when all masks will be removed.

Is it a calumny on modern history to observe that such reversal of order has in the past hundred years assumed enormous proportions therein, more particularly in the social sphere? Yet there was no lack of warnings by great minds, by such an ever faithful Catholic as Ozanam, such a misdirected Catholic as Lamennais. The defense of the poor and the oppressed, zeal for justice, peace and liberty, the crusade against the tyranny of money, against the enslavement of body and soul to economic interests—the earth was strewn with innumerable Christian parts abandoned. They were picked up by the adversaries of the Christian name. It was of the first importance that the play should continue; the producer willed it so, even though frenzied actors were to denaturalize such parts by corrupting the text and perverting the action.

Elsewhere it will be observed that for a century past the part of stimulators turning intellectual milieu towards religion was occasionally more effectively played by great romantic, writers or a few "accursed" poets than by the representatives of classic apologetics. Need the part played by the mummy be mentioned? It has long been held by the character "Order and Progress."

The "parts" mentioned relate after all to what I have described (p. 14) as historical *utility* values: the masks or characters to *truth* values. A character is the bearer of a name, representative of a form, an idea, a conception of the world; such name and form have in themselves absolute significations, are, considered in themselves, the occasion of truths and errors discoverable above time. Parts and characters are indifferent: it is those forms which are of the first importance. If a mask of iniquity seizes hold of a part of justice, that part is spoiled; and so long as it is spoken by such a mask it will remain more or less spoiled. The attempt may be made to turn to account whatever good it may retain; it is a betrayal to applaud the name under the sign of which it runs its course. If a mask of justice assumes a part of iniquity, it spoils itself and causes, the name it bears to be blasphemed: the name itself remains holy. To blaspheme it is madness. In the universal saraband the temporal task of the Christian is unceasingly to try and prevent such a confusion of parts; by striving to become what he is, he frees his own character from parts of iniquity and at the same time recovers the parts of justice from the masks of iniquity.

Notes for Religion and Culture

1. "Many symphilics devour the eggs of ants, others suck their blood, others again lay their eggs in the larva. Nevertheless, the colony of ants maintains and carefully feeds its guests in order to obtain the liquid for which they have such a marked preference. This liquid is not a food, but a sweet, and the ants sacrifice their young to obtain it, often even to the point of endangering the state." F. Buytendijk, *Psychologie des animaux* (Payot, 1928), p. 161.
2. I am applying here to Christian culture in general the expression used by John of St. Thomas with reference to the infused moral virtues. Cf. *Curs. theol.*, Vol. VI., disp. 16, a. 7, §29.
3. Charles Journet, *Vie Intellectuelle* (March 1929), p. 439.
4. *Le Mystère de l'Église*, 3rd ed. (Saint Maximin, 1925), p. 22.
5. This matter deserves a special study to itself. The least to be said is that such legislation puts into the hands of men and of the state a weapon of terrible danger. It remains that this method of assuring the mastery of man over Nature is, like the others, of an entirely negative kind and shows, as they do, a general tendency in the direction of death. The recent Encyclical *Casti Connubii* gives the reason for these being condemnable in themselves.
6. *Summa Contra Gentiles* (*SCG*) III, c. 37.
7. Cf. my *St. Thomas Aquinas*.
8. The first volume of *Das Kapital* appeared, as is well known, in 1867; the other two volumes were published, after the death of Karl Marx (1883), in 1885 and 1894, respectively.
9. Cf. *The Syllabus* of Pius IX in Denzinger-Bannwart's *Enchiridion Symbolorum*, 16th and 17th ed. (Fribourg.-im.-B., 1928), p. 466, 1703. [The text of the condemned proposition is as follows: "*The human reason, without regard to God, is the sole arbiter of truth and falsehood, good and evil; it is a law unto itself and sufficient by its natural resources to procure the good of men and nations.*"]
10. *Ep. ad. Macedon.*, c. 3.
11. *St. Thomas Aquinas*.

CRISIS IN THE WEST

by PETER WUST

Editor's Note

Peter Wust, whose work here appears in English for the first time, was born in 1884 in the village of Rissenthal in the Sarre country. Of Catholic parents and upbringing, he came later to succumb to the agnostic atmosphere prevalent in Germany at the beginning of this century.

His subsequent development is well illustrated by an incident which Charles du Bos recounts in a recent article (*Vigile*, No. 2, 1931): in 1918 Wust went to Berlin and was there received by Ernst Troeltsch. The news of Germany's defeat had just come to hand; Troeltsch, in giving it to Wust, added—"the external catastrophe has come about—but it is only the delayed consequence of our inner weakening since the death of Hegel. Since Hegel's death what have we seen but the gradual draining-away of our native belief in the power of the spirit to mold the world's history?" Whatever may be the truth of that remark, its effect on Wust was to set him at the service of a metaphysic where ontology occupied a central position, as of right, and where man would be no longer that being "severed from his ontological roots and his transcendent objects," described by Maritain in his *St. Thomas Aquinas*. At the same time, thanks to the work of Ernst Robert Curtius and Hermann Platz, Wust was making contact with the new tendencies of thought in France. Paul Claudel came to meet him on the road of his philosophical inquiry.

In 1920 appeared Wust's first work, *Die Auferstehung der Metaphysik* (*The Resurrection of Metaphysics*). Besides a great number of essays and articles he has so far published three other books—*Die Rückkehr aus dem Exil* (*The Return from Exile*), where he wrote of the enfranchisement of Catholicism from its feeling of inferiority in Germany and its entrance into the full tide of intellectual life. *Naivität und Pietät* (*Naivety and Piety*) appeared in 1925, and *Die Dialektik des Geistes* (*The Dialectic of the Spirit*) in 1928.

The introduction to Wust's philosophy given here is based on the last two books. In these the crisis or judgment that is today being passed on modern man for the neglect of certain essential aspects of his nature is worked out in full. The essay *Crisis in the West* is only a sketch of a vast subject, but it can well stand by itself and be read independently of the introduction, although the reader will find useful English variations on Wust's theme in Part II (p. 69), where Watkin makes comparisons between Wust and Wordsworth, Blake, Ruskin, D. H. Lawrence, and Coventry Patmore.

T. F. Burns

An Introduction to the Philosophy of Peter Wust

I.

The nature of man is the witness of truth, witness of itself and its origin and of the nature of the universe, a witness whose testimony can never be *permanently* set aside, perverted or silenced. The preconceptions of an individual, a society or an epoch may indeed refuse to admit its evidence—the disregarded witness becomes the judge and passes his sentence of condemnation on those who refused his testimony. Such a judgment is the crisis (here to be taken in its original and literal sense, i.e., judgment) of which Peter Wust writes in this pamphlet.

For centuries Western thought has tended to admit only the evidence of discursive and analytic reason, the *ratio ratiocinativa*, the clear conceptual reasoning of judgment and inference. The deeper, if dimmer, intuition (Wust calls it *Vernunft*, as opposed to the more superficial *Verstand*) which apprehends the hierarchy of values with their corresponding degrees of reality—the primary spiritual facts which the discursive reason must take for granted—has been rejected as subjective: nothing but human volition, belief or emotion. The result is a logical machine working in a void—a suicidal skepticism, and, finally, the exposure of humanity naked to those sub-rational, vital, and animal forces which, however indispensable and valuable in their subordinate place, cannot without disaster take control of a being who, after all, is not, and cannot be, a mere animal.

In one of those moments of illumination when, from the depths of the spirit, the voice of truth makes itself heard above the opposition of an inadequate theory, Bertrand Russell—distinguishing in man *instinct* (the vital, animal forces and functions), *mind* (the discursive, analytic reason, Wust's *Verstand*) and *spirit* (the profound super-rational intuition, Wust's *Vernunft*)—pointed out that mind, supreme, well-nigh omnipotent in the thought and life of modern man, is by itself a solvent, a destructive force. To escape its ruin man must go forward to spirit, by which he apprehends those deeper values without which no constructive thought or life is possible. Here, for an instant, Russell's glance exposes the radical defect of modern thought, the danger which threatens modern civilization. Unhappily he has not been able to maintain that momentary insight. Vaguely conscious that the rationalism to which he had pledged himself so deeply was radically imperiled by his incompatible perception, and that religion, against which he is so deeply prejudiced, loomed ahead, he has turned his back resolutely on the unwelcome vision and entrenched himself more firmly than ever in his refusal to admit anything beyond the purely formal, atomistic logic of a ratiocination *bombinans in vacuo.*

What for Russell was a passing and neglected insight is the starting-point and center of Wust's philosophy. This may be described as a metaphysical anthropology for which man is the measure of all things, not in the Protagorean acceptation that truth is but man's subjective opinion of it (the distinction is made by Wust himself) but inasmuch as his nature reflects every level of reality from mechanical matter to God. And, because his nature thus reflects every level of being, man is able to apprehend every level, though in varying measure. Only the middle levels can be apprehended with any clearness. Of matter at the bottom of the scale of being, or God at its summit, man can only know what they are not, not what they are.

Spirit, as experienced in the contingent and relative human spirit, is relatively creative and personal. Therefore the ultimate ground of reality must be an absolute spirit—absolutely creative and absolutely personal. There is no room for any impersonal substance—whether conceived as consciousness, abstract reason or blind force. Uncompromising theism, such as is taught clearly and consistently by Catholic theology, is thus the primary datum of a metaphysic true to the implications of the psychological human fact.

At the opposite pole is nature as opposed to spirit—a region of determined events which owe their coherence, order and objective rationality to the fiat and control of the Creative and Conserving Spirit.

Between the purely objective sphere of nature and the pure Subject-Spirit, God, lies the human spirit—with whose analysis Wust is chiefly concerned.

It is in man that spirit in the strict sense, creative personality, first appears in the scale of being. Man is a relative creator insofar as he distinguishes the general from the particular aspects of being, thereby freeing himself from bondage to nature's concrete *hic et nunc*, and penetrates to what Wust calls their "inner form," which is practically the "idea" in the Platonic sense. This "inner form" man expresses in the "secondary forms" which he shapes as his self-expression—whether mental (e.g., the concept), or objectivized in word, deed, or artifact.

Expressive form is thus the distinctive feature of man as active spirit. This is, after all, but an amplification of that school of art-criticism which sees in art the manifestation of significant form. In nature, forms are usually so chaotic in their unrestrained luxuriance that they present no significance to human contemplation. The artist selects from the mass those forms which, to his vision, convey significance (in Wust's phraseology, reveal the inner form). Nature, in favored moments, performs the task by accident, and we suddenly find in some natural scene, for example a particular effect of sky and trees and a hilltop with horses ploughing, what seems a picture of human workmanship. It is the selection of these natural pictures which distinguishes *artistic* photography from mere record-making. For Wust, though he never formulates it in these terms, man is essentially the artist. He is a creator in the sense that the artist is a creator.

Man also is a relative person, inasmuch as he is conscious of himself as an independent, unique and self-possessed center of action. He is relatively "*a se*," from himself, inasmuch as he is the original source of his creative activity. God—the absolute Spirit, the absolute Creator, and absolute Person of absolute aseity; Man—the relative spirit, the relative creator, and the relative person of relative aseity: this is the comprehensive formula of Wust's metaphysical anthropology.

But because in man spirit, creativity, personality and aseity are only relative, he is never wholly his own; his *entire* being is never possessed, understood and actuated as an independent self-conscious ego. The ego (the *Ich*) is always bound to something greater than himself and exceeding his comprehension. That something is the order of nature still present in himself, no longer a blind mechanical order of happenings, but, because it is the nature of a spiritual being, spirit-nature, a force of love which binds man willy-nilly to the cosmic order of which he is a part, and ultimately to the God who created it and him. This spirit-nature, the *it* (the *Es*) in man as opposed to the ego (the *Ich*), is not altogether easy to grasp—the more so because "whist elsewhere *seems* to identify spirit with personality and opposes it to nature. But Wust is the first to admit, indeed to insist, that we are here dealing with something which exceeds comprehension, and therefore clear formulation.

Besides the spirit-nature, the bond and urge of a cosmic love, the *Es*, there is in man a further nature, another *Es*, his physiological life, which belongs as such to the lower nature. For both natures, the *its*, the spiritual and the physiological, are ultimately united in the one body-spirit self. Wust insists on the fundamental unity of man. Its co-existence with the three factors he has just distinguished cannot, he admits, be made fully intelligible.

A complex being—two natures and one ego—yet all three one ego in the strict sense of the term. Wust's meaning is true and important, however obscure his formulation. I will try to make the point clearer: Below man is non-mental nature. Insofar as it is matter it is a non-mental energy.[1] But, as we have seen, it possesses significance and rationality. Man finds order, rationality and significance in the sub-human world. Wust calls this "objective spirit or mind," as he also calls the significance, the form, imprinted on human artifacts. It is, in short, form. In man the formal principle is a conscious and reasoning ego, the self, actively manifested in *Verstand*. The physiological nature in man, the energy or energies he shares with beings lower than himself, is one "matter" to be informed by the self: the spiritual energy, his higher spirit-nature, is another "matter" which must also be informed by the self-conscious personality. Matter-life, experienced by outer and inner sensation—Wust's *bodily nature*; the spiritual life, immanent in man yet transcendent of man (perceived by *Vernunft*, intuition)—Claudel's *anima*, Wust's *spirit nature*; the reasoning self-conscious personality—Claudel's *animus*. This is the trinity in unity which composes man.

This formulation will not, I think, do violence to Wust's meaning, though in some points it goes beyond anything he says and supplements what he has left too vague. His meaning is the more obscure because he never states clearly in what sense the self-conscious reason is the ego. On the one hand he tells us that the entire man is the self, on the other it is the reason that is distinctively personal.

To sum up and, I hope, make myself clearer: (1) The entire man is the self; (2) he is a self in virtue of the relation of his entire nature to the radical ego at the root of his psychic powers, the apex or *fundus animae* of the mystics; (3) *normally* that radical ego is manifested clearly in self-conscious reasoning. It is, however, manifested more obscurely, because passively, in sensation and intuition, most passively but most radically in mystical experience. We may say that the human self manifests itself passively in his sensual and in his spiritual experience, actively in his reasoning and rational volition. Perhaps it would have been better had Wust called the self-conscious reasoning not the ego but the active manifestation of the ego, which is, I think, what he really means.

For Wust the unity of the soul is pre-eminently seen in the phenomena of memory and conscience. In memory because, despite the admittedly pathological phenomenon of dual personality with its double series of memories, it witnesses that the remembered experience belonged to the self which now remembers it. In conscience because conscience witnesses: "I am responsible for that past action, because *I* did it, it belonged to *me*." Yet within this one self the three relatively distinct entities—the physiological *Es*, the spiritual *Es*, and the conscious ratiocinative ego (roughly Russell's instinct, mind, and spirit) exist in a state of tension. The animal force attracts man to the lower pole of his being where he approaches closest to nature, his "animality," *Animalität*; the spiritual force draws him upwards towards pure Spirit, effecting that bond with God which Wust calls man's "sacredness," *Sakralität*. Hence the tension which moves while it torments the history of man both individual and social, the spring which sets in motion the dynamic or dialectic of the spirit. This tension between the animal-vital and the spiritual poles of man's being, his animal life and his spiritual life (cf. St. Paul's antithesis between life in "the flesh" and life "in the spirit"—although St. Paul's life "in the spirit" is *super*natural), is founded upon the ultimate metaphysical tension of created being between the poles of nothingness and Absolute Reality. But only in man, because he is many-leveled, does this metaphysical tension issue in a practical tension of diverse possibilities and divergent directions.

When spiritual self-consciousness first dawns in man on the background of his double nature, it produces the primary emotion from which his spiritual-intellectual development sets out—astonishment—which from another point of view is reverence, before a reality—implicitly, at least, God. Our English term "awe" expresses the union of both aspects in one indivisible act. There follows what Wust calls the primary, better perhaps the primitive, naivety—which consists on the one hand in a harmony between the three factors of human nature—the two "natures" and the conscious ego—on the other in a correspondence between man's expression and his nature. This primitive naivety or simplicity—for Wust the terms are co-extensive—cannot be permanent. For it is still an indeliberate semi-conscious instinct. As the mind awakes and develops, the conscious reasoning, which is the active manifestation of the ego, must assert itself and transform what was originally instinctive *acceptance*, uncriticized and undifferentiated, into the fully conscious and deliberate possession and expression of a personality.

The goal of the process is the second naivety, in which the harmony between the three factors is restored by the conscious affirmation by the active self of the spirit-nature, the love uniting man with reality and so with God and the conscious correspondence between his expression and his nature, now thus informed by his personality. To this second naivety, the naivety of the perfectly wise man, who is therefore also the saint, corresponds a piety which is the conscious reasonable counterpart of the instinctive natural piety of the child and the childlike primitive. It involves piety towards oneself, in the first place, that is reverence for the spiritual value of one's own personality, as opposed to the egoism which seeks the superficial profit of the individual—regard for *what* I am by the mediate or immediate gift of God rather than for the fact that it is *I*, not another, who am what I am. "By the grace of God I am what I am" is the formula of piety in this aspect. It further involves piety towards nature as the work and expression of the Creative Spirit, towards one's fellows as members of a spiritual society, and, above all, to God. Were this goal infallibly attained by the individual and by society the tragedy and tension of humanity would be absent. But, in fact, man's will, free only with the imperfect and preliminary freedom which can deny as well as affirm the power and command of the cosmic love which binds him objectively to God—and the universe in God—may and does go astray during the process from one goal to the other.

Man may choose to identify himself with the animal physiological force. He may, and this is the subtler, more deadly temptation, identify himself with the self-conscious reason, with its clear analytic ratiocination and correspondingly limited aims. Volitionally this is the attitude of "Promethean defiance" which makes man his own end, and treats his secondary aims as absolute values, intellectually the attitude of the "Gnostic" who will accept only what can be logically demonstrated and clearly understood. It is the "false subjectivism" which deflects the true development of the spiritual subject in his apprehension of and integration within the objective order of being into a deification of the subject and, therefore, a self-imprisonment.

As we have seen already, the reason is the active manifestation of the self, the subject of experience. To confine oneself to the sphere of reason is to confine oneself to the active form of the subject while rejecting the sensible, or, at any rate, the spiritual reality it should inform. It is the noetic counterpart of the egoism which values the subject as such, that my and mine which for the mystic is the soul's deadliest foe. It is the subjectivism which of its nature condemns an individual or an epoch to emptiness.

"*Il faut payer par la tristesse, la désolation, l'orgueil d'avoir pensé.*"[2] This despairing quotation of a contemporary agnostic is a half truth that just misses its mark. Not the pride of thinking is the cause of modern despair, but the pride of expecting thought to be self-sufficient, the key to reality: the pride which refuses to accept as given the spiritual realities or the sensible material which the activity of the subject can never confine within its own so limited categories, though these, being abstracted from and determined by an external reality, give us knowledge of being, within their scope of reference. When I conceptually explain, I make the object of thought to that extent mine—*master* it, so to speak, by my activity. When I accept what I cannot clearly explain I passively receive what is at the same time beyond me and realize the presence of the transcendent. To accept only the former and refuse the latter is therefore the pride of an impossible self-sufficiency. We ought, indeed, to explain everything we can—a false passivity would be but a slothful quietism—but always humbly accepting experience which escapes our comprehension—that is, in fact, all the ultimates of experience.

The will being free, man is never compelled to take the wrong path. Indeed, Wust goes so far as to say that man, in virtue of his free will, retains habitually a "universal determinability or adaptability" which enables him to start in another direction at any time. This we think exaggerated—the power of native disposition being more than the simple emphasis of one aspect of interest, attention, or activity to which Wust would reduce it. But, granting as we must that free will is never lost, and that within the limits of his vision and powers of execution man can turn his will in another direction, in practice man will choose wrongly even against his lights. The effects of his free will become, Wust points out, a doom, or fatality, which it is hard, though never impossible, to resist. If, therefore, man chooses to entrench himself within his ego and its *clear* perceptions, thus deifying his individual purposes and the notions he can prove, he will not attain that final balance of his nature, and that simple trust in God and His world which must necessarily exceed clear understanding that constitute the secondary naivety and ultimate piety of the saintly soul. He will, indeed, be unable to resist the objective order of the universe and of his own soul, which will automatically avenge itself in his frustration, dissatisfaction, and interior disharmony. "He must pay for his pride by sorrow and desolation." But subjectively he has failed.

Man, however, is not a solitary individual. Just because he is a unique partial representation of God, and because his disposition inclines him to one-sided emphasis of one aspect or value of reality, he is intrinsically a social being, a member of a community of fellow spirits. This community, "*nexus animarum*," is constituted by three factors. There is a "*commercium spirituale*," or "intellectual intercourse," mediated by a common world of expression and significance, mankind united by common languages and art forms, by a common logic and corpus of sciences; in general, by mutual understanding, its methods and its instruments. There is a "*motio physica*," a nexus of physical inter-relationship—men share a common physical environment which renders them physically dependent one on another. And there is a "*motio metaphysica*" or inter-relationship of wills. No man can achieve any purpose whatsoever by himself. The volitions of other men, either in present actuality or in their effects, condition mine. For in these three forms this bond of souls embraces time as well as space, binding one generation with another as well as the members of each generation between themselves. In virtue of this triply-constituted communion of spirits, the free choices of the individual become for good or evil the objective destiny of his fellows. After his death not only do the effects of his choices remain, but insofar as they are incorporated in objective works—institutions, writings, works of art, speculative systems, etc.—they constitute an "objective spirit or mind," which, when brought into contact with the living intelligence and will of others, lives again for them as a force influencing for good or evil their own deeds and achievements.

Moreover, every human spirit, being unique, makes a unique contribution to this Kingdom or Society of Spirits. Every soul reflects and represents a unique aspect of the Infinite Spirit of God, which thus, for its complete human reflection and representation, requires the entire society of human souls from the first to the latest born.

Although the steady addition to the kingdom of souls of new spirits, and the steady addition to the sum of human achievement from generation to generation, constitute a unilateral progress throughout human history, that progress is from another point of view broken and turned about, as though by a natural fatality, rectilinear progress bent to a circle resembling the "everlasting return" of nature, through the operation of that "false subjectivism," impious self-glorification and proud rationalism refusing to accept what is not clear to the limited reasoning of the human ego, which, infecting society as a whole, in virtue of the triple nexus just described, carries it away from its goal of pious union with God and the world in Him to the *cul-de-sac* of an intellectual and spiritual void and anarchy. For the order of values has been rejected, and the forms of being decomposed by the disintegrating analysis of a ratiocination (*Verstand*) cut adrift from the synthetic view of intuition (*Vernunft*). The metaphysical intuition which apprehends the integral values and fundamental forms of being beyond the comprehension of the analytic and discursive reason is conditioned by an attitude of faith, being, indeed, a sacred contact with the Divine, the reception, so to speak, of a natural revelation of God to the soul; and this attitude of faith, the piety which is the bond and cement of human knowledge and social order, must fail a society dominated by this rationalist and subjectivist current. Moreover, since the discursive reason is by itself an empty form and the ego cannot affirm itself in the void, when man has turned away from his metaphysical-spiritual pole to which the spirit-nature, that energy of spiritual love, with its direction to God and his integral universe of being and value would attach him—the pole of "sacred-ness" or "piety" (here *Sacralität* and *Pietät* may be taken as identical)—he must inevitably turn to the vital-physiological pole of his animality. Reason now becomes a mere tool in the service of a vital egoism, the brutality which wars for power and the means of enjoyment, the luxury which is more bestial than the pleasure of brutes because, unlike theirs, it is not restrained by the limits of natural well-being. As we have seen already, the pious man values himself simply as what God has made him, the impious as himself, the subject for his own sake. Hence an impious society must be a complexus of self-affirmations—never inwardly reconciled—however self-interest may dictate external cooperation. Though the objective *nexus animarum* is as indestructible as the order of nature to which it belongs, subjectively it is denied, and love becomes at most a pleasure of the body, a satisfaction of the desire for power or a bond of mutual self-interest. Thus the loss of piety is for society and individual alike the loss of man's *raison d'être*—the reduction of his life to emptiness and irreconcilable discord.

"Godliness" (piety, ευσέβεια) "is profitable for all things having the promise of the life that now is and of that which is to come."

The truth of this text, which might serve as a summary of Wust's message—piety being understood in that complete sense in which he takes it—is thus visible in the intellectual, spiritual and cultural decadence which follows upon the loss of piety. Such a process is sketched in this pamphlet—and the possibilities of its arrest discussed. Living faith in God as the Source of Reality—the perception of that reality as a whole with its values—gradually disappear. Since the incomprehensible facts revealed naturally by God through the intuition; primary values, first principles, the soul, God himself, and the "inner forms" even of material objects are denied because they are not to be explained in terms of discursive reasoning, that logical reason is left alone with its relentless analysis which "murders to dissect." Correspondingly all understanding is lost of that sanctity which attaches to objects, to "things" as created by God and therefore a scripture written by His hand, an "objective spirit" reflecting the Absolute Spirit. Modern man is thus left "in these days so far retired from happy pieties" without even the natural immanental piety of the ancients "when holy were the haunted forest boughs, holy the air, the water and the fire," and Keats' fellow romantic must cry out upon the desolation of his contemporaries:

> Little we see in Nature that is ours;
> We have given our hearts away, a sordid boon.
> Great God! I'd rather be
> A Pagan suckled in a creed outworn;
> So might I, standing on this pleasant lea,
> Have glimpses that would make me less forlorn.

"Forlorn" because alone in a world which can no longer be trusted as fundamentally good and in harmony with the highest values and aspirations of the soul, with a spirit divided against itself because no hierarchy of values is recognized to give its life unity and direction, and the harmony between its three fundamental powers has been lost—such is the condition of modern man. He may indeed escape from himself by living in a superficial zone filled with noise, excitement, and variety. But the inner discord and emptiness remain: the repressed hunger for the things of the spirit—for God—grows more urgent.

We may not agree in detail with Wust's view. Personally I am disposed to think that he attributes too much to the evil will of man, where the fault rather lies with that inevitable one-sidedness of human development which, as he himself points out, compels man to advance by action and reaction—a too exclusive advance in one direction followed by an equally exclusive advance in another. Moreover, he seems to me to undervalue the positive aspect of the rationalist and secularist movement. In his *Dialektik* he points out the evils which attend a too exclusive trust in intuition (*Vernunft*) to the detriment of discursive reason (*Verstand*). And may it not be that the ages of faith, too *exclusively* pre-occupied with the realities which exceed rational comprehension, God and the soul—St. Augustine, the typical representative of this movement, would know nothing besides—neglected too much the more superficial but necessary sphere in which the critical analytic reason is at home? Nor perhaps is the circle of complementary reactions after all a circle. We would rather regard it as a spiral returning to a higher point than that from which it set out. The religious movement of Christianity, for example, as Wust would be the first to allow, did not simply repeat and restore the religious movement of antiquity destroyed by the earlier secularism which began with the Sophists. Thus the combination of the two movements of human history pointed out by Wust, the rectilinear and the circular, results in a series of spirals, a spiral staircase by which, if humanity ascends slowly, still it ascends. But, however this may be, Wust has certainly laid bare the mortal disease of modern civilization, and the radical insufficiency of rationalism, whether as an epistemological method or a practical guide. He has shown how it has severed man from the universe, from his deeper self and from the God who made and reveals Himself in both. And he has firmly grounded his diagnosis in a metaphysic which, centered in man's nature *in its totality*, presents a synthetic view of God, nature and man, deep enough to do justice to man's deepest perceptions and needs and wide enough to embrace, as by a bird's-eye view, the movement of history, as it reflects and reveals the inner movement, the dialectic of the human spirit.

In the magnificent introduction to his *Dialektik des Geistes* Wust depicts humanity as an ocean tossed ever to and fro, as he explains later, by the conflicting powers of his being, his animal nature, his spiritual nature, and his active reasoning ego. But that ocean is not like the primal-chaos ocean of Babylonian myth—its boundaries have been established from the beginning by the hand of its Creator who "walketh above the waves of the sea" and whose Wisdom "gave the sea its bound that the waters should not transgress His commandment." The objective law of spirit-nature, as Wust is careful to insist, is not to be broken by man's subjective errors and sins. And, after all, this human sea may prove a mighty stream flowing surely, if slowly, into the pacific ocean of God's kingdom of spirits. "Their waters roared and were troubled: the mountains were troubled with their strength." But "the stream of the river maketh joyful the city of God."

II.

In the following essay Wust, as a German writer, takes the bearings of his thought relatively to German writers and thinkers—as Goethe, Dilthey, Herman Hesse and Max Scheler. For English readers it may be helpful if we compare him with Wordsworth, Blake, Ruskin, D. H. Lawrence, and Coventry Patmore.

Wordsworth, like the other romantics, represents a revolt against rationalism, and what Wust says in his pamphlet of the German romantic movement is applicable to its English counterpart. But Wordsworth is of peculiar significance for the student of Wust because he represents and stresses what Wust means by piety (*Pietät*). His reverence for things, for human ties, for the soul, as vehicles of a divine power is precisely what Wust describes and demands. And, like Wust, he finds this piety preeminently in children and simple peasants. In fact, Wordsworth's position would be altogether satisfactory were it not that in his creative epoch he tends to a vague pantheism which treats the vehicle of divine immanence as the body of a purely immanent world-soul, and when, later, he decisively adopted Christian theism, his choice was rather a reaction from revolutionary excesses than the internal development of his original perception. However his poetry at its best remains perhaps the best English commentary on Wust.

Blake represents the deliberate rejection of discursive reason (the *Verstand*) in favor of intuition or, as he called it, imagination or inspiration. On the one hand, he is a powerful witness against the tyranny of "rational demonstration" taken as the sole criterion of truth, on the other hand, he proves the danger of the contrary excess, its total rejection. His work comments on and justifies the chapter in which Wust describes the powers and limitations of *Vernunft* and its need to be "policed" by the *Verstand*. Blake refused that control and became unbalanced, inconsistent, finally almost unintelligible. But he supports and illustrates Wust in emphasizing the intrinsic connection between egoism and rationalism, in insisting on a return to the simplicity of childhood and in noticing the femininity of intuition (he calls it man's emanation) and the masculinity of the reason (man's specter).

From Ruskin we can expect no metaphysical contact. He shared to the full that dislike of metaphysics which, as Wust shows, has proved so fatal to "modern thought." It is in his insight into the process of secularization begun at the Renaissance, his view of the inner decadence masked by a superficial progress, that Ruskin stands by Wust's side. In particular he saw the fundamental weakness of the romantic movement as Wust sees it, its lack of religious faith. Like Wust, he bitterly opposed the mechanical industrialism of modern civilization with its divorce from the realities of life and nature and, like him, understood the supreme necessity and value of piety in Wust's sense of the term, the piety of the simple peasant. His *Praeterita* is largely the loving and sorrowful record of pieties vanished. Indeed his entire life-work was a protracted and unsuccessful battle against the decay of piety in the modern world. His chapter "Modern Landscape," in the third volume of *Modern Painters*, anticipates, some seventy years earlier, Wust's lament over modern faithlessness. "The profoundest reason of this darkness of heart is, I believe, our want of faith. There never yet was a generation of men, savage or civilized, who taken as a body so woefully fulfilled the words having no hope and without God in the world as the present civilized European race. A Red Indian has more sense of a Divine existence round him, or Government over him, than the plurality of refined Londoners or Parisians.... Nearly all our powerful men in this age of the world are unbelievers; the best of them in doubt and misery, the worst in reckless defiance, the plurality in plodding hesitation, doing, as well as they can, what practical work lies ready to their hands." And his criticism of Sir Walter Scott, taken as the typical British representative of the Romantic movement, confirms almost verbally Wust's account of the romantic reaction, as exemplified by Goethe. His attack upon modern industrialism and economics is based upon its blindness to the sacred element in things, its refusal to admit values not to be reduced to quantities, its treatment of men as money-getting and money-spending machines; and his criticism of contemporary "science" is for a similar blindness whereby it hoped to explain things by the quantitative analysis of their material—all effects and manifestations of the denial of faith and intuition. But Ruskin, starting with an inadequate religious system, and, as we have seen, *rejecting metaphysics as subjective cobwebs*, was vanquished in his struggle with the age, lost his own faith and went down in despair and madness, fighting to the last against the triumphant self-satisfied rationalism that he did not know how to overcome. The tragedy of Ruskin is the epitome of that tragedy of western culture which Wust depicts.[3] Moreover it confirms his insistent diagnosis that the rejection of an objective metaphysic is the radical error of modern rationalism.

Not altogether unlike is the lesser but yet very real tragedy of a more modern writer, who has battled against the mechanical valueless civilization of the modern world—the late D. H. Lawrence. His witness endorses Wust's revolt against the deification of the discursive reason. "Real knowledge comes out of the whole corpus of the consciousness. The mind can only analyze and rationalize, set the mind and reason to cock it over the rest, and all they can do is to criticize and make a deadness. I say *all* they can do." In fiery, indeed hectic tones (as Wust points out, reaction is necessarily one-sided) Lawrence denounces the emptiness of the rationalist talking in the void and the utterly hopeless deadness of the civilization he has produced. His attack on industrialism and machinery is indeed the echo of Ruskin's. But whereas both agree in a diagnosis of the disease which is substantially Wust's, they differ as to the remedy. Where Ruskin gropes in the dark, Lawrence is sure and, seizing upon a half truth, demands a return to life-living intuition and the reality it grasps. But of the life and intuition of spirit, the *Vernunft*, he is ignorant. By a fatal error he confuses it with the abstractions of conceptual reasoning—the *Vernunft* with the *Verstand*. He thus approaches by a different route Bergson's identification of instinct and intuition and repeats Rousseau's demand for that return behind the natural awakening of humanity whose inherent impossibility Wust explains. Nor is he true to his own maxim, as enunciated in my quotation, for he seeks the real knowledge which he rightly opposes to conceptual abstractions not, as Wust, from the metaphysical avenue of spiritual intuition but only from the lower physiological avenue of sense. Thus for Lawrence the sole life to be lived is the life of physiological nature, the only "real knowledge" its sensual perception, Russell's instinct. This life and perception he finds in their purest, most intense form in the experience of sex with its strange *mystique à rebours*, an ecstasy of union with the lower vital nature, an ecstasy, therefore, which mimics the higher ecstasy of union with the life of Spirit. Hence "his ending" too "is despair," for though he certainly attains life and reality they cannot satisfy the demands of a spirit or do justice to the total witness of human nature. His inadequate solution however may help us to understand the completeness and necessity of the integral solution propounded by Wust.

But there is another teacher who never surrendered to modern "rationalism," and, however impotent his voice to shake the solid bulwarks of the foe, never yielded an inch of his ground. Fragmentarily, almost allusively, and with meaning veiled in enigma, myth and allegory, Coventry Patmore proclaimed the bankruptcy of analytic reason and mechanical science as a philosophy for individual or social life. The permanent need of piety, the witness of the soul, the objective reference of man's spiritual intuition, with due respect also to his physical nature and its experience—everything for which Wust raises his voice in the arid wilderness of chatter and machinery which maddened Ruskin and dismayed Lawrence is championed in Patmore's abrupt, broken, often cryptic utterances. "A strange age of 'science' in which no one pays the least attention to the one thing worth knowing—himself! It was not always so.

Scire te ipum was the maxim of all ancient philosophy; the stupidest little Greek knew more of man and therefore of God who is 'very man' than...all our men of science put together." These words might almost have been written by Wust. "Exclusive study of material facts seem to lead to an absolute *hatred* of life. 'Science' makes a boast of death and the dryness of its bones. What the world calls Mysticism is the science of self-evident Reality which cannot be reasoned about because it is the object of pure reason or perception. Rationalism begins at the wrong end: Religion rationalizes from the primary and substantial Reason and explains all things. Rationalists take zero for their datum and, do what they may, they can make nothing of it."

But perhaps there is no more forcible presentation of Wust's case or one that makes it easier to understand than the story told by Martineau to Baron von Hügel and related by him in his Edinburgh address on the "Central Needs of Religion."[4] An American propagandist of rationalism who had come to doubt his position, asked advice from Martineau. At Martineau's suggestion, he spent respectively six months among the Catholic peasantry of Westphalia (that *milieu* of traditional Catholic piety of which Wust speaks in this pamphlet and which surrounded his own childhood), and six further months among the rationalist medical students of Berlin. He reported from the former, ignorance, roughness, superstition, bigotry, but in face of the fundamental realities of life "a depth of insight, an assurance of action, an at-home-ness of conviction, a magnificent swiftness, purity and massive-ness"; from the latter "wide knowledge, polish, suppleness of mind, tolerance," but in face of those same realities "the nimble 'enlightened' students were utterly helpless, without insight, action, conviction of any kind." Here, in a nutshell, we have piety accepting realities beyond the comprehension of the discursive reason and the rationalist enlightenment which rejects them. Not all the gain on one side, neither by itself completely satisfactory. But can we hesitate for a moment where the balance lies? The former group represents Europe before the enlightenment, at the beginning of the process depicted by Wust, the latter Europe at its close.[5] God grant us a Europe uniting the values of both. But a deep well is better than a shallow pool. For the well merges at its base into the subterranean waters, the narrowest[6] form of religion communicates with the infinity of God.

Perhaps the testimony of these witnesses against what the historian Guglielmo Ferrero has called the substitution of quantitative for qualitative civilization may help English readers to appreciate Wust's diagnosis of that process, its causes, and its possible cure, as he states it in the present essay; and may induce them to study in his other works the philosophy on which that diagnosis is based and by which it is more fully explained.

E. I. Watkin

I. *Humanity During the Classical and Christian Eras: The First Two Phases of Its Decline*

It is an axiom of modern intellectual history, long accepted as a dogma, that in the course of the great era upon whose last phase we have now apparently entered, man has been discovered as an individual. The truth of this proposition need not be disputed. Only we must add that by this discovery of man as an individual is meant man detached—one might even say forcibly torn—from all the sacred elements of being; man, that is to say, who at least subjectively, in his intention and conscious thought, appears as dependent entirely upon himself, to a certain degree *in puris naturalibus*, if we may borrow a well-known theological concept.

A closer inspection of this modern type of man—entirely self-dependent and self-aware—especially in that ultimate form which we meet with everywhere today, is, to be frank, productive of grave uneasiness. No longer has he anything of importance in common with that older type of man who still remained within the bosom of the Church, incorporated into the mystic unity of sacrifice and love. Both in knowledge and will a law unto himself, in his self-sufficiency he repels even the Hand which, stretched forth lovingly from out the obscure background of life, affords or at least proffers, the possibility of redemption even to the most hardened hearts.

Hermann Hesse recently typified the outlawed humanity of our day by what is by far the most impressive symbol yet conceived. He shows us man under the form of a *Steppenwolf*, roving restlessly hither and thither in the endless and loveless desert that is Western civilization, and hideously crying his hunger and thirst for Eternity. A howling, hungry wolf is a natural thing enough, God knows. But a howling human animal, crying for Eternity? What then? Is it not a terrifying metaphysical phenomenon, at which we must shudder with apprehension? Emphatically there is something unique about the howl of pain uttered by the human animal who has lost his bearings and suddenly realizes how deeply the metaphysical thorn is driven into his flesh; for it means that henceforth he must reveal that soul which he has failed to reveal in love and in reverence, until now believing it capable of being explained away on materialist, naturalistic or other lines, in a horribly distorted shape.

It will be our ungrateful task to study this metamorphosis of Western man, and to demonstrate that it is since his withdrawal from the unity of the Church that there has gradually been evolved that final type symbolized by Herman Hesse as the wolf. With this end in view, we shall in the first place endeavor to sketch in somewhat greater detail five leading types of Western humanism. We shall then examine closely the fifth type of the series, that is, the positivist and historicist[7] type of our own time, as being that from which a reaction in the direction of a fresh intellectual era seems today to be preparing.

On the threshold of Western intellectual developments stands the man of classical antiquity. The assertion sometimes put forward that the man of the classical age is in reality nothing more than the purest form of the rationalist *homo sapiens*, must once for all be emphatically contradicted. We should rather say that the man of antiquity is the *homo naturaliter obediens*, man naturally submissive to the sacred sanctions of being. In any case, the puzzling fact remains that the classical type of Western humanity has, up to and including the present day, preserved its mysterious fascination for all who followed after it. It is true that as a type it is non-Christian, or pagan. But it cannot for a moment be denied that even now, in spite of the long development of Christian humanity, spread over a period of two thousand years, classical man still retains an incomparable charm, which never releases those who have once fallen under the spell of its beauty. The Church herself has never attempted—nor indeed was it possible—to deny the existence of this charm; indeed, she so closely associated herself with the classical type of humanity as to provoke the reproach—even today unsilenced—that Catholicism is from one point of view nothing more than the idealized form of the old belief in the holiness of things.

Where, then, is the essence of this wholly mysterious charm to be found? I do not think that it is necessary to go very far afield for the explanation. It is their wholly unique, frankly childlike reverence for things that still today brings the two sister peoples and sister cultures of antiquity so very near to us, so that we are conscious of an indefinable pang of regret whenever we look back at them. The ancients—during their best periods at any rate—take things so simply, so sanely, and so genuinely, as natural facts, that, as a result, after more than two thousand years, every rhythm of their verse and their prose, and every line in their plastic art, reveal to us—so aged and anxious and mentally exhausted—the dewlike freshness of eternal youth.

Now it may possibly occur to some bright person that at certain periods, notably in the nineteenth century, we too manifested a similar intellectual pre-occupation with the impersonal *thing*, and that it therefore follows—but it is unnecessary to complete this train of thought. Ancient realism and modern positivist materialism are such poles apart that any attempt at a comparison between the two is bound to appear a systematic profanation of the classical attitude to life.

The decisive factor here is the manner of approaching an object, the purity and the innocence of the eye beholding things. And how wonderfully pure and single must the eye of the ancients have been—up to and including the time of their highest intellectual achievement, at any rate—that they saw things so clearly and with the directness born of reverence; a vision of which we are, unfortunately, no longer capable. For this reason, therefore, we must speak of the pious realism of the ancients as something in complete contrast with the impious, irreverent realism of our positivist age.

This, too, is the reason why all modern attempts to resuscitate the spirit of antiquity have never achieved more than a temporary and superficial success. For it is precisely the objective piety of the classical outlook that is essential to the success of all such attempts at resuscitation. And that outlook cannot so easily be recaptured.

The foregoing remarks have already indicated the lines on which we are to seek for the essence of classical humanity. I would like to inform sophisticated twentieth-century free-thinkers that the pagans of old had at least this "natural piety," and we have lost it. "Yes," they may reply, "but they prayed to Zeus and Poseidon and to a multiplicity of gods, and that was folly." Of course it was folly; but the actual prayer itself was not folly. On the contrary, it was the ancients' supreme act of childlike wisdom. Their whole life was fashioned and hallowed to a liturgy, and from thence it derived its sheer greatness and its monumental quality, and that character of sacredness before which even today we still feel ourselves obliged to linger in reverence, for from the flame of that unique consecration a spark yet glows. Classical humanity still stood for a realism that was naturally religious, at any rate before skepticism and profanity (ἀσέβεια) had as yet made their appearance, and before the noble unity of a civilization based upon natural religion had dissolved in decay and corruption.

One thing, however, we must not forget in our review of ancient man. It would be a mistake to fall into the one-sided sentimentalism of the school of Winckelmann and yield credence to the belief that the realist and cosmic optimism of the ancients was, after all, so utterly pure and unalloyed. Every type of humanity, as soon as it develops a serious side to its nature, becomes overshadowed by the cloud of pessimism. And, therefore, even the divinely joyous ancients dimly apprehended that sin and guilt, sacrifice and salvation are things that belong to mankind universally. They did not, it is true, plumb the depths of the soul; indeed, it was this very lack of profound and accurate spiritual knowledge that for so long made them resemble grown-up children. Yet their slumber was broken by flashes from these dangerous spiritual depths. This is apparent in their myths and mysteries, most forcibly perhaps in the tremendous legend of Prometheus. In this, as if by some secret instinct, they—the noble, grown-up children—touched upon those final mysteries of the spirit which reveal themselves to us in their most impressive form in the phenomenon of titanic self-glorification.

Now, when the decline of the earliest type of Western civilized humanity set in, or to all intents and purposes had become an accomplished fact, there suddenly occurred in the very midst of this decadence the most astounding miracle of all time—the appearance of the *homo perfectus*, the *homo absolutus*, the spiritual ancestor of humanity. Halfway through the decline of classical civilization that event took place, which, seen with the eye of faith, must be regarded as the most revolutionary occurrence in the entire history of the world.

We are today, one and all, too apt to forget the fact that history, in its deepest sense, does not consist merely of secular happenings, but that it is always at the same time a sacred process, a spiritual happening. For it is only on the surface that history is a *motio physica* of wars, battles, national disorders, political catastrophes, and so on. Below, in the depths that are accessible to the mind alone, it is a truly majestic *motio metaphysica voluntatis*, a passionately stirring will-drama of the spirit. And, if this is so, then the really decisive factor in this will-drama will be that tremendous tension which continually exists in one form or another between the organism, compound of all human wills, and the absolute Will of God.

Now we learn from revelation that in the dimness of remote antiquity human history began with just such a grave tension, revealing precisely that dialectic movement which we experience today. As a result of the first transgression, the spirit of discord suddenly precipitated itself into the head of the human organism. At the same time a tremendous upheaval of the human organism as a whole occurred, which effected a sweeping change in the aboriginally clear and straightforward relation between God and man. As a result, a greater atonement became necessary, an *ἀναχεφαλαίωσις* or reintegration of the race under a new head, that the disharmony arising out of the first fault might be removed.

The most truly epoch-making occurrence of that sacred history which is wrought in the depths of the human spirit, the action that was to bring this state of tension to an end, took place in the midst of time. It was Christ's act of redemption. Since, however, we have lost our understanding of the metaphysics of history, this fact of redemption in reality of central historical importance will scarcely appear to us as historical. This was not always the case. At first, of course, in the actual moment of its accomplishment, this spiritual and sacred event was recognized in an act of faith by but a few people. Yet this handful immediately began to diffuse such a glow of faith that, as if by a single great miracle, henceforth continually operative, the sun of Christianity rose out of the dark night of paganism, and an entirely fresh chapter of history was begun.

Now it is a very remarkable thing that the greater the degree of responsiveness manifested by humanity towards this supernatural fact disclosed by revelation, the greater became its capacity for plumbing the depths of human nature, that ultimate background hitherto veiled in darkness of all human history. As Dilthey once observed, it is the dimensions of his history which best teach man his nature. This dictum is even more profound than a *historicist* like Dilthey could realize. And it is therefore best verified in the record of the progress made by Christian self-knowledge. Once the Christian world of the first centuries had set itself energetically to work to view human history in its entirety—to contemplate with the eyes of faith that portion of history which until then had remained hidden from the eyes of the understanding the whole fundamental essence of human nature, which had hitherto been shrouded in obscurity, was suddenly lit up.

This, then, was the quite unique and marvelous achievement of Christian humanity; the childlike cosmic realism of the ancients was not destroyed, but most admirably completed and perfected by a supernatural realism hitherto unknown. As a result, the whole architecture of being stood suddenly revealed with startling clearness before the eye of the Christian. This eye, with the strengthened visual power imparted to it by faith, now not only perceived the aspects of this world with a far greater depth of spiritual insight than the ancients had possessed, but also discovered, as never before, that most profoundly spiritual structure of humanity whose lines prolong themselves to eternity. It is true that Buddha also possessed an insight into this spiritual depth. Nevertheless, his view of the world, measured by the Christian's depth of vision, was nothing more than a dim conjecture of the ultimate mysteries of the soul. With Christianity came to the human spirit a full awakening, and the vision of the far horizon of human self-knowledge. Christian self-knowledge meant the discovery for the first time of the complete extent of man's metaphysical structure, and of the entire actual and potential range of his history.

Unfortunately at the present day—so great has been the aberration of the human mind—the man who upholds such a thesis at once exposes himself to ridicule. It is the crying scandal of the modern mind, which owes its present Promethean greatness to the spiritual and intellectual awakening of humanity affected by Christianity, that it has scarcely kept in remembrance even the actual historical fact of the discovery of all those spiritual continents which were then opened up for the first time.

It is especially noticeable in this connection that the Christian discovery of the spirit was not originally undertaken as a purely theoretical task with that intention. On the contrary, Christians had from the very beginning scarcely any other purpose in view beyond the solving of the purely practical problem of their adjustment, in the light of their faith, to the new objective world presented by revelation, in order that they might generate a new being within themselves. Their main task was the creation of the new man by his incorporation into a supernatural reality. And then, out of this new life by faith, there developed a new vision as well, and, simultaneously, the complete whole that is the Christian culture of the Middle Ages.

This phenomenon—full of instruction for our contemporaries—is most clearly perceptible in the history of mediaeval ethics. Alois Dempf and Othmar Dittrich have recently pointed out that the ethical theory of the Middle Ages, which penetrates far more deeply than modern ethics into the personal foundations of man, is actually explained by this unquestioning preference of practical life to all theory. It was primarily by actual religious practice that man learnt to what profound depths theoretical ethics must penetrate before it can attain such fundamental phenomena as, for instance, freedom. The same thing applies to mediaeval mysticism, and already today it is safe to assert that since we have lost both faith and practice we have become blind to all the wealth of spiritual experience.

At bottom, however, the primarily religious orientation of mediaeval man was already foreshadowed by the naturally religious *pietas* of the ancients. It was simply raised from the natural to the supernatural plane. Belief in the supernatural mysteries of revelation now transformed the naturally religious attitude of the ancients towards immanent being into a piety that was in the strictest sense at once natural and supernatural. From this it follows that in spite of everything there exists a far more intimate spiritual relationship, from the point of view of religion, between the Christian of the Middle Ages and the man of antiquity than between the man of antiquity and one of us moderns. It almost seems as if a single great wave of faith welled up out of antiquity and spread over the Christian humanity of the Middle Ages, receiving, to be sure, at this latter stage, after the short interval of classical skepticism, a purely supernatural dynamism.

It is just this spiritual affinity between the classical man and the mediaeval Christian, inasmuch as both recognized the paramount importance of religion, that we must keep well in view if we are to grasp in all its bearings the transition to the specific forms assumed by modern humanity. For the decisive factor in this great process of reversal is the loss, despite the resumed familiarity with the spirit of antiquity which characterized the Renaissance, not merely of the supernatural religion proper to mediaeval Christianity, but also by degrees of the natural religion of the ancients. The revolution that produced our modern type of humanity is, judged by its final effects, in the last resort a radical rejection of piety in any shape or form.

It is true that in the Sophist movement antiquity had already suffered the first impact of a similar form of spiritual *tantalism*. But this first tentative rationalism was incapable of completely subverting the piety of the ancients. Even through Stoicism, the most pronounced system of classical rationalism, there runs a clearly perceptible vein of the old religious dynamic. So much is this the case that even a man of the world like Cicero, when compared with a certain type of modern intellectual, is most emphatically a religious man. At the moment, however, when the complete disintegration of the old piety seemed dangerously imminent, there had already set in the new and infinitely stronger current of Christianity—stronger in that it drew upon a supernatural force—and thus, out of the flagging classical spirit was generated the new spring of a new spiritual age.

But with the appearance of the specifically modern type of humanity there suddenly comes into existence a really unique situation, as a result of the twofold work of destruction which now begins to go forward. For the first time there arises the tremendous danger of a collective annihilation of religion, both of the natural religion of the ancients and of the natural-supernatural religion of mediaeval Christianity. We are now in a position to appreciate quite clearly the peculiar significance of that terrible howling of the wolf-man who appears at the end of this long process of development. The axiom *corruptio optimi pessima* applies to collective history as well as to the history of the individual. The fall of the saint is a very different matter from the fall of the average man. In the same way mankind's fall from the lofty spiritual height of the Middle Ages must be in another category altogether from that of the ancients, for their religious level was, after all, but a natural one. The howling of the wolf that we hear today is, therefore, the distinctive cry for help uttered by the man who feels by instinct that he has lost both the classical and the Christian piety, the cry for help of a man who, as a metaphysical being, now feels himself really cheated out of the ultimate reason for his existence. It is the cry of the man, now self-dishonored and spiritually bankrupt, who may perhaps rapturously await the approach of a new revelation, but who, after the absolute revelation of Christianity, will await it in vain. In this way he may come to feel that unless he himself returns to the Christian message, the universal defeat of the human spirit will draw appreciably near. And in all this is to be found the element of metaphysical terror which is voiced in his very cry of distress. For that cry is itself a self-manifestation of the metaphysical depths which exist even in this man who is spiritually bankrupt; and the irony of it is that such a man is always incapable of interpreting this unconscious metaphysical manifestation of his own being in the one and only sense in which it is susceptible of interpretation. Here we find verified, almost literally, the profound ideas which, in 1849, in his work, *Sickness unto Death*, Kierkegaard propounded to the entire nineteenth century, as if in a single great sermon after the manner of Savonarola. We can, indeed, truly say that the crisis of the spiritual sickness is reached when the dying man no longer recognizes himself as moribund. It is the point where the paroxysm of fever turns, as it were, into spiritual delirium.

Three distinct phases of this peculiarly modern development of humanity must now be distinguished. In the first of these the supernatural idea of God gradually grows dim, and slowly but surely the supernatural order of life fades from the field of vision. This process extends from the beginning of the Renaissance to the Deism of the eighteenth century. The second phase is the comparatively short interlude formed by the German idealism of Goethe's day. We ourselves are in the final phase. This evolves a positivist and historicist humanism and ends with the total uprooting of man.

It should be borne carefully in mind that it is during the course of the first phase—during the development, that is, from the Renaissance to Deism—that the really decisive crises occur. That is because it is during this period that the destruction of the religious unity of the Middle Ages is accomplished. This fact is usually ignored, because at that time, in spite of the inner decadence, an astonishingly high level of culture was attained, while the fruits of decomposition did not become apparent in any way until the second, nor fully until the final phase. It is scarcely admitted that the level of culture characteristic of the first phase is in reality to be attributed to the still consciously effective operation of the mediaeval religious dynamism. And yet a link still remaining with the Christian spirit of faith is indubitable. No doubt that link is not the same for the man of the Renaissance and, for example, the Deist. The former, it is true to say, still belongs to the supernatural order of life. The latter has already sunk to the level of purely natural religion. Moreover, the whole of this revolutionary movement is at first restricted to the intelligentsia. The extension of the movement to the masses only follows very slowly, and at a considerably later date. It was not until the nineteenth century that it became an accomplished fact. And even then it actually affected the industrial classes to a far greater degree than the peasantry.

Perhaps the feature that characterizes the first phase of the modern spirit, extending from the Renaissance to the development of Deism, is the definitive substitution for the life of faith of a life that finds its end in secular culture as such. Whereas, in the best periods of the Middle Ages and of antiquity, the cultural achievement is, so to speak, the automatic result of a life steeped in the liturgical consecration of religion—natural in antiquity, natural-supernatural in the Middle Ages—at this point the center of gravity is suddenly and fatally shifted. The cultural achievement becomes the primary consideration, the sanctity of religious fellowship and the life of faith of secondary importance. Already in antiquity we find this change of gravity in the transition from Aeschylus to Euripides. For Aeschylus dramatic art was still part of a liturgical life; for Euripides it had already become an end in itself.

This displacement of emphasis in Renaissance man as between religion and culture may be studied in the Camaldolese dialogues of Cristoforo Landino. He describes how, in the year 1468, several members of Lorenzo the Magnificent's Platonic Academy met in the Casentino for philosophical discussion after the manner of the Dialogues of Plato. The Abbot of the monastery was present. The Christian spirit still permeated everything. The members of the party attended the conventual Mass in the morning, and the supernatural still had a place in all their discussions. But in spite of all this a neo-pagan current was perceptible in this intellectual elite. Christian earnestness had yielded to an aesthetic idealism, and thereby the change of orientation characteristic of the age stood revealed.

However the man of the Renaissance may have pictured to himself his increased delight in secular culture as a return to antiquity, he failed to perceive that in reality he took only a connoisseur's interest in the fragrance and bloom of the old civilization and had little understanding for that fundamental piety from which the fair fruit of human culture had sprung. This delight in culture as an isolated and self-contained achievement inevitably effected a cleavage within his soul between his Christian belief in the supernatural and a classical culture which he had already, in his conception of it, at any rate, profaned.

We are now in a position to understand why the problem of the creative genius will henceforward be experienced far more intensely than hitherto. This truly modern malady is already apparent in the great spirits of the Renaissance, in Dante, in Petrarch, in Michaelangelo, in Botticelli. It is true that the first victims of this disease of modernity recover after long struggles their place in the religious fellowship. But we already find the tremendously significant symbol of Michaelangelo's "Night" heralding Hamlet and Faust. And the time will soon come when the artist will no longer find his way back to the foot of the Cross when he has laid down his brush. He will no longer find, in the symbolism of his work, atonement and relief for the discord which it has engendered in his spirit, but can only follow the path of tragedy to its end, whether it be despairing suicide or the oblivion of madness.

From the Renaissance onwards the Christian conception of God recedes steadily into the background. The God of Deism is but a pale shadow of the Christian Father-God; the Christian consciousness of sin has almost disappeared, the earnestness of the Christian life has degenerated into the comfortable optimism of the respectable Philistine. And this development will go irresistibly forward until the last trace of faith in God, supernatural and natural alike, has melted away like snow before the sun.

The final dilution of the inherited faith of antiquity and Christianity is represented by the fourth type of man, in the second phase of secularization. It is the humanism of Goethe and his age. Again there is talk of a resuscitation of antiquity. And what is actually attained is but the last remnant of the faith that still survived from that idealism of the reason, itself little better than a ghost, which had characterized the Enlightenment. It is true that at times Goethe's work breathes something of that delicate perfume which marks the Catholicism of the Rhineland. But, when we look more closely into it, we see that it is merely a pleasing play with aesthetic categories; the tremendous, supernatural substance is lost; we are but faintly reminded of the metaphysical depth from which once sprang as a serious reality the life of an entire age.

And now there pass across the stage the first really tragic figures, those who feel obscurely that the aesthetic idealism of Goethe and the ethical idealism of Kant and Fichte are not sufficient to restore a vital content to human life. But the circle of immanence has closed in, and no sortie can any longer pierce the lines; Kleist, Hölderlin, and Novalis fall as the first precious victims of the age.

The great assault of the Romantics on the bastions of the Enlightenment fails. The positivist and historicist nineteenth century has become inevitable. The tragic shadow of the age of Nietzsche already looms ahead.

II. *The Last Phase of the Decline: Modern Man*

Now appears before us the fifth type of humanity, the completely uprooted civilized man of the closing nineteenth and early twentieth centuries, who, with his ideal of a perfectly uniform and standardized internationalism, is preparing the destruction not only of Christianity but of human culture in general. It is man living a life *in puris naturalibus*, from whom every remnant not only of religion but of metaphysics also has been eliminated, and who, admitting nothing but the abstract law of Things, will recognize the religious convictions of mankind merely as natural phenomena witnessing only to the laws that have produced them.

This human type, the structure of which is so difficult to grasp, has evolved, on the one hand, from the Anglo-French Age of Enlightenment, and, on the other, from the reaction to it that developed during the eighteenth century, that is to say, the aesthetic and ethical idealism of the age of Kant and Goethe. Positivism and historicism are, as it were, the progeny of these two movements, which are inwardly akin through their common deistic origin. The God of Deism, the mere world-builder, the *architectus mundi*, was the last lingering shadow of the Christian Father-God. As soon, however, as the process of abstraction went a step further, the world was bound to appear as a mere piece of machinery, and this mechanistic conception of the universe was that of positivism. From it there also developed an early type of historicism.

But a second form of historicism developed out of the movement of German idealism, which had resumed contact with antiquity, and, later on, out of Romanticism, which attempted to find a support in the Christian Middle Ages. The latter form of historicism was of course intended to offer a certain degree of opposition to the positivist conception of the world, but actually in the end it was swallowed up by the positivist conception of universal law governing all phenomena, and thus was finally accomplished the complete ousting from history of its sacred element, or, as Berdyaev aptly puts it, "the winding-up of the Renaissance," the complete disruption of that intellectual unity which still survived in the Enlightenment.

The inner affinity between positivism and historicism, which, existed from the outset and survived later after a certain amount of conflict, is to be found in the reduction of all phenomena to an abstract law, by which such phenomena are stripped, on the one hand, of their qualities of form and value, and, on the other, of every element of mystery. Everything that strikes us in an object as constituting its form and inner essence is dissolved into relations, and everything that presents itself as a mystery is denied as illusion. Positivism now sets about developing a unique system of metaphysics, based upon the so-called human capacity for illusion. This extraordinary metaphysics of illusion starts off with the attack upon anthropomorphism. It may be true that the Christian Middle Ages had exaggerated at times the part played by anthropomorphism in human knowledge. But in modern times the fact has been overlooked that there is a positive side to anthropomorphism without which the spiritual form of things is bound to remain unrecognizable. In eliminating the subjective sources of error we must on no account lose sight of the fact that the subject, viewed as a spiritually conscious entity, i.e., as πρόσωπον, a person, must not be allowed to disappear completely, since otherwise the form of things is of necessity lost or unrecognizable. The metaphysics of so-called illusion, however, as found in positivism, has for its goal in this direction the complete destruction of the forms whereby being manifests itself. And the most remarkable point about this particular metaphysical system is the circumstance that it actually ascribes positive value to this process of the destruction of forms, inasmuch as it insists that it is only by the rejection of all theological or metaphysical conceptions of the universe that the real, actual, positive universe will become visible, comprehensible and controllable, a reality "freed from illusions" in every sense, because it is freed from form and values.

The insistence of science that perception should be as much dehumanized as possible was therefore, properly speaking, an aspiration towards an utterly despiritualized reality, which was to present only an absolutely calculable mechanism. The beginning of this tendency is already typified by Descartes's discovery of analytic geometry. However important in the abstract this discovery may have been for mathematics, it became, so to speak, the prototype of the relativity mania which characterizes modern science. Just as in the first case the mathematical forms were reduced to their numerical ratios, so the whole domain of the forms proper to being was to be resolved into similar relative values. It is hardly to be wondered at, then, if gradually space and time became the sole great irreducible factors of existence, the overcoming of which human thought set before itself as its almost exclusive aim.

This effort of positivism to get rid of all so-called illusions contains implicitly the first form of historicism. This is first apparent when the soul, like nature, is stripped of substance and form and regarded as explicable by a soulless relativist psychology. A further step is taken when the endeavor is made to account for the dominant features of culture as mere combinations of mechanical laws. As soon as the combinations are recognized the so-called illusions are exploded. And the release from illusion, too, depends upon a progressive reduction of everything to mechanical laws.

Sharply opposed to this early type of historicism we find the second type. In opposition to Comte and Taine stands Dilthey, the father of the new tendency, everlastingly repeating his protest in identical terms. This protest is actuated by two distinct motives, the one scientific, the other romantic and sentimental. From the scientific point of view Dilthey opposes the view that psychological phenomena can be explained as combinations of physical laws. He points out that there must exist in the field of psychology a twofold method of knowledge—besides the explanatory method, the comprehension of spiritual significance. In this suggestion of Dilthey's we have the first important protest against the demolition of form characteristic of modern thought. Fundamentally it is an appeal to the spirit, an appeal, moreover, on behalf of that method of comprehension which was the rule in the Middle Ages and in antiquity, but which, since the beginning of modern times, has been increasingly relegated to the background. To understand how important Dilthey's thesis has grown today we need only glance at the actual position of psychology, which is passing through a very critical stage, and of those other sciences of the spirit whose former position is menaced from this point of view.

The second motive—the romantic and sentimental—of Dilthey's protest, and at the same time of the second form of historicism, is to be found in his retrospective romanticism. Destiny had placed Dilthey in a world from which positivism had banished God. But his personality, which needed a religious principle, found itself thus cheated of its highest good. Spiritually too weak of will to make good, by building up a complete system on the basis of his leading idea, the great deficit of his age, which he had correctly divined, he steeped his mournfully retrospective spirit in the past of German idealist faith. It was the last system to offer a certain remnant of belief in values, and from it he steadily followed up the receding footprints of faiths past and gone. By this process he attained one fairly important result at least. He demonstrated that the metaphysics of illusion of Comte and his precursors was fundamentally erroneous. It was Dilthey who recognized that what Comte hailed as progress was a phenomenon of progressive decadence, a destructive manifestation of the steadily growing modern skepticism.

His contemporaries, it is true, saw his position in a different light. They spoke derisively of the discord between Dilthey the scientist and Dilthey the poet. And in this mephistophelian sarcasm at the expense of Dilthey the poet there was conveyed everything that since the development of the positivist metaphysics of illusion had become the common intellectual property of cultured people. In just the same way others had already set about playing off Plato the poet against Plato the scientist interpreted in terms of Kant, with the idea that in this way they could jettison what they called the poet and retain only the scientist. But the poet in Dilthey had not judged so badly. He had grasped the fact that man cannot live without a belief in values, and that, least of all, is the higher life, of the spirit possible without them. And, though he so far yielded to positivism as to term these religious forces "myth" and "illusion," yet he regarded these illusions as a beneficent and fruitful necessity, whereas for the opposition party the welfare of humanity lay in emancipation from these so-called illusions.

Inasmuch then as he looked sentimentally backwards to the earlier ages of faith, Dilthey was a historicist of that second type of which we have spoken; he recognized the necessity of the forces of which faith is the source, but lacked the courage to make the decisive act of faith. He understood what it was that his contemporaries lacked, but he did not live before his time. On the contrary, he endeavored to explain away both the presence in ages which were spiritually robust of the energy of faith, and its absence, in ages which were spiritually stunted, on purely psychological grounds as the inevitable effect of subjective disposition. That is to say, he was a pragmatist of culture, a characteristic product of the period since the Renaissance.

In this way Dilthey's sentimental brand of historicism dovetailed into the earlier positivist type. Thus, the second form of his historicism was not only untenable in itself; it sterilized perceptions which had set him on the right track, so that ultimately he returned to the earlier form. Through weakness and human respect he betrayed the best of himself to the all-pervasive power of positivism. For a determined attack upon the subversive positivist metaphysics of illusion he lacked two indispensable qualities, courage and the childlike simplicity that would not have allowed itself to be led astray by the spurious scientific pride of the age.

Here I must permit myself an observation apparently irrelevant, but without which it will be quite impossible to understand in its true nature the spiritual void, the appalling "profaneness" which characterizes the humanity produced by modern civilization. We have already seen that positivism includes a peculiar metaphysics of illusion, which, strictly speaking, is concerned with two points, the part played by anthropomorphism, here regarded as purely destructive, and the specific "sacredness" inherent in every operation of the human spirit, which does not merely subserve out conservation as living beings, but ministers to man's higher spiritual activities. It is unnecessary here to go more deeply into the positive as opposed to the negative significance of anthropomorphism. But the second point, though actually less frequently considered, plays a very important part in the history of modern speculation. The entire illusion-metaphysics of modern philosophy since Kant—both the negative as well as the positive or cultural-pragmatic systems—constitutes in its very erroneousness one of the most instructive products of modern thought. I therefore propose to carry this line of thought a little further. I would draw attention to the fact that in St. Bonaventure the famous doctrine of the *concursus Dei* is far more profound than in later speculation. Admittedly a distinction must be drawn between the natural *concursus Dei generalis* and the supernatural *concursus Dei specialis* of grace. While accepting this extinction in principle, Bonaventure postulates, for all higher non-supernatural spiritual activities, besides the ordinary divine cooperation, a special cooperation, which is not supernatural, it is true, but which, all the same, has a special significance and imparts a peculiarly sacred and mysterious character to these spiritual functions. Later, in part from a fear of making concessions to pantheism, in part from the desire to maintain a firm boundary between nature and super-nature, this doctrine, though witnessed by the profoundest experiences of all creative spirits, was almost wholly abandoned. I would emphatically insist that this denial of a special divine assistance initiated the fatal development which has resulted in a profanation not only of man's higher knowledge but of culture generally. This brings us to the question of "scientific impartiality," the tranquil light of reason.

Impartiality, "a tranquil light," these are certainly required, but they must not be confounded with the positivist indifference to values. On the contrary, the true impartiality, the tranquil light of a knowledge untrammeled by unworthy bias, is the highest degree of wisdom, that is to say, the highest degree of the spiritual love of values, the finest and purest conceivable tranquility and holiness of spirit. The destructive metaphysics of illusion characteristic of modern philosophy has in its gradual development not merely destroyed the positive element of anthropomorphism, to replace it by the deification of the machine, but it has also represented its principle of indifference to values, which ultimately is nothing more than a very shallow philistinism, as wisdom, spiritual tranquility, and freedom from every kind of so-called illusion. It has attempted the well-nigh sacrilegious identification of its principle of indifference to values with that profoundly significant ethical purification which is the indispensable prerequisite of all higher cultural achievement, and a natural parallel to the supernatural purification of the saint. The ultimate ground for this, however, is that a genuine psychology of the metaphysical substratum as personal no longer exists, but has been replaced by a mechanical psychology of acts. The concepts expressed in the terms "myth" and "illusion," "abstract poetry," and so on, are in themselves witnesses to the disastrous misconceptions entertained by philosophy on this point of such decisive importance, at any rate since the transcendental dialectic of Kant and the metaphysics of illusion sponsored by positivism and historicism.

Unfortunately I cannot extend this digression any further. Those, however, who would understand the thorough-going intellectual snobbery that characterizes the type of man produced by modern civilization, from the standpoint from which alone it can be understood—his complete lack of any sense of obligation towards holiness or ethical value—should keep this point carefully in mind. The great significance of Goethe's personality, in spite of all his neo-paganism, is entirely due to the fact that he never permitted his intellectual creation to be completely secularized in this respect, but in spite of constant lapses always felt himself obliged to a certain consecration and purification of spirit, to prepare himself to receive the noble and holy gift of his art.

Bound up with the question we have treated so cursorily is the relentless conflict that still rages between what are termed the pure scientists and the poetic scientists. That difficulties exist in this connection I have no wish to deny. But it cannot be over-emphasized that the campaign waged by the modern positivist spirit is and will continue to be directed fundamentally against every type of ἐνθουσιασμός. This is quite natural. For the very concept, as the derivation of the term implies (ἐν τῷ θεῷ εἶναι, "to be in God," is strictly its fundamental meaning), flatly contradicts the positivist attitude towards the world. There scarcely remains a trace in modern man of that reverence for the higher zone of the human spirit which was felt by the man of antiquity, not to mention mediaeval man's reverence for the supernatural. Today the frigid, value-indifferent philistine holds almost undisputed sway. If, therefore, we are to be frank and to call things by their names, we must acknowledge that things have come to such a pass that today the noblest spirits of earlier ages—Plato, Plotinus, Augustine, and so many others—are spurned as out of date, as illusionists, visionaries, romantics, poetic natures, insufficiently cool—that is to say, not indifferent enough, for nowadays only the disillusioned are tolerated. The ages of inspiration and intuition are gone by, and already things have reached the pitch where a philosopher may quite calmly announce that unfortunately he has had no experience of intuitive powers operative in himself.

We have now, however, an inkling at least of what is wanting in Western civilized man. Positivism and historicism between them have nearly everywhere produced an identical human type, which outwardly appears of almost terrifying uniformity, but which inwardly is divided, sentimental, and so possessed by the phobia of illusion that he falls into a blind panic if he perceives anywhere a phenomenon which appears in the least incompatible with his mechanistic and naturalistic categories.

This human type is uniform—astoundingly so, indeed—but chiefly wherever the modern gospel of disillusionment, or, more truly, of the desecration of being, has been accepted in an almost childish—we cannot say childlike—spirit, as a matter of course. In its extreme form this type was, of course, only to be seen before the outbreak of the great European catastrophe, for afterwards this universal fatality startled more or less even the most humdrum from the pillow of civilization. And yet it persists today, to this extent, at any rate, that many people still imagine themselves at the recommencement of the good old times, if only, they think, tranquility can once more be restored.

Previously, however, the type was everywhere rampant. It was indeed such a wonderful age, so safely mapped out according to program, and so remarkably free from problems. Apart from the little social problems in Ibsen's plays, the insignificant difficulties of a Norah produced by the ennui of civilization, what was there really to worry about, unless one were a misanthropic monster like Kierkegaard or Nietzsche, Strindberg or Dostoyevsky? Perhaps there were some problems after all—the labor question, for example. But a smoothly-functioning state machine was taking action to prevent this particular question from becoming too acute for the present. And, after all, it was a rather unfair question—something with which people did not care to occupy themselves, because it disturbed their peace and quiet. The gathering storm-clouds of war, to be sure, constituted another problem, which people discussed at intervals. But for the most part such discussions were not serious but academic, in the style of the as-if philosophy, because in so guaranteed a period nothing of the kind could possibly happen. Generally speaking, there was no such thing as reality; so people learnt from the works of the neo-Kantian philosophers. There are no such things as stars in the sky, Natorp was then teaching; they exist solely in the heaven of astronomers. And there is no such thing as real history either. In 1914 or 1915 an over-zealous disciple of Rickert declared in all seriousness to those who were trying to puzzle out the meaning of the events which were then maturing that they should wait until at a later time the historians should have spoken. For, he argued, history is not to be sought in the events that occur from day to day; it first originates in the historian's system of categories.

In general, reality was law, or, strictly speaking concept, nothing more. The good God—well, He was dead at last. At the most He existed only in theological systems. Since the days of Kant metaphysics had been finally defeated; it was merely the pathological history of defunct metaphysical epochs which repaid study. Man, on the contrary, it had now been scientifically demonstrated, was merely the last link of a long chain of animal evolution. This human type was made uniform by its official progress through education-factories, which were the same everywhere. At the most people were distinguished—and the distinction was certainly important—by the number of years spent in their education or by the number of books that they had read. They were everywhere uniform, with a uniform emptiness and philistine superficiality. For it was easy to find an explanation for everything, when one had acquired the expert's glance, which could always be obtained, moreover, for a consideration. And all puzzles were solved, except a few minor details such as, for instance, the phenomenon of life, which, however, it was hoped would shortly be produced in a test-tube. In fact, in earlier days people would never have believed it possible that so much could have been achieved by following the positivist prescription.

Above all, the days of the great historical cataclysms already lay far behind. One had to go all the way back to Napoleon if one wanted, from the depths of a capacious armchair, to experience the agreeable and aesthetic sensation of a genuine historical thrill. The frontier posts of the European countries were so firmly wedged in the ground. Beyond doubt, they were planted there for eternity. Yes, everything was stable, amazingly stable, and as for historical movement—well, there was a certain amount going on, of course, but that was in the far distance, in the Balkans—among races that had not as yet tasted sufficiently the blessings of European civilization.

I know that in all this I shall be accused of exaggeration. For only a very few men have really suffered from the spirit of this period; the majority felt themselves at ease in this superficial uniformity. And the impression left by the sketch I have given will only be heightened by the necessary inclusion in the picture of the fact that almost everyone was unconscious of the mental atmosphere he breathed. However, to meet the charge of exaggeration I will recall two utterances of prominent men of the day, which belong to the time shortly preceding the catastrophe.

On December 31st, 1913, the eminent Berlin lawyer, Joseph Kohler, wrote the preface to a book that bore the title *Recht und Persönlichkeit*. At the end of this preface he triumphantly spoke of the victory won by the modern mind. With particular pride he pointed out that war, like private revenge, had been, so to speak, left behind, thanks to the great strides made by modern reason, which, as Comte had already said, must finally succeed in abolishing all irrational outbursts of violence. The fury of war, in Kohler's opinion, had been banished to the Far East, where it was lingering out its last days. Perhaps the Berlin savant wrote those proud words on the last night of the year, oblivious of the fact that with the stroke of twelve at his back the hands of the great clock of world history had swung forward to the fateful year 1914.

That is all very well, you may object, but Joseph Kohler was something of a visionary, with a head full of other things besides jurisprudence. Very well, then. Let me remind you of the words of an eminent statesman, who at that time held in his hands, to a certain extent, the fate of the world. It is impossible to suggest that his mind was feverish or eccentric. That man was Sir Edward Grey. Have we already forgotten the words spoken by this sober calculator when, at the moment of the declaration of war, he sought to reassure the German ambassador by remarking that of course England would call a halt when she considered that the time was ripe?[8] Were not such words more or less equivalent to Joseph Kohler's? Were they not amazingly typical of the positivist spirit that characterized the civilized man of this period, who had lost all understanding for the ever-impenetrable irrationality of world history?

Hitherto we have spoken only of the external uniformity of this civilization and of the human type it produced. It is time to consider them from within. Here we discover, in spite of the uniform surface, a really terrible lack of direction and of communication between man and man, between soul and soul. There was but one bond of union: science, which explained, and explained away, everything. Inwardly man was as free as a bird in the air. Not only was religion solely the affair of the individual, but each and every kind of conception of the universe was equally his private choice, varying from day to day, often even from hour to hour. And these conceptions of the universe, countless in their number and variety, were marketable like any other commodity. They were very seldom deeply rooted in the soil. Some there were, even, which were put on for important functions, like an order or dress coat. At such times people intoxicated themselves with the perfume of their eloquence, just as if they believed what they said, only to lay their views aside again the next morning, when they had fulfilled their purpose. An amazing riot of conflicting views was the order of the day. Woe to the young man who at this period entered the anarchy of the intellectual world. He must have fancied that he was starting on a long sea voyage, so tossed about was he from one conception of the universe to another.

Shortly before his death, Dilthey, in complete despair, uttered his memorable remark on "the anarchy of values" in which we were obliged to live. But this anarchy of values was only revealed when the storm at last broke. Men, both great and small, stood like frightened children on the shore of time, while the fearful hurricane raged itself out and the waves swelled mountain-high. For the first time men could clearly measure the bankruptcy to which the positivist spirit had led mankind. The confusion now reached its climax. The division was revealed between man and man, indeed, in every human heart. A few retained their old pride in science and took refuge in the naturalistic wisdom of the stoic. Everything is fate, they said, and the only thing to do is to submit and keep a stiff upper lip. Others recognized the want from which humanity was suffering; and they took refuge in a realm of form. But they only prized the form for the sake of its pragmatical value. They took no account of its content, or, rather, they lacked the genuineness, the energy, the courage and the childlike quality which were necessary before they could accept the content. Others, again, looked round regretfully for old discarded forms and collected them with an extraordinary devotion and love. I need only recall Anatole France and his museum of religions at the Villa Said. And then there were those who did not merely turn reflectively towards these various views of the universe, but put them into practice, one after the other. They staggered to and fro between Buddha and Christ, between Lao-tsze and Francis, unable to find foothold or rest. But at the end of all this was the dreadful howling of the wolf. The spirit dwelling within the human animal shrieked aloud its testimony to the fact that man is not merely the final link of an animal evolution but the beginning of a wholly new kingdom, the Rubicon behind which there is no return.

Since Hegel, however, the philosophy of immanence had completed its circumvallation wall of fatalism, and it was in vain that the human spirit attempted to break through it. The philosophic interpreters of the contemporary outlook now taught, to be sure, that we must take account of human personality. But when they came to the point where the circle of immanence should be pierced, and the way to the transcendental laid open, they shrank back afraid. It is in the earthen vessel alone that we find the heavenly treasure in its entirety, was the prudent opinion of one of them. There is something satanic in existence, declared another; but—so he immediately modified his pronouncement—we must not, like the Christian mythology, take it seriously as a reality. We could go on piling up example upon example to prove this phenomenon of despair, this advance to the edge of the supernatural, and terror-stricken recoil. Men could not well go beyond Hegel, for that would have meant throwing themselves into the arms of Christianity. A tragic spectacle indeed, this humanity outside the Church, this man of the early twentieth century who has been so completely uprooted. Again and again we are forcibly reminded, as we contemplate him, of the great Danish writer Kierkegaard, who already, by the middle of the nineteenth century, had so profoundly analyzed this malady of despair in all its metaphysical symptoms, in all its disquieting forms and phases.

Are men mature enough today to understand his message at last? A few perhaps. A reaction has certainly set in. But the great masses? We can hardly doubt that they must still pass through a very long development before they can measure the extent of that tremendous annihilation of values which has taken place, step by step, during the last three or four centuries. At whose door does the blame for this annihilation of values lie? What really is its ultimate and profoundest significance? The answer to this question is shown dearly enough by the foregoing analysis of modern intellectual history. But I will shortly restate with the aid of a picture what is the only possible reply.

I have often sat meditating before an Italian bookmarker, which I discovered between the leaves of a Dante. On this bookmarker there is a very original little picture. In the midst of a flowery spring landscape stands a tall cross. Christ hangs upon it, His downward glance movingly expressive of the anguish He suffers. At the foot of the cross sits a man wearing a cowl, his face supported in his hands, and softly sobbing to himself. He is Francis. Everywhere around him and around the cross there is loneliness—dreadful, terrible loneliness—for all men have fled, and he alone has remained. Beneath the picture are the words, *L'amore che non è amato*, "Love that is not loved." Further comment is unnecessary. *L'amore che non è amato.*

III. *What Are We to Do?*

Our reflections hitherto have directed our glance backwards to the widespread ruin left by the Western Enlightenment. But we are now faced with a serious question. What can we do, we whom Providence has placed in this situation, if we intend not to allow ourselves to drift passively down the stream of events, but rather to check this progressive decadence?

To answer this question seriously we must first of all clear up some preliminary questions which appear to be blocking the way to a solution of this fundamental problem of the age.

The first of these preliminary questions is this: is it still possible in principle to arrest a destiny so overwhelmingly powerful because it is the result of an accumulation of energy which has proceeded unchecked for three or four centuries? This is no idle question. The pessimism in both life and culture that has existed ever since the beginning of the nineteenth century is sufficient proof how far Western man has lost his old belief in the power of the mind and free will, which still dominated the eighteenth century, with its boundless confidence in reason. Contemporary fatalism, as manifested, for example, in the historical philosophy of Oswald Spengler, has proclaimed to the entire world that man must be regarded as simply the passive channel through which flows a stream of cosmic process wholly determined by natural law, which leaves no room for personal action.

If, in reaction against this conception, a handful of idealists take refuge in an equally one-sided method and attempt to hide with a few cheap idealistic declarations the tremendous burden of fatality which at present presses so hard upon us, this rash idealism is just as blind as the blind fatalism it combats. We have but to consider the difficult problems involved by the modern economic system, indeed by the entire machinery of that civilization which we serve, to realize that this potent destiny which we ourselves have prepared cannot be averted by an airy wave of the hand. Even the man who withdraws from the contemporary world into a lonely Thebaid soon discovers that the tentacles of civilization reach him even there, for the monasteries of today make use of the comforts of modern civilization, however determined their rejection of the spirit which that civilization represents.

Or consider the Machiavellian principle of autonomy accepted as the political principle of the modern state. How could a Christian statesman today absolutely reject this political bestiality, and build up his state entirely on the foundation of the Christian ideal of love? Obviously he could not, for by such an attempt either he would gravely imperil the existence of his country, or his own career as a statesman would speedily be cut short by an all-powerful public opinion.

We are therefore compelled to recognize both alike; the objective burden of destiny, on the one hand, and, on the other, the power of ideas, freedom and personal action. But we must not ignore the constantly shifting relation in which, historically, these two factors of liberty and fate stand to one another. The opinion of Hegel, for instance, that history consists of a beeline progress towards freedom, must be emphatically rejected. There is no constancy whatever in the relationship between these two historical forces, liberty and fate. On the contrary, the latter force, fate, is always developing by its own momentum until the opposing force, freedom, seems reduced to the minimum of a mere potentiality. The marvel is that this mere potentiality of freedom though faced by a fatality grown so excessively powerful is sufficient to enable the human will to rise superior to fate, and, at times, with such catastrophic force that in one night, so to speak, it uproots the jungle of poisonous growths fostered for an entire age by a destiny whose sway had known no check. This occurs whenever personalities inspired by a fervent belief in their mission intervene at the right moment in the causally determined course of events. The example of a man like St. Francis in the thirteenth century should prove to us how erroneous is the doctrine, recently advanced by Max Scheler, that ideal factors are impotent in face of real factors; that is, we regard the former not, like Hegel, as ideas acting impersonally, but in that concrete form in which alone ideas normally take shape, namely personalities, inspired by a powerful faith, which have always been, through the world's history, the agents of the Eternal.

We have only to look about us to find contemporary examples of the spiritual energy which at times a single man can infuse into his age. In Italy, for instance, Mussolini appeared, and Italy followed him. In Russia Lenin, and Russia abandoned the lethargy of Oriental mysticism and took his path. I am certainly not suggesting that in future the world must travel along one or other of these two routes. These two figures, both of daimonic power, are simply examples of what man's personal will can accomplish when face to face with a destiny apparently overwhelming. They further prove that in principle nothing prevents humanity from returning to the Christian road, if hereafter personalities arise who will make the Christian spirit an effective factor in world history with that enthusiasm which alone has from the beginning accomplished the miracle of freeing man from the burden of his animal nature and leading him upwards to that hallowed summit which rises above space and time.

It cannot, of course, be denied that at the present day a peculiar difficulty stands in the way of such a possibility. We have already seen in our preceding inquiry how profoundly the piety innate in human nature has been destroyed since the power of Christian faith was defeated. We must therefore ask whose mission it shall be to become, amidst the indifference of Western humanity, the leaven of a new energy of faith, the salt of the earth. The mission of Christians generally? That is impossible, for the Protestant Christian of today has been, to all intents and purposes, robbed by a liberal sciolism of his full belief in Christ. Movements of regeneration within Protestantism, such as that led by Karl Barth and Friedrich Gogarten, only confirm this terrible fact. Fundamentally, therefore, in the midst of the universal intellectual and religious chaos, only the Catholic remains to undertake so responsible and sublime an apostolate in the Western world of our day. And when we remember that the forces of destruction broke in fullest fury upon the center of Europe, the region of Teutonic culture, we may say that the brunt of responsibility rests on the shoulders of German Catholicism, on that section of the Catholic people which lives in the heart of Europe, and which, ever since Luther and the Council of Trent, has had to put up one single unbroken struggle to preserve its Christianity and Catholicism.

This fact, however, complicates the whole situation still further. For this mission of a Christian apostolate to the Western world falls precisely on those Catholics who in the course of the long struggle for their spiritual and intellectual existence have themselves lost something of the original spontaneity of their faith and Christian life. It is true, no doubt, that among the peasant masses between Cologne, Munich, and Vienna faith is still everywhere genuine, strong, and practical. But among the urban proletariat the situation is entirely different; for the worker in the towns, because he is more intimately bound up with the machine of Western civilization, is strongly attracted by the current of international indifferentism. The position of the Catholic intelligentsia is more difficult still, though it is they precisely who should take a very special part in this great Christian mission. The clergy are hardly capable by themselves of undertaking and carrying out successfully such an apostolate. For the clergy—chiefly concerned, amid the universal movement of secularization, to maintain intact the purity of the faith—have on this account been obliged to a certain extent to let the modern world go by, and can no longer even understand its language. The educated Catholic laity, however, is for the most part either itself infected in some degree with the poison of modern religious indifference, or else, where this is not the case, usually lacks at least that theological equipment without which it is practically impossible to engage with any hope of success in the mighty intellectual struggle of today.

It will, however, be better perhaps to leave all such considerations on one side, and calmly ask ourselves another question. What actually can happen? This question has nothing to do with empty prophecies, such as are in vogue nowadays. We would simply consider a few eventualities of future development, and perhaps in the prospect of these we shall find the answer to our main question, what are we to do?

Now, first of all, it would be possible to allow things to go quietly forward in the direction they have taken for the last three or four centuries, the steady downward trend of intellectual and spiritual secularization to proceed unchecked. We should then look calmly on while the positivist spirit of the age reinforced still deeper its dogma of the mere immanence of being and propagated it steadily among the great masses of the people. The inevitable consequences of such a nihilistic apostolate are scarcely doubtful. The example of Moscow should have proved to the most blind indifferentist that where the purely fatalistic principle of *laissez-faire* is given full rein events will work out their inevitable logic and produce the fall of Western civilization. For when man loses faith in the power of positive ideas, things begin to dictate to him the law of their intrinsic development, and—amazingly enough—always find nihilistic personalities to carry out their work of destruction when constructive personalities are wanting.

We might, indeed, ask what it matters, after all, if Western culture is destroyed. It would not be the end of the world. World history would merely assume a fresh aspect, by the shifting of its center of gravity from Europe to some other continent. And the Catholic could go further, and add that even if Western culture were destroyed, the Christian work of salvation and its natural-supernatural institution, the Church, would survive the ruin intact.

No Catholic worthy of the name would attempt to deny this last contention. For him, the Church of God—*portae inferi non praevalebunt contra eam*—stands fast as a rock amidst the ebb and flow of temporal movements. And yet we, too, we men of the Christian West, are called upon to assist, by our action and our sacrifice, in assuring the stability of the Christian sanctuary in a non-Christian world. This indeed belongs to the supernatural aspect of our Western history. But from the natural standpoint also we are faced by a demand no less grave. For "man must make history," as Willy Helpach aptly put it; that is, it is not permitted to any man or race to renounce the will to heroic action, so long as even a spark of life remains in that man or people.

It is, of course, possible to visualize another possible development. History is, after all, not only the work of the human will. It represents a certain cooperation between the human and divine wills, a mysterious interplay between the providence of God and the intentions and deeds of men. We might therefore ask whether God's providence may not someday intervene directly to effect a decisive turn in this downward process? God could indeed raise up among us great saints, men and women, who would set an example to their age of supernatural life actually lived, and, at the same time, by their personal sacrifice, mystically effect, as it were, a vicarious redemption from the tremendous load of universal guilt, whose weight prevents our contemporaries from ascending to a higher level of spiritual existence.

Has not this perhaps actually happened in France? Was not the spiritual life of nineteenth-century France penetrated in its entirety by the silent, one might almost say anonymous, sanctifying work of quite simple people, who offered themselves to God in order to make atonement, not for themselves alone, but for their country and their age? And were not these souls genuine springs of spiritual power which, as time went on, watered the land which Voltaire and his fellows had laid waste? Already we can estimate how much the revival of the Christian spirit among the Catholic intelligentsia in France owes to the holy life and work of such a man as the saintly Curé d'Ars. Do we not meet everywhere with the profound traces of his activity? Those who have read Huysman's *Cathédrale* or *En route*, or Bernanos' *Sous le Soleil de Satan*—I have no intention whatever of excusing or concealing the jansenistic blemishes of this latter work—will understand the extent of France's debt to this single man. And they will also understand what it means. It means that for humanity there is not only a degrading solidarity of fate and guilt, but a solidarity of goodness also, and that whenever a human being in silent self-dedication devotes his life wholly to God, the general level of personal conduct around him immediately begins to rise, whether or not we are conscious of the effect.

Why then, we may ask, should not God raise up among ourselves also some great figure, like, for instance, St. Francis or St. Dominic, who through the miracle and grace of his character would bring about at one blow the great reaction, which the weakness of our hands and the poverty of our souls makes it impossible to effect by the natural way of isolated actions. It would surely be a mistake if we men of little faith denied the possibility of such an amazing intervention of Providence. But it would be equally mistaken to sit still and placidly await such a miracle of grace in order thereby to get rid of all personal responsibility. That would be as disastrous a fatalism as that described above. It is true, *spiritus ubi vult spirat*; we can never force the Spirit's miracle of grace; we must hope for *it*, wait for it, beg for it. But we must never make such a hope the pretext for sinking into a mystic lethargy, for shirking personal effort. We ourselves must begin to take action, and only then may we justly expect that God will act with us. We must ourselves try to prepare for the new outpouring of the Spirit.

This brings us back to our question, so pregnant with responsibility: What are we to do? Immediately we are faced with a fresh difficulty. It is that great alternative which faces us in the first place as Catholics. This alternative arises out of the intrinsic opposition between nature and supernature. Catholics of every age have had to wrestle with it. Today, however, an unambiguous decision on this twofold relationship, a clear and resolute choice between these factors, seems more urgently requited of us than ever before. We have already seen clearly enough the extent to which the world of today is "disenchanted," to speak the language of Max Weber, that is of the modern mind itself; "atheized, de-Christianized" in the Catholic terminology. The originally fictitious *status naturae purae* today no longer seems a fiction; it seems to have become very real. Subjectively indeed—that is so far as the attitude of modern man is concerned—it has actually become a reality, among wide masses of the people. In consequence so wide a gulf has opened between the natural and the supernatural order that it might seem impossible to bridge it. Is it then to be wondered at, if one party in the Catholic camp urges a policy of wholesale retreat to the *status fidei*, kept uncontaminated from all modern culture, though the desecrated world be thus left to take its own way to destruction? The Catholic's primary duty, they urge, is to secure his personal salvation and the purity of his faith; everything beyond this is the concern of Providence, and that self-regulating development of modern culture which has now lost the faith for good and all.

Obviously such a counsel of despair could not pass uncontested, and inevitably it has given rise to an acrimonious dispute within the Catholic camp itself, on the line of action to be adopted in this critical juncture. Those opposed to the policy of wholesale withdrawal plead for a courageous apostolate to the modern world, they advocate a firm advance from a position which might justly be termed a form—if only partial—of Catholic Stoicism. And, however seriously the demand for the preservation of faith at any price must be taken, from another point of view it represents a surrender to the power and fatality of our desecrated modern culture, and the extremist policy of retreat *intra muros* manifestly involves a stoic despair.

But a further question arises out of this controversy within the Catholic camp. Will not our disputes about the line of action to adopt result in bringing all action to a standstill, and ultimately in making it impossible? In actual fact, has not this controversy gradually weakened the initial vigor of German Catholicism, until today it is in danger of being entirely paralyzed? And, meanwhile, has not this internecine conflict between Catholics so poisoned the atmosphere that not only are those who stand without beginning to turn away again disappointed, but among Catholics themselves a disquieting uncertainty is becoming noticeable, an uncertainty that, unfortunately, has already produced many distressing consequences?

Of what use, however, would it be to settle this great question of the relation between nature and supernature, between culture and Christianity, theoretically, unless we also grappled with the practical demands of the times? At a crisis like this the most urgent necessity is to act. It is no time for theorizing, still less for theorizing over a problem that is one of the most difficult that theology has to consider, which in practice must be settled differently for every case, situation and individual. But here we are back at the question: What we are to do? What are we, each in his place, to do at a crisis which must decide the fate of an entire epoch?

In treating this serious question of conscience we must no doubt recognize the truth contained in the "catacomb" policy. Every important modification of the general ethos must proceed from the profoundest depth of personalities whose interior life endures unperturbed however the tides of contemporary opinion ebb and flow around them. Modern morality has entirely forgotten that the wellspring of all ethical change must be sought in the interior depths of the soul, and that, therefore, the root of every ethic is embedded in a radical stability of disposition, in the ground once more become unconscious of the acts which manifest a moral and moralized nature.

Operari sequitur esse; action follows being: this maxim also holds good for the being that has been and is constantly being produced by our action. Thus the first duty of the Catholic of today is to comply as strictly as possible with the demand of the secessionists so far as the preparation of his own soul is concerned. He must not at first presume to think of anything but of strengthening from day to day the life of faith in himself, as the early Christians did amid the decadence of antiquity. And the more cheerfully and earnestly he works at this primary task of personal preparation, the more sure will be his success. This, however, entails much more than would appear at first glance. For it means that we must eradicate in ourselves the critical, indeed hypercritical, spirit with which even Catholics, as partakers of the modern mind, are filled. It means that once and for all we must avert our gaze from the temporal aspect of the Church, which, like a creeper, covers with its rank growth the eternal, and in the tendrils of which we are in daily danger of becoming entangled. As Catholics, we must try to recapture the quality of reverence, reverence for what is eternal in the Church. The criticism we must then employ upon the temporal accretions that surround the eternal nucleus will then become of itself different from what it has been of late years in certain quarters. Even if in individual cases we find much to displease us, we must accept with complete trust the general line of development that runs through the Christian tradition of the centuries. Such a confident and positive attitude, however, is possible only if with childlike joy we identify ourselves with the unity of faith. If we will do this, all the obstacles arising out of modern social distinctions will automatically vanish. The man who kneels in church before the gracious image of the Mother of God is not divided by his intellectual culture, be he statesman, artist, or thinker, from the intellectually less cultivated man who kneels beside him, for he shares with him the same supernatural atmosphere. Indeed, he feels at once that the mere presence beside him of the relatively less cultivated man passes over to him something of his being, so that a union is effected between them, in the very substance of the soul, which no method of intellectual cultivation that modern pedagogics could devise, however ingenious, could produce.

Moreover—and here also the uncompromising secessionists are in the right—this personal preparation involves of itself a certain apostolate. It is always the being of a personality, which has the greatest power to attract his environment, if the latter is inwardly weaker. Moreover, it is the being of a particular quality (*ad hoc*) that chiefly performs this miracle of attraction; the serious, genuine being, which is no mere show, but lives in the center of the self—is objective, childlike, happy, and trustful, fed by the central energy of faith itself.

But how absurd it would be if in sight of a personality that has thus molded not isolated deeds but its very self, we continued to torment ourselves with the question whether we ought to undertake the official task of evangelizing modern culture or not? The problem is already in a fair way to solution the moment we set our hand to the plough and seriously undertake our own moral and religious purification. Inevitably the effects of our new interior life and personal disposition will reveal themselves in our action upon our environment. The alternative, Christianity or culture, now loses its meaning. Every view of the universe immediately generates its specific cultural energy. Why, then, should Christianity—which, after all, is no mere view of the universe arbitrarily adopted, but the junction of man's nature and supernature with an objective, natural and supernatural truth—be unable to effect what is within the power even of purely subjective conceptions of the world?

To be sure the faith of the Catholic can never be pragmatic. From him above all is demanded a being genuine through and through. He must never content himself with the flower when the root and stem are of supreme importance. Yet if he complies with this primary demand, inevitably, given certain conditions, his tree of life will begin to bear its buds and flowers, for such is the nature of every living plant. There can be no doubt that Fra Angelico had in the first place to become Fra Angelico the saintly friar, and that with all the ardor of his Christian and childlike spirit. But it is equally unquestionable that once this condition had been fulfilled, or rather while it was being fulfilled more and more every day, the artist within him was putting forth—and could not do otherwise—the splendid blossoms of his art.

Why should not that which was possible centuries ago be possible again today? The intrinsic laws of history and of the human soul are the same at all times and in all places. We may indeed ask ourselves how long it will be before that great process of secularization is reversed whose final phase we are now witnessing. But a question like this is, after all, thoroughly un-Christian, born of an impatient anxiety over this world. Christian faith does not live by sight, but by belief in the Invisible. And, therefore, it always involves Christian patience, that is to say, the long deep breath of Eternity. But it is actually possible to answer the question here and now. This process of regeneration will be accomplished in the very hour when we Catholics unite in the serious reform of ourselves. When we have one and all effected this self-reformation, each in his own place, at once, inevitably and simultaneously, a force of attraction, natural and supernatural, will be generated so potent that none of those standing without will be able finally to resist it. No doubt the difficulties involved by the opposition between Christianity and a de-Christianized culture will not be disposed of at one blow. But they will begin to disappear, and a new age will dawn.

Yes, what are we to do? What am I to do, and what are you to do? It is, of course, impossible to answer the question in detail. But a general answer is easy. It will be this: *crede et fac quod vis; ama et fac quod vis; ora et fac quod vis.* Believe and do what you will; love and do what you will; pray and do what you will. And that in turn means—get on in every respect with your own work. Make *yourself* Christian: completely Christian. Then look around you, and perform the work that has been given you, according to your capacity. But wait in patience. For it is only the sowing that is your business. Leave, with childlike trust, the gathering of the harvest to the generations that God has called to that magnificent task.

Notes for Crisis in the West

1. EDITOR'S NOTE: It is, however, sub-divided into *matter*, in the strict sense—non-living energy, and *life*—living energy. Wust, I think, makes too little of this distinction.
2. E. L. Woodward, *The Twelve Winded Sky*, p. 68.
3. Cf. Wust's account of the "tragedy" of Dilthey, below, p. 96ff.
4. F. von. Hügel, *Essays and Addresses on the Philosophy of Religion*, 2nd Series.
5. Of course this is but a very rough statement. Discursive reasoning achieved *enormous* triumphs in the Middle Ages. We have only to think of St. Thomas. It was, however, confined to certain aspects of the intellectual life and to a comparatively small elite. The masses were frankly barbarous. Moreover, the scholastic movement represents, in one aspect, the birth of rationalism, though a rationalism still controlled and integrated by faith and intuition, With the nominalists the work of disintegration had begun.
6. Narrow in its exclusion of non-religious interests or blindness to the positive values in other creeds.
7. TRANSLATOR'S NOTE: *Historicist*, i.e., regarding objective truth as merely the relative and temporal expression of the historic process.
8. Lichnowsky, *My Mission to London, 1912–1914* (New York: Doran Company, 1918).

THE NATURE OF SANCTITY

A DIALOGUE

by IDA FRIEDERIKE COUDENHOVE

Foreword

The author of this dialogue, Ida Friederike Coudenhove, is of Austrian origin and was born in 1901. She is representative and indeed one of the leaders of the Youth Movement in Germany, more particularly of its Catholic manifestation, and is closely associated with the group headed by Romano Guardini.[1]

Her line of thought is symptomatic of a vitally important trend in young minds today. Religion, institutional Christianity, Catholicism is being widely challenged for its alleged inability to provide a consistent way of life within the modern world. Whatever its worth in the past as a regenerative, educative force for the individual and society, it is no longer in touch with human conditions, needs, ideals: that is the indictment. This has come as a challenge to Catholics and has had the effect particularly in the younger generations in France and Germany, of calling from them an effort precisely towards a vindication of the vitality, inclusiveness and coordinating power of the Faith. It is impossible to take religion as a matter of the routine observance of "church parades," as an ethical system consisting mainly of negations, as a body of doctrines held by the mind only. With many other hitherto accepted facts of life it is being put to the test. But it remains that the only test is to live it:

to be fully alive and aware of life, with religion as the condition and completion of existence. What difficulties and questions that enterprise raises, when we see it carried to its ultimate conclusions in the life of a saint, are dealt with in this essay.

T. F. Burns

The Text: The Nature of Sanctity

A: We have just passed the Feast of St. Elizabeth. I wanted to keep it in mind with as much happiness as I have every year in the past—but this time I could not. An obscure discomfort came upon me when I thought of her, as if there were something amiss, a touch of unreality between us. So let us talk about her for once quite honestly and critically, setting her in the clearest light, and then see if the mist surrounding her will disappear.

B: Well, tell me first which St. Elizabeth you mean, so that we may know whom we are talking about. Is it to be the St. Elizabeth of the colored pictures, of the sentimental poems and plays, that picturesque figure of almost sickly romance best known to us in the pose of the "miracle of the roses"—the model patroness of yesterday's charities and today's social works: in short, that St. Elizabeth who really stands as a symbol or a badge for a whole category of beautiful and edifying qualities, a banner, a catch-word, the synopsis of a whole program?

Or are we to talk of the historical Elizabeth, daughter of the Arpads and the Meranians, wife and widow of the Count of Thuringia, the extraordinary penitent of Marburg whose mysterious and entrancing personality no one has yet quite "explained," no, not with all the piety of Catholicism nor with the historical criticism of Protestantism?

A: You touch on what has become very doubtful to me. But my difficulty goes further. I do mean the true, historical Elizabeth, and I feel ashamed and conscience-stricken that we should have reduced this unique woman, this rich and living personality, to such a banal picture as you describe. She was a human being, in more senses than one, a marvelous, queenly creature, pure and radiant, such as seldom lights up the long centuries. Naturally, in her day, a personality so brilliant and so rich could only be explained by the miraculous—an extraordinary person in those days was perforce accounted a saint, unless he belonged to the Devil—and so it came about that an unfamiliar halo and a place in the Calendar were bestowed on her.

True, she was devout, exceptionally so; I have no intention of toning down the picture as some people attempt to do for St. Francis, her greater brother in spirit, making him into a mere inoffensive nature-worshiper and so falsifying him. But this piety of hers is not the most essential thing in her, it is only the garb of her time; it is not *her* soul but the great soul of the Middle Ages. Every strong intellectual or spiritual current had then to flow along this, the only available, the only known channel. In this sense alone does piety belong to her of necessity—an external necessity of history, of time, and not arising from the nature of her own being. How right Lulu von Strauss-Torney is when she concludes the epilogue to her fine life of St. Elizabeth (which is not at all rationalistic, but deliberately retains the most childish embroideries of her legend) with this pronouncement: "She was at first only the kindly ghost hovering over the Wartburg and looking down upon us from its walls. She became the stiff figure under the canopy, with the halo on her brow, the brocade mantle of legend upon her shoulders. Then the saintly glow faded and a childlike figure of womanhood trod with simplicity, head meekly bowed, the bread of charity in her hand, her cloak thrown around a crippled child. She lifts her head and smiles. And see—it is the eternal human face, the face of one dead yet living." That is better said than I could say it. When I read it I felt a tightness about my heart: we have no courage, we Catholics, to see "the eternal human" face, least of all in our saints. Our fathers knelt with childlike faith before these visitants from another, better world; and they were right because that was their sincere faith. But it is wrong, because it is insincere to keep these tinsel haloes.... Why do we say "Saint" when it would be enough to speak of great men, heroic examples, kingly leaders? Why do we not dare to understand that it is their human personality which makes these mighty dead impressive and immortal? No one would deny that their Christian piety gave strength to them, but honestly, quite honestly, was it not also the deepest and subtlest danger to their splendid humanity? Did it not destroy, and suppress, and forbid much that would otherwise have blossomed magnificently? Must we not ask ourselves about many of the saints: what would he not have become without his "sanctity"? And do you not think the answer would often prove depressing and disturbing to the Christian? Look—I have it now—what troubles me so acutely and constitutes so powerful an indictment in Elizabeth of Thuringia is this: she was never wholly herself, was not allowed to remain herself, because she had become, as you and yours understand the word, a "saint." The Elizabeth of the poets and the painters is a wistful dream of her humanity, without tribute to the certainly great and heroic, but also murderous power of the asceticism of her day, the asceticism of the Church. Of course it is idle to imagine her without this asceticism, it is finally part of her picture. Nevertheless, I seem to see her image as perplexingly double, as if two pictures were painted one over the other.

I see the human Elizabeth, pious, God-loving, indeed devout, but human all the time...the gracious lady of the Wartburg, wife and mother, in her happiness, in her kindliness, and her bitter, undeserved grief. It is she who lives in the hearts of children and of the simple people; she whom everyone can understand and must love, be he Catholic, Protestant, or outside the Christian pale, for she confronts him like a figure in a fairy-tale, a dream of the human heart, like Parsifal and the Holy Grail.

But beside her, a threatening shade, almost eerie, a ghost amid all this brightness, stands the "Saint." Or do you really think it necessary, valuable, or beautiful, that she should have been subjected to that dread figure, Konrad of Marburg, the incarnate spirit of gloom and harshness and terror; that she should deny her race and blood, and even forget her motherhood, the most binding of natural ties, for the sake of an unnecessary "love of one's neighbor" (more correctly termed, love of strangers); that she should let even her charity be laid on the rack of her obedience to the gloomy Magister; that she should pray to God to free her from love of her little ones?

This second period of her life is hard and incomprehensible; it repels and hurts. And, mark you, this second Elizabeth is not sung or painted. She seems to me a defection from an ideal, not the ideal of her time, true, not even known then, but one which for us stands high and supreme above all others: a pure, rich, upright human personality. This ideal she sacrifices—without understanding what she is giving up—to the ideal of her day, no not only of her day, it is the ideal of Catholic sanctity, which means the annihilation of values, the loss of personality and the destruction of every fresh green shoot of Nature. Yes, I must say it, the impression is irresistible that Saint Elizabeth, the ascetic of Marburg, destroys the beautiful and gracious lady of the Wartburg, fetters everything most lovable and precious in her. And she is not a solitary instance of this self-destruction.

B: You mean that the human Elizabeth and the saint were two conflicting personalities, not in the sense in which in each of us the sinner strives against the child of God, but as it were two competing ideals: that of natural human nobility and that of the Christian, in his most perfect manifestation, the saint. You say that in this melancholy, tragic struggle, the saint won, supplanted and destroyed her opponent. Have I understood you?

A: Yes.

B: I should like to prove to you how mistaken you are. Certainly there were two forces in Elizabeth as in every child of man—what Plato of old called the "two horses." But that has nothing to do with your problem. No, the saint in Elizabeth is only thinkable, is only possible, in the flesh and blood and with the mind and heart of the human Elizabeth. The saint is, so to speak, the natural Elizabeth raised to the highest degree, her ideal figure formed and chiseled out of the precious stone of her humanity, inseparable from it. How can I express it so that an exaggeration may show you what I mean? She is the human Elizabeth and more, raised to the limit, the utmost possibility of her being, completed and perfected. Elizabeth is the saint just because and just inasmuch as she was the human being. She is a splendid proof of the old dictum *gratia supponit naturam*. She became so holy in all the respects that you reckon to be against her human nature just because she was so intensely human. And, moreover, not she alone. What you just now more or less stigmatized as the "Catholic ideal" of sanctity is a conception which demands thorough revision. Your view of its unique character, its origin, its detailed characteristics, and your general impression of it cannot pass unquestioned. Or are there no misconceptions in this sphere?

Misconceptions of sainthood! They would supply material for a book, not merely for an evening's conversation.

But as a beginning I would say just this: that we, today, with all our refined spirituality and our scientific study of religion, our accumulated experience of innumerable Christian generations, our intensive ethical culture, our superior psychological and pedagogic methods—combined with our religious literature, our retreats and systematic meditation and all the rest of it—that we, with all this machinery at our disposal and such a mass of good will, should see so few really great, convincing Christians amongst us (of course we cannot pass any final judgment, but we are told to know them by their fruits) is, I venture to say, due to one simple but sufficient cause: we are not human enough to be saints. No, right from the outset, from an utterly false notion of piety, we dare not let ourselves become human beings. A human being is made not born. We do not let our children grow up into real, healthy men and women, we wish them to be simply and solely Christians—and we forget that grace needs a deep, reliable, healthy, natural ground if it is to take root and bear a hundredfold; that otherwise the "supernatural" remains in the air, is unnatural, a phantom without strength or life blood, and will therefore disappear before the first onslaught of a real power, springing from strong, natural roots.

We talk of spiritualizing, and fail even to grasp that the word itself implies that there must first be something to spiritualize. Visit the Galleries in Munich and Basle and see the saints depicted by the mediaeval painters. Look at the gay, robust figures of Lochner, Dürer, Holbein, and Hans Baldung Grien and the many nameless painters. See how, for all the halo of unearthly glamour which invests them, they stand against the landscape of their own country, "with strong and sturdy limbs planted on firm and enduring soil"—men of flesh and blood; in recognizable costumes of Nuremberg, Cologne, Bruges, or Florence. And then go across and look at the saints of El Greco, clad in timeless "garments" floating in vague, cloudy regions, with shadowy greenish features and emaciated hands which could hold neither weapon nor distaff; bathed in weird light, stiff, or writhing in feverish ecstasy—their gaze ravished into Nowhere. These, indeed, are no longer men, but neither are they angels—man is not meant to be an angel—they are gruesome chimaeras, arbitrarily put together, with bodies hung on them like ghostly sheaths already withered and falling, never created by God.... Compare these pictures and then perhaps you will know what I mean.

And Elizabeth? The essence of her humanity is that she is a great lover, a generous heart of incomparable capacity for self-giving. And the essence of her Christianity is that she is a saint—and that means literally the same thing, a great lover, a heart with an incomparable capacity for self-giving.

That Elizabeth, the woman, was a loving heart, and more than that, a loving soul, you allow. That is proved by all the accounts which we have of her. Loving, not using the word with that faded significance which today mostly attaches to the term love, that is, when it is not charged with sensuality—as if we knew love only as sentimentality or lust! Not "love" then, of the idyllic, pathetic and "poetical" sort, but that great love in which passion burns, unmeasured, dangerous. A loving soul: that means that in her love there lived that spiritual element which raises it, so to speak, to a higher dimension, and gives it a new quality of danger and finality, because it lifts it into the sphere of the permanent, indestructible, irrevocable, inalienable. Do you begin to feel how perilous it is, what courage is needed to risk such love?

You also spoke of danger, but as if speaking of a stealthy disease. That is far too mean and poor a view. Certainly the passion of Christianity is dangerous, but as an avalanche is dangerous, or a slowly descending landslide, or the spring flood of a suddenly awakened sea, sweeping away all boundaries and marks of ordered life and renewing the face of the earth.

Elizabeth could love. The story of her marriage with Ludwig grips one's heartstrings so powerfully at times that one almost wants to stop reading, even the unadorned frank statements of eye-witnesses—whether it be the depositions of her maids or in the life of Ludwig—because it is as if one were assisting uninvited at the confidences of two people who are alone together. Wenck, indeed, once maintained that these statements are not reliable, that they are proofs of a popular revolt against asceticism, and must be understood as an attempt to translate the saint into human categories and especially to adorn her with the affecting traits of most devoted wifely affection. But his argument seems to me completely unconvincing. Even if we grant that individual details are "legendary," nevertheless they reflect a truth which shines with overwhelming evidence through all the ornamentation and is in complete harmony with Elizabeth's character and way of life: the fact of her happy and holy marriage. When we remember how childishly young and without choice in the matter Elizabeth was when betrothed and married, like most royal daughters of her day, and how impersonal such marriages were, arranged solely from dynastic interests, and ennobled only by the wife's Christian obedience and the common desire for offspring, then this marriage does indeed seem a miracle of tenderness. The love of Elizabeth and Ludwig was a most pure friendship, an intimate accord of souls who from childhood had so grown together, that it was assuredly no empty word, but the expression of something real when they called each other, even after marriage, "dear brother" and "dear sister." How deeply confiding is the noble way in which, as a matter of course, Ludwig accepts Elizabeth's actions and that unrestrained Hungarian passionateness which was incomprehensible to his sober, German mind. How great a freedom he allows her, and what respect, in days when a woman was entirely under the tutelage of her husband, he shows, in allowing her to keep her rule of food at his table, although it amounted to a reflection on his own conduct. What a depth of understanding between these two, even in the secret places of the religious life where each of us is left alone, is contained in that simple phrase: "The angel of God was often the messenger between them."

The "spiritual" taste of today, which always mistakes a weakness of nature for the supernatural, will be tempted to conclude this was a "purely spiritual" love, a non-sensual affection, and that this precisely is its "edifying" feature. Those who really believe such an attitude a part of sanctity should ponder such episodes in Elizabeth's life as these: her fever of anxiety when she was still but a child, lest she should lose the affection of her betrothed; how she pines and droops under this consuming anxiety, and how happily she blooms again when he sends her a little mirror as a love-token. Unbounded, and contrary to many people's notions of perfection, is her pain, her yearning grief, when Ludwig has to leave her—for battle, on a journey, or feudal warfare, for the Emperor, for court-service, or bound for Rome. Then she cannot be parted from him, follows him for days in all weathers, puts on widow's weeds. So passionately does she cling to the sight of the beloved, so much does she hunger for him, so deeply even to the heart's core does she know, does she feel, the bliss of remaining for work or rest, in the warm, living presence of a beloved being. And boundless is the passion of her joy, her starved longing for his tenderness, when he returns—impetuously, heedless of his retinue, she throws herself into his arms and cannot let go of him, so insatiable is her joy at the sight of him. The naif chronicler tells us: "She kissed him right heartily with more than a thousand kisses on the mouth." She is so entirely human, burningly, hungrily, tenderly human; unrestrainedly yearning for warmth, nearness, caresses; whose deprivation was a sore burden to bear; the blissful possession of the present, a delight wellnigh infinite. Such is she; *Saint* Elizabeth, already at that time the saint of charity, of penance; nursing the lepers, obedient to Konrad von Marburg, going hungry at the princely table to obey the rule imposed upon her food, scourging her body, rising from bed in the night to pray for hours, chilled to the bone, until her husband, fearing for her health, imploringly draws her back to his side.

Do you really still contend that holiness must make for inhumanity, destroying human warmth and beauty in the heart? Elizabeth does not seem to have known any of that fear which torments so many today, and has for so long tormented believing and pious souls (who can say how much it torments and worries them?), the fear that a true love of God is not compatible, with "real" natural, burning love of a human being; with a love that fills the whole self and not only the "soul," or what is understood by that—for who can say that with a really great love the blood too does not catch fire from the white-hot soul? A love that knows the pain of parting, anguished longing and unappeasable loneliness; a love that hungers for caresses and must express itself in caresses, even maybe with that boundless measure of blissful joy which Elizabeth, the saint, showed. Do we not often think of all that as "sensualism" in a derogatory sense—as of the flesh and the world? If we would only take our standard of perfect and imperfect from the actual lives of the saints and not from learned abstractions "drawn from" them, many would be saved great inward anguish and conflict.

It remains true no doubt that destructive forces threaten behind these great and holy powers and that the soul must always be watchful or maintain a religious discipline and responsibility before God. The chronicler never loses sight of this, his entire account of Elizabeth's married life reflects his own warm and simple humanity, depicts it as at once tender and austere. "The love and devotion which they bore to God subdued all undisciplined and inordinate desire and excess. The fire of God's grace drove out all sloth and indolence."

And Elizabeth also knows that other tension to which the love of every Christian is subject; a tension and a peril which only we, the bondsmen of Christ know, and not the world. We know that the holiness of our love is in peril, not from what is lower than itself, but what is higher. Or, to put it better: it is not endangered from below, but our love, which seen from below, from the level of the human, is a height, a peak, the highest in human life—nevertheless "lowers," exercises a pull downward, when seen against a much greater height; a height so great that by comparison the highest earthly love is shallow, a void—may even be a fall, the more sheer, the higher it is in itself. Here we must let Kierkegaard speak, for he has experienced it as very few. The actual experience of this tension became the catastrophe of his outward life, and the turning-point in his inner life, when, to find the right path, he broke off his betrothal.

> Learn and never forget this melancholy lesson: the truth of our earthly life is that no love between human beings can be or should be perfectly happy, dare be quite secure ! For, from the divine standpoint, the happiest love between human beings has always a danger, of which a merely human conception of love knows nothing, the danger that the earthly love may grow too violent and impede our relationship with God, the danger that our relationship to God may claim the happiest earthly love as a sacrifice, although humanly speaking all is well and no danger threatens from any quarter.
>
> From the possibility of this danger it follows that even in the happiest state of love you must be on guard: not lest you grow tired of the beloved or the beloved of you, but lest you or the beloved or both should forget God.

That Elizabeth experienced this reality of the Christian life the following striking legend shows. Once during Mass her gaze fell on her lord in his festive array, and she was so deeply moved by the beauty of the sight that she quite forgot the Holy Mass until roused by the sound of the bell. She turned her eyes again to the Altar and perceived the Host to be bleeding.... And it is told that she long remained weeping and disconsolate over this sign, so that Ludwig could scarcely comfort her.

That is the tension of Christian life; felt at times as a heavy burden, the shadow which clings to all earthly good when seen in the light of faith. Because of this the Christian view of the world *appears* so much darker than the pagan; appears checkered with a darkness the more intense the brighter faith's light shines upon it. The beautiful, the noble, and the excellent can become temptations *because* they are beautiful, noble, and excellent—temptations not towards the base and ugly, and not for base natures who are tempted by other things and in other ways, but for those who, with open hearts and delicate sensibilities, with great reverence, and yearning desire to approach these high things because they are so good. This is the "pilgrim's temptation," to weary of the road, and to build, before the time, a refuge in the creature, for warmth and protection against the troubling immensity of the invisible, the call of eternity. But we have no right to evade the suffering in which this situation continually involves us, by turning in childish spite against these good things, railing against them as base, or contemptible, and declaring flight our only salvation. What is most alive in us does not believe it, and secretly stretches out its hands towards them, the good and gladdening gifts of God; and this secrecy can become a danger indeed and ruin the soul. Nor are we justified in declaring these things, the innocent creatures of God, free from sin only to condemn the desire and hunger of mankind for them as sinful and shameful, something that must be rooted out and smothered. Of course there are really dangerous things and really sinful desires, but we are not speaking of these now. Just as there is a true beauty and excellence of created things that comes from God, so there is also a right response to them in men's hearts, healthy and strong and noble. The worthier the man, the stronger his response will be, the stronger his desire and hunger for created happiness, because it is the mirror of eternal values.

How comes it, then, that we Christians so often forget what the pagan world knew? Have you read in the *Phaedrus* that moving passage where it is said that every earthly beauty is a similitude of the eternal beauty, so that indeed only those who have already gazed on the Godhead can recognize it...but the unsanctified and perverted will not easily be brought to see beauty—"for he is blind and knows not how to adore"?

No, this tension is not between good and bad, but between the lesser and the highest good; it is not the struggle between light and darkness, but between the candle and the sun; not between nature and corruption, but between the natural and the supernatural, not between man and devil, but between man and God. It is a part of our humanity and our relationship with God. It cannot be removed, only denied, or evaded, or bravely and humbly borne. Certainly one can cut the knot and force an unreal solution. We spoke just now of flight—but then the desire still remains. We can, to be sure, put on a contempt of the "world," which poisons and enfeebles our desire, but such peace is built on a lie, and works great ravage. We can kill our human sensibility, to make ourselves proof against the pain of the conflict—but these are the methods of Stoics and Buddhists, in my opinion not the right attitude for a Christian who must still be obedient to his manhood, the manhood God has given him....

A: That sounds well, and I should like to believe you. But I feel a slight uneasiness as I listen. There must surely be something that is not good, something defiling and defiled, something guilty in even the purest and loveliest "earthly" things; otherwise we should not always find that God strikes them as if in anger and destroys them utterly—even where there can be, perhaps, no question of "punishment for sin." I believe, and I think I believe it more deeply than you, that the things of the world are good and that man has a right to them. That is my complaint against sanctity as you conceive it, that it seems to depreciate and question them. But it seems to me that man can only keep this right, this joy, by a faint defiance of God; that he must hold it as a fortress which God threatens, and which God finds an inexplicable delight in destroying.... That is a situation the consciousness of which goes back long before Christianity; it is what the fear bred of innumerable experiences called "the jealousy of the gods." You see in this also it was easier for the ancients: jealousy of the gods, that interpretation of a fact experienced by us all is clear and illuminating, it puts the gods moreover in the wrong, gives them the inferior role, and men the heroic.

But the Christian, since he has a God to whom he cannot attribute jealousy, must argue in the contrary sense: "These innocent creatures are not, after all, quite so innocent. There *must* be something in the things themselves which provokes the divine wrath, the divine condemnation...." We have, you see, only to take one step further to land ourselves in the dualistic war between spirit and matter, between God and the world, in which being born is in itself sinful, and the finite as such unclean.

B: And where does the first clause of the creed come in? *Factorem coeli et terres, visibilium omnium et invisibilium*? I believe untold mental bewilderment and spiritual difficulties arise from our inability to make up our minds to take these words seriously, and to the letter. The jealousy of the gods...there is a good deal to say about the Christian interpretation of the fact that you speak of. But of that another time—for the moment just this: we spoke a few minutes ago about the tragic opposition between finite good and absolute good. When a man falls between them, may it not be that what we are tempted to call the "jealousy of the gods" is God's solution of the conflict? That He knows the hour when His own precious gift will be our danger and will defeat His purpose—and that He then destroys His creation and takes it away from us? And we rack our brains for deep and fantastic reasons, would like to put Him in the wrong as jealous and cruel, and wrap ourselves in the heroic gloom of a tragic guilt.

You have brought me now to another point I had not thought about—the question of man's rights to things. I think "rights" a very dangerous word. "Man" has a "right" to—yes, shall we say, to life, to "happiness" (another very questionable notion, this happiness) to a family, to a healthy body. We may perhaps lay down this "fundamental principle." But the concrete, individual man—where is his right? You or I, he, she—in relation to each other in society, and the state, in any community, even in the Church—there we certainly have "rights" and can, may, and must often assert them and fight for them. But as against God? Man has not even a right to faith, that God should be obliged to grant it him, he has not even a right to the most intimate and absolutely indispensable condition of his sole eternal salvation: to Grace. That is implied in the very word. It is hard to believe but so it is. How much less right have we to the things which are not necessities of life but extras—even though these extras may mean one hundred times more to us than life itself? Everything is a gift, every thing. The commonest as the rarest; that I have two eyes, that today the sun shines—these are gifts no less than that I have my baptismal grace or the incomprehensible joy of a true friendship. Our thinking of them as "rights," our claiming them without gratitude, our complacent security may deserve God's lightning in the midst of our seemingly pure human happiness...and the far-flung glare of such a portent may warn others; a sign from the Lord that no man's possession is signed and sealed, but a new gift which we receive anew every day, and every day may lose.

A: But that is as if we were walking on thin ice and with every tread there was a faint threatening crack. It means we must believe ourselves walking on a swaying bridge over a dizzy abyss of nothingness.

B: No, not quite that; for if indeed the support of a creature breaks under us—as may happen any moment—the only abyss into which we can fall is the Hand of God.

A: What has become of our St. Elizabeth?

B: I was thinking of her. Her life is an excellent example of what I mean. Were we not speaking just now of the touching beauty and happiness of her married life, that married life which was everything that the union of two people can be, a fruit of finest stock, grown on the sunny side of life, in a peaceful garden? It was blessed with children, and was not merely a narrow domestic happiness, but the pledge of a whole country's prosperity, an example to a whole people and many courts. What more do you want? It seems as if not even the purely human dangers attached to so many loves were there—that narrowness and exclusiveness which many strong passions bear within themselves like the germ of mortal disease, presaging no good end in spite of present happiness.... This danger, to which perhaps the woman is more liable than the man, never seems to have existed for Elizabeth in spite of all her passion and surrender. Just as Ludwig had his very protracted and fairly complicated military undertakings which took him constantly away on

Saxon and Polish expeditions, or on journeys with the Emperor, Elizabeth had her great works of charity inspired by all the fire of her unbridled, exuberant nature: her hospital in Eisenach, the great food distributions, her sick and poor. These do not merely take up her time during the long absences of her husband—though we cannot but feel there is a something of a relief and compensation in this unresting activity. They also occupy a large part of her daily life when he is with her, neither hindered by his presence nor disturbing their happiness in being together. This independence, this division of interests, to be at home thus in regions where the beloved is ever but a guest, this reserve of solitude in the midst of union (which is perhaps felt as hard and strange in hours when the longing for perpetual union stirs with an overwhelming force but which is the salt that preserves our love from sloth and shallowness), all these Elizabeth, it seems, possessed and guarded from her youth up.

What was there in such a marriage to displease God? Or are we not driven to the conclusion there may be other motives for God's refusal than displeasure and punishment? For this dreamlike beauty, this hallowed and luminous joy did not last long. It is shattering when we think how young she was! Scarcely twenty years old when the blow fell.

Ludwig took the Cross. You know the touching story how he did not dare wear the Cross on his coat "that his dear hostess S. Elspeth be not aware of it and be distressed and affrighted thereby, she loving him beyond measure and with her whole heart."

And how one evening, she searched in his pocket, found the fateful sign there, and sank down "frighted to death," she carrying then her third child? There follows the heartbreaking farewell, when Ludwig's firmness through all the lamentations must excite our admiration. Do you remember how she "in great pain and grief" rode for a day with him, after his mother and all others not belonging to his company had turned back, but when she attempted to part from him her heart was so heavy with sorrow that she went the next day's march with him too, because the bond of great love and the might of her suffering constrained her to forget the world and be with him, and she did not know if she should stay with him or go, until his knights had almost to force him to send her home. And then she turns home in tears and mourning like a widow. She puts on weeds, and from that time on knows no pleasure, and commits herself to God's hand in solitude and grief.... Only think with what difficulty and how sparsely news came through, what confused and fantastic ideas those left behind formed of the distant lands and the strange heathen countries.... We can assume, too, that a heart so closely united, felt and trembled at every danger, every distress he must undergo. She brought her last child into the world without being able to let him know—it was a difficult time, truly, for the poor young wife.

Endlessly long must her days have been, an aching burning void, in spite of her dear children and the new-born child, in spite of her active care for the poor and hungry.

But the worst, the inevitable is coming. Ludwig succumbs to a fever in Brindisi. Nobody dares to tell her. It is strange perhaps, that no inkling of his death tormented her. But her starved, waiting, hoping love was too firmly clamped to belief in his return...he must, must, surely come back.

At last the old Countess Sophie dares to tell her.

Look well—here her "humanity" is revealed as in no other feature of her life—unbounded and passionate as was her love, is her grief now—unbridled, unreasonable, despairing. "Dead, dead, dead is all happiness and pleasure in life." Screaming and weeping she rushed through the castle "like a person demented." Of what use here any abstract maxims—how a perfect Christian must "take up his cross"? Idarnarie Solltman is quite right; if anyone had come to Elizabeth at this moment with pious phrases about God's Providence and the meaning of suffering—she would simply not have understood. She, the saint, founders in the boundless sea of her sorrow, and all the dark waves submerge her.

Tell me, is she not lovable in the comfortless abandon and misery of her woe? It is, in truth, a bad thing in the face of a living catastrophe like this to philosophize and annotate. But what I wanted to show you was only how human Elizabeth the *saint* was, how much more human feeling, flesh and blood and passionateness in the most human sphere she had than most of us would dare to have, even if we could.

A: So far you tell me nothing new. But the death of Ludwig is the end of the gracious *woman* Elizabeth. Now the life of the saint really begins, of the professional saint I should like to say; the fanatical ascetic of Marburg, the disciple of Meister Konrad. Until, worn out...I nearly said "by this senseless business," she dies—a strange, nunlike shadow of her former self—at the age of twenty-four.

B: You have touched upon a crucial point. That is what, apparently, nearly everybody feels who studied her life—that Ludwig's death seems to divide it into two parts which sharply diverge. Only the interpretations differ. Pious hagiographers, let us say of the last generation, remark with satisfaction that the Countess can now live her "true" life. Protestant historians regret (as you do) that this catastrophe wholly unbalanced the inner life of the girl, always at high tension and endangered by its own intensity, that she is no longer on guard against herself, and a "feverish striving after superhuman holiness" begins, bringing her soul no peace, her body to an early grave. Also the best Catholic biography that we have (that of Maria Maresch, the Viennese historian) puts the finger on this break: "The great problem in the life of S. Elizabeth," she calls it, "the spiritual development of the Countess into the Franciscan."

The book is a very good critical study, historically as well as psychologically, but this one thesis I am unable to accept. It seems to me too clever, too "interesting," too psychologically developed, too reasoned. But we shall come back to that later.

Maria Maresch, too, sees in Ludwig's death a complete break with her youthful and married life. Now begins "a new phase in her life": that of the widow, the penitent, Sister Caritas, the saint no longer of earth. And she gives her contention a subtle psychological basis: this revolution, this violent leap into a totally new life comes "from a deep instinct of self-preservation in this oppressed soul" who was at home only in her love for Ludwig, and who now stands homeless between two worlds, who cannot bear to continue her former life after the catastrophe, and therefore must alter her inward and outward way of living.

Here I can no longer agree. It is an exceedingly attractive and tempting reconstruction, but I am afraid, artificial. I see in Elizabeth's life an absolutely straightforward development, only perhaps that at first her way lay through green mid-summer woods, afterwards through wintry barrenness, and so more visible to our eyes. But it is one single line. She did not become a Franciscan first on that Good Friday in 1229 or 1230, when she laid her hands on the bare altar of the Minorite Church at Marburg, and Brother Burckhardt cut off her hair and put the rope girdle round her. It was only the full blossoming of the bud, that was all.

Just glance back at the records. From tenderest infancy all the outlines of sainthood as we know it are there: penance, poverty, charity.

What her women and former playmates seem to remember best of her childhood days are a lot of tiny significant traits, self-denial in her play, sometimes concealed with childish cunning, sometimes bravely done as an example. At the time of her greatest human happiness, when newly married, we hear that the young princess chastised her body with fasting and scourging, that she made her servants smite her in her room, especially on Fridays and fast-days, that she indeed put on purple and gold brocade at times to please and do honor to her lord and his friends, but underneath she wore the hair shirt. She seeks hard and coarse work, she the wife of a prince, sits with the maids and spins wool—and that meant more in the Middle Ages with its strong class consciousness than it does today. To obey the rule forbidding certain food, she often went hungry all day at her own table, though so young, indeed not yet fully grown, and bearing a child every two years. Was that not a truly hard penance? And look at her care of the sick and poor. It is something wholly different from our sensible and practical welfare work and organized charity. It is inspired by an altogether personal and unquenchable thirst, one might almost say pursuit, of the hard and the unpleasant—a pursuit, in fact, of self-conquest. Think how she seeks out the lepers, even the most scabrous, how she openly or in secret takes the lowest and most disgusting services on herself—yes, she steals such opportunities and hides away with them, and when her women catch her at it, as if at some mischief, she laughs like a child who has played a trick on them. And her poverty! A long, long, time before the vow of that Good Friday, when the first gray Brothers, the troubadours of God, made their appearance in Germany, her heart went out to Holy Poverty with the dreamlike certainty of a bird set free returning to the forsaken nest. As a young bride, trembling at the poverty of the Crucified, she takes off her crown in the Church, to the vexation of the Court, even of the pious and austere dowager-countess. Naively exact, the legend relates how she took off every useless and worldly vanity, crown, bracelet, silk band, colored veil, plaited sleeve, and clothed herself in wool and "vile" linen.

She wore fine clothes only to please her husband, and hardly was he gone, and she no more under this obligation, than she seized on the poor clothing, as though at last she might "have a holiday." The first Minorites came to the court shortly after her marriage, and she chose Brother Roger as her confessor. Then she hears for the first time of Brother Francis, far away in the land of Italy, and it is a recognition and meeting in spirit—you know the legend, how Cardinal Hugolino persuaded St. Francis to send his old beggar's cloak to the devout Thuringian princess, and how every time she had a special petition to make to God she put it on her shoulders.

She is such a child, and poverty is so much her heart's desire that she plays at "being poor"—real play, as children play at "being grown-up." So at least I understand the story how she sat with her women, took off her ornaments, put on poor clothing and a clumsy kerchief on her hair and told them: "So shall I be clad if by God's appointment I suffer poverty."

Later legend saw in this episode a prophecy of her fate. I see in it the spirit of a child who says in serious play: "when I am poor"; just in the same way that another says, "when I am grown-up." It is touching to see how the princely child pictures poverty—which she is going to learn so thoroughly later. Do you know the story how she confided to Ludwig how beautiful it would be if they were both quite poor, so that he had to plough and she to milk, and if they had "only" a yoke of land and two hundred sheep—making the more practical husband laugh aloud and say that that would be splendid poverty indeed with two hundred sheep? In the same way she "plays" at being a poor woman when, after the birth of her child, she goes to Church for the first time, to be churched, and walks secretly (not therefore for edification) dressed as a peasant woman with bare feet, and presenting the offering of the poor. She does the same on Good Friday, mingling with the crowd and offering small candles and coppers as poor women do—causing displeasure to some who find it unfitting for a princess to make such trifling gifts.

To sum up: her great and wide charity fills her life from the beginning. As a child she steals everything in the house that is not a fixture, and takes it to the poor. Her life at the Wartburg is filled with unceasing service to beggars, cripples, nursing mothers, travelers. Right at the beginning of her married life occurs the story of the leper whom she puts in Ludwig's bed—to the very natural horror of the mother-in-law. Almost as well-known is Ludwig's humorous reply, meant however to be taken very seriously, when on his return from court duty at Cremona his irritated stewards inform him that Elizabeth's indiscriminate bounty to the beggars has wasted his possessions: "Let her give, in God's name, and do good to the poor, as long as we keep the Wartburg and Neunburg!"

And Elizabeth takes full advantage of this magnanimous permission. Yes, her "good works" were anything but a reasonable, practical charity organization, and *our* charitable associations which bear her name would soon expel her from their membership. It was an almost wild, almost dangerous passion, which Konrad von Marburg, with iron severity, forced into a practicable channel by a bitter and endless battle against her nature, though not against her will. Just as one compels a beautiful, untrammeled waterfall to work a power station.

While pestilence, famine and war, floods and bad years impoverished Germany, she built the hospital at Eisenach. While the Count away at the court could not provide for it, she invited a hundred poor people daily to eat in her presence; gave away the jewels out of her coffers, and probably all the costly ornaments that her proud ambitious mother had sent as dowry with her little daughter, betrothed at the age of four, whose fairy-tale splendor astonished even Count Hermann's showy court. She gave everything away regardless, with both hands, to the poor, for them to sell.

Among the most endearing of the Wartburg legends are those in which she appears, by a miracle of God, before her guests, "more splendidly and beautifully arrayed and adorned than a Queen of France," though she had literally no decent garment left in her chest, and did not know how she was to appear in the hall without shaming her lord before ambassadors from a foreign court.

After Ludwig's death she really can do *less* than before. It is true she spends all the revenues from her widow's estate on the poor, and lives herself on what she earns by spinning wool for the convent at Altenburg. With the excellent motive of preserving this source of supply, Meister Konrad prevents the final legal alienation of her property, and cuts down in every direction her personal charity, indiscriminate and passionate. You will remember she was only allowed to give pennies to the beggars, and with childish cunning, as we must call it, and rebellious obedience, has silver pennies made. Then she is only allowed to give loaves, and at last only slices of bread. So the zenith of her almsgiving, if one reckons by the size of the gifts, was actually *before* Ludwig's death.

You see, do you not, that all this was not an asceticism forced upon her from outside, a painful and violent distortion of her personality, due to the external catastrophe which laid her life in ruins? It belongs to her nature and demands a simpler and more profound explanation.

A: I would gladly accept the explanation which you refuse. This penance, this extravagant desire to spend herself in the service of the poor and needy sprang from the craving to forget, the thirst for oblivion felt by a soul wounded to death. It is so over and over again; how much of the most valuable spiritual, intellectual, artistic, or social work whose fruits we enjoy thoughtlessly and with easy conscience, springs from the aching sorrow of wounded hearts seeking and finding a narcotic in ceaseless, excessive service, just as weaker men seek a physical narcotic in some drug!

B: Let me postpone the answer to that for a moment. Her asceticism is capable of yet another explanation. Maria Maresch tells the same story, and her explanation is as follows: All through Elizabeth's life there is a thirst for humiliation and abasement. She must surely have had a reason for this. Only some threatening danger could initiate such a conflict. This danger must therefore have come from *within*, and the demon's strength can be gauged by the sharpness and relentlessness of the struggle he called forth. The writer continues: Elizabeth was the daughter of Andrew of Hungary, the Arpad, and Gertrude of Meranien; she inherited, like all members of these violent, ambitious families, the racial curse of "the will to power." She learnt in childhood the tragedy and bitterness of this thirst for power when her mother was horribly murdered during a rising in Hungary. Under the influence of grace she resolved to root out this dark inheritance in her nature by an iron discipline. During her widowhood she once said to Konrad that she "must heal and compensate for that which had gone before"—and on these words Maria Maresch builds her theory. I remember verbatim the sentence with which she concludes her explanation, since it once impressed me so strongly as the final revelation of our saint's soul. "She wanted to heal and make compensation for one extreme by another, to quench the burning lust for power and possessions, so deep-rooted in her family, by abasement and self-denial so deep and so unbounded that she bore even the blows of Konrad of Marburg. That is the creative idea which informed Elizabeth's life."

It is a profound, a great, an appealing conception, but I can no longer subscribe to it.

It may well be that her entire stock, proud, blood-guilty, and held fast by the bonds of the world, obtained remission of its sins in her, the spotless victim, thus permitted to bear in this pure young scion "holy fruit" in the eyes of God. But I do not believe that Elizabeth was at all conscious of this—I mean, that she intended to conquer the racial inheritance in herself, and that her heroic austerity sprang from a purpose of compensation and self-discipline. Moreover, to my mind, she is too naive, too unstudied; indeed, I cannot believe that the racial curse ever existed in her. Her words to Konrad can bear another interpretation (oh, these patient texts that admit any possible interpretation!) and I know of no single situation in her life, no word or gesture, that, for me, points to an inner struggle of this kind. I do not believe, either, that this is due to the "gilding" added by venerating followers. With a host of saints we see the scars left by the struggle which achieved their sanctity, and they shine like trophies, but in *her* portrait as we know it, is there not an altogether unique tint, a light indescribably fresh and tender, for all the reckless strength of a heart that knew no bounds to its love, its courage and its endurance, a radiant simplicity, artless and limpid, like the purity of a child who knows nothing of guilt, struggle and victory? It is not easy to believe that she was exposed to any great inner danger of this kind. None of her "heroic deeds" seem to have been wrested from her in conflict with her nature. I have already told how she steals her penances as a magpie steals a glittering object, or a child pilfers apples—just as impulsively, naively, instinctively.

If she had been rigidly training herself to overcome her nature, "hating her own tendencies," as Maria Maresch says, then her impulses would not have run away with her obedience quite so often. Meister Konrad had no easy task to tame the fire in her! It is forever breaking out again, against all her good resolutions; he forbids her to go near infectious cases, and she brings them secretly into the house, begging her maids not to complain of her to the strict Magister—and when he discovers it she allows herself to be beaten with hard blows. But no sooner has he gone away on a preaching tour than she has found some other poor waif to hide in her hut, share her bread with, and on whom to pour all the treasures of her love.

Can one say that her path always lay against her inclinations? It seems, however absurd it sounds, that she really felt quite differently about things from the normal human being, and that she would have needed more patience, mastery, and strength to lead a "reasonable" life than she did for what even in those days was a fantastic and irrational one. And this, not because she had an unhealthy or unnatural taste, but because a living power was driving her, the overwhelming force of her fiery, untamed nature. No; her deeds are the expression of an inner necessity, not a habit learnt in obedience to an alien standard.

I can find no trace in Elizabeth of a conversion, a re-orientation, an inner revolution in any sense whatever. If I am to find a psychological problem in her life, it is not in the discontinuity, but on the contrary, the astonishing simplicity and continuity in her character. She actually belongs to that category of saints who today are less highly esteemed, those who really seem somehow to have come "straight from heaven," the "born" saints.

Our sympathies go out much more readily to an Augustine, a Magdalene, a Charles de Foucauld; or to those who were not indeed sinners in the full sense of the word, but worldlings—Francis, Ignatius, the great Theresa, or Madeleine Sémer—we are grateful precisely for this dark chapter in their lives. It is the link of a chain connecting our lowliness with their height.

In this great and lovable family of converted hearts and minds Elizabeth has no place, and it would be arbitrary to class her with them. She was almost born with a halo round her "dark and lovely face"; or to speak as a Christian, she received it at her baptism, like every one of us. Only she never lost it again.

A: Why do you take away from the saint the *one* feature which would have reconciled me to her halo? Everyone respects a hard-won holiness; it is impressive, and nobly human, even if one cannot sympathize with the form the struggle assumed.

So she became a saint by following her abnormal nature? Is that holiness? In that case what seems great and difficult in her efforts would be neither difficult nor heroic—not even meritorious; and her perfection only the cheap victory of one who had no difficulties. I see in that at most an injustice of fate, not to say God, but not an edifying or soul-stirring drama.

B: I expected that answer—it always comes. It is true that the expression a "born saint" at first offends us—but why should God not lavish gifts upon man as He wills? Why should He not sometimes show us how He planned man to be originally—how rich and beautiful and lovable He made our much-abused nature; how it is possible to be *naturaliter Christianus* and yet a human being; just as, in those converted saints, He shows the power of regenerating grace, the elasticity and curability of human nature, how indestructible is man's nobility, how abiding and sure the faithfulness of his Creator? Why do we accept the second and not the first? Why does the first rouse our resentment when actually it should rouse our pride with the thought that we belong to the same noble stock from which such fruit can spring? It often fills me with surprise to see how deeply the economic—capitalistic is the truer word—mentality and its valuations have corrupted even our ethical and spiritual ideas. Here is a typical example! We see in the possession of grace and in the natural virtues of such people only "private property" in the bad, capitalistic sense of the word, derived from *privare*, i.e., that what they have is withheld from us others, indeed robbed from us. It is an undue share of things to which all have rights, which is selfishly enclosed and shut away from us in those privileged persons. Is it not so? Instead of seeing that in the Kingdom of God there is no private property but only that fellowship of the saints to which St. Paul constantly returns. What each possesses belongs to the others, and necessarily so; in strictness it is not a case of one man giving himself to others. He is simply the vessel into which God pours his fullness; the port into which God can run His rich cargo; he is not only God's means of giving, he is the gift. He is, above all, God's gift to us, to every one who knows how to receive, to accept a present, rejoice and give thanks. He is a letter written to us, and instead of reading it, we are annoyed because the message is written in his life instead of in ours—though it is for us.

From the same capitalistic spirit comes also the question of the "merit" of the saints—better say their cost. In our eyes a thing is only well earned if a man has worked for it himself. To receive gifts, to exchange gifts, is suspect.... Can you not see that the *price* of the sainthood of St. Mary Magdalene and of the sainthood of St. Elizabeth is at bottom the same—the Blood of Christ? And that the Divine choice involves its human cost to the chosen, which he must pay, namely, the greater sensitiveness of the noble-natured, an increasingly severe testing of his worth and endurance, of his generosity and purity of heart?

Again, the saints, and this saint too, get—to speak vulgarly—"nothing out of it" during their lifetime. They are certainly not consciously aware of their sainthood; it is not a psychological fact that you can experience—any more than grace itself, for that matter. For them it is, rather, a painful and mysterious fate, and to the world a scandal, for it is part of the "hidden things of Christ." It is not as if the saint admired and enjoyed his own halo—he is not conscious of the rays which invest him, making him a beacon above the sinful world, he suffers but the scorching heat of their purifying flame. Neither did I say that being a "born saint" implies the absence of all difficulty! (And if it did, would that be enviable?) Had Elizabeth a path of roses? This supposition betrays at least a complete lack of imagination, and depends on the assumption that pain and punishment are identical—that the only battle, heroic battle, is against sheer evil. Of course Elizabeth had her daily battle, like all of us, against daily faults, but that seems to me the least interesting thing about her. Her real warfare was on another level. Must I put it plainer? Do you not believe that the struggle with God, the struggle of the wrestler Israel, may be harder and more terrible than the struggle with the devil? No, the sainthood of a saint is as little an injustice against the rest of us as the fact that a man is a doctor is unjust to the patients he has to cure.

To be sure, you have an excuse for your attitude. There is nothing more exasperating than the behavior of people who take their lack of temperament and their apathy for Christian perfection—who look down on the honest struggles of humanity with a "How *can* they?" These people believe themselves gentle and humble because they take with a smile an insult to the pride in which they are naturally deficient; are obedient because they have neither initiative nor desire for the burden of responsibility and hold themselves purer than others and "detached" because they have never felt the warm generous impulse that lifts man out of his chilly, petty self, and throws him into the arms of another. That a shallow and purely external concept of perfection confuses such types, unfortunately only too common in this age of pigmies, with the lofty ideal of genuine holiness, has enormously contributed to discredit the latter in the eyes of the healthy and courageous.

A: I come back to my question more bewildered than ever. Everything we recognize as unusual, inexplicable, and yet admirable in Elizabeth you call the fruit of an inner impulse; and moreover it seems that you call this inner impulse her *sainthood.* And you say at the same time that it was in the flowering of her fine, noble humanity that she became the woman she was, and no other. What do you mean, then, by this word "sainthood," in which I am disposed to look for the key of the riddle; which is both human and inhuman; which you do not first discover in her works, the works being themselves its fruit; which is not social service for "humanity," nor yet the ethical, pitiless self-mastery of an overstrung and dangerous nature?

B: Now at last we have come to the heart of the question. But I can only answer by giving an opinion, which is nothing more, and pretends to be nothing more than one opinion among many. You can, of course, find many definitions in books; but the saintliness of the saints is perhaps differently reflected in every believer's conscience, as in turn Christ's holiness is differently reflected in every saint. But you are right, the holiness of the saints is the solution of the riddle, of all we cannot or perhaps will not understand in them; it is the key to all their secrets. And so we will see whether we cannot unravel the mystery of saintliness with the clue provided by a human, but saintly, figure. If we can understand sanctity in Elizabeth, we can understand it in others also.

The saint is a friend of God. The phrase has been handed down by the age-long tradition of the Church—valid and official currency. He is a man who is in the relation of a friend to God, and God to him, a special, personal, intimate and vital relationship, different from that of the ordinary God-fearing and God-seeking believer of good will. A friend of God. The term friend includes a whole range of meanings, from the most vapid convention to the utmost, most tremendous intimacy. Understand it here in its fullest and richest significance, as denoting something altogether exceptional and extremely precious: a person, no, two people have dared, to take each other into the inmost sphere of their lives, to stand together before God, to have a right to each other, as far as a Christian can claim a right over another. Friendship in this sense is nothing else than love, in the unique simple meaning of that word which we have so unduly narrowed down and confined to particular manifestations. The saint is, therefore, a person whose relationship to God is one of personal love.

To the saint God is not "a necessary postulate," an abstraction, not an unimportant matter-of-course, nor yet a mere comfortable and comforting Truth; but something real, or rather—*the* Reality. To him God is not the "Sovereign Power"—the *Summum Bonum*—Law or the Absolute—in no sense some Thing, but Some One, not It but He; no, not even He but Thou. The rest of us also believe in a personal God, and that distinguishes our religious position from every other. We wish to love Him, we wish to serve Him—and God in His mercy accepts that because we have nothing else. But the saint's love of God is different. Our love of God is like our love of our neighbor. The seed was, we know, planted in our hearts at baptism, but, like a seed, it lies buried and invisible in the earth, rich no doubt in possibilities of flower and fruit, but so far as lifeless, bare and rigid as an actual grain of corn. And when we see the love of the saint like a rose-tree in a splendor of luxuriant blossom, our courage begins to fail. Then reason comes to console us: Love of God is after all no matter of "feeling," but of the will only; a good will suffices, affection we can confidently leave to the sentimental. Believe me—nobody rejoices more than I in the truth contained in these familiar words; it would be a poor look-out for most of us if God required more than that we should try, as best we can, painfully and stumblingly to do His Will. But I believe all the same that we dismiss the problem too lightly when we turn the truth that a good will is sufficient into the exaggeration that it is the only right attitude, and everything beyond that unimportant, mere decorative trappings. Do not misunderstand me, "feeling" is, I maintain, often most unduly depreciated. In such discussions it is allowed only one meaning, and that not its most important or most worthy. It is confused with sentiment; and understood as a vapid, sweet froth, a temperamental indulgence, "pleasure" or "enjoyment" in love, such as the serious man whose love is a matter of "will," neither needs nor desires. It is true that this kind of feeling exists, but besides this inferior sentiment and "will," there is a third way of loving: emotion as a vital force, a reality which must invest the will if it is to catch fire and not remain only the "will to love," but become actually love. There is, therefore, emotion of great power, of high quality, of profound depth, of creative energy. Is not so-called "earthly love," when genuine, "feeling" too? And yet it is poles removed from that insipid, color-wash sentiment to which people try to drag down the word. Is love then a "pleasure"? Is it not, with all its bliss, one of the heaviest, most painful burdens a man can carry; a charge on all our energy, full of tension, of fear and trembling, of problems and claims, of profoundest earnest and melancholy, of anxiety and reverence? Is it ever simply an attitude of will, chill to the very core, directed solely by common sense? No, it is more than that—a unique and living thing—and not the most subtle psychological apparatus succeeds in explaining, analyzing and labeling it. But it is a fact, and we know it, and we cannot explain it away by putting will on the right hand, "superfluous emotion" on the left. It is enough, certainly, in God's mercy, that I, as I have not this great love for Him, but only the desire for it, should serve Him with a loyal will—but it is by no means the same as love, is the slow and toilsome way, not the goal.

Such an attitude of will is good, necessary, sometimes the only necessity, but the foundation stone can never be the cross on the pinnacle, and I do not see why, for my own personal consolation,

I should exaggerate what is necessary and *therefore* precious, into the only precious thing, as if there were nothing higher, no summits far above me.

True, I can serve God and serve Him loyally without the great love of the saints; I can serve Him as the faithful servant, the loyal vassal and soldier who willingly gives all his strength to his Lord, and his life too, when it is needed, but who would never *dream* of entering into the King's presence, who would draw back in confusion at the hint of a confidential talk, still more of a caress... He is content to stand on guard his life long, and work in the knowledge that the Master knows about him too, and that he is allowed to do his work. I believe there are many such Christians to whom God is a genuine reality—but always only He, the Lord of Lords; never Thou, never the Friend, never the Beloved. Even this is a great and a beautiful thing. Only think of the grand worship of the Old Testament, whose relationship to God is almost wholly of this kind. It is, indeed, love, but the love of the servant, the follower, strong as life and faithful to death, but not the love of the Friend, love of Love.

The saint, however, is the friend of God, the lover in the great heroic sense. Perhaps when we know something about a great human love we realize a little what our love to God is *not*. Then for the first time we see the appalling difference between the living fire, the capacity to do and suffer, the thirst for self-sacrifice of the former—and the pettiness, chilliness, and satisfied ease of the latter.

Seen from this standpoint so much becomes intelligible in the character of the saints which to mere critical reason seems unnatural or even untrue. We read of a St. Aloysius who had to be ordered to turn his thoughts away from God because his weak body could not bear the continual strain—and we shake our heads and to escape the necessity of passing a judgment, doubt at least whether the report is reliable. But no such wondering doubts of their psychological truth are stirred by such lines as the following.

Rather, everything alive in us seizes upon them with gratitude, for they sound like an echo of our own hearts:

> How shall I then hold back my soul
> That it no more may touch thine own;
> Or lift it over thee to things above?
> Ah, gladly would I drag it down,
> In darkness lost, to some far deep.
> In darkness lost it could no more vibrate—
> When deeps in you are trembling.

Why can we only understand here and not in the other case?

Or consider the saint's *humility*—the real fear for his salvation which seems to us so superfluous, the consuming remorse for sins which scarcely seem sins to us, the life-long tears over this and that mistake that seems to us so natural and not worth worrying about, the profound conviction of personal unworthiness, even when the rest of the world is already on its knees in reverence. Such humility seems to us mistaken, something intrinsically impossible, forced, unjust. Yes, if he were not a saint one would detect in it the most revolting form of crooked and perverted vanity.

But who does not know the passionate, inarticulate confession of the heart bowed to the dust, abashed and trembling, because it is so utterly unworthy of the love given to it, unworthy of choosing, and being chosen by, the friend? Does an undeserved love not show up our defects and faults in a light incomparably more glaring than all the reproofs and scorn of our enemies? Oscar Wilde once achieved this happy phrase: "No human being is worthy to receive love. Love is a sacrament we ought only to receive on our knees with 'Lord, I am not worthy,' on our lips."

What then, when a man apprehends as a living reality with the whole of his startled soul the tremendous fact: that God wishes to be his friend...that God has called him from eternity to this, to be His own, and not only that he should be God's, but, far more difficult to understand, and infinitely more difficult to believe, that God will be his? Do you think that that man will study moral theology to reassure himself of all the sins he has *not* committed? Can he do otherwise than remain tremblingly aware of his infinite and unalterable unworthiness, in silent adoration of a choice which he can never, never understand, but by whose reality, notwithstanding, he lives every hour of his life?

That is why the humility of the saints is so immeasurably deep, so passionate, so alert, so unforgetful, inexorable, and implacable—and so fearless withal, so calm; without tormenting shame or "inferiority complex," without flight, subterfuge and contortion. For they know for sure that the Lord has taken this very Nothing that they are, this poor wretched nothing to His Heart, laid His kiss upon it, and made it His friend: *quoniam voluisti me*. What is the cold philosophical humility of those who recognize their littleness before the greatness of the Cosmos—after all, simply a difference of quantity—when compared with the glowing humility of the lover?

I come now to what is perhaps the most important feature in the character and life of all saintly people—a feature which Elizabeth exceptionally displays in exceptional relief and intensity, namely a life of sacrifice, penance, self-denial, poverty. Here I must be allowed wider rein, there is much here that calls for discussion. There is a stumbling block here, and not only for those to whom sacrifice is an irritation and a folly. Here lies the root of much spiritual danger for those who seriously seek to imitate the saints, but who see only their external actions and misinterpret them. Here is the core of the many fatal misunderstandings in our popular versions of asceticism; of endless scruples of conscience and heart-burnings for sincerely religious people, of endless perversions and distortions. What does sacrifice mean in the life of the saints?

For we see the saints sacrificing all, every earthly good in the human experience: property, honor, marriage, home, family, learning, work—everything. And so completely, so insatiably, so extravagantly! Flinging away with both hands! And we either turn away shocked and dismayed as at something unnatural, some pathological self-mutilation. Or we draw the conclusion that what was sacrificed must be of little or no value. How bad, how base and worthless that must be which the saints in their sublime, God-given knowledge despised and forsook, and how inferior those people are who seek and hold fast to such things! How culpable we are, how corrupt our nature must be that we hunger thus for things which the saint shuts out from his life! In both criticisms sacrifice is understood as a negation, carries an unpleasant suggestion of compulsion and extortion, destruction and refusal of life. It is a word that stirs uneasy fears, as if something dark, fanatical, cruel, and hostile lurked behind it, against which everything in ourselves that is young, strong and shining struggles in self-defense.

At most we admit sacrifice only as a spiritual and mental exercise, to train a strong will, and achieve an iron self-control which will temper and fashion our natural instincts into a pliable instrument for the spirit's use. Certainly it has this purpose, and it is a very important and valuable one, but there is much, very much more in it than that. I might almost say that to understand what sacrifice means we must go back to the pagans. For them it was a solemn and festal, a glad and beautiful affair; and only a valuable thing, indeed only the most valuable thing was good enough to offer—the first-fruits of field and herd, the unblemished fruit, the choice, the rare, the precious.

Even behind the darkest abuses, the sacrifice of children and kings, this conviction which we have so completely forgotten, is discernible. A sacrifice is a gift, chosen because it is precious, for the offering it is anointed, crowned and garlanded, and the priest is clad in festal raiment, himself garlanded, incensed and greeted with songs. But what need to quote the pagans. Have you not noticed that the Church herself sacrifices with lights and songs, amid flowers and incense? Or what is implied by that symbol of the Benedictine spirit, the never-ending liturgy of praise, but that the monks make their offering, the offering of their lives, as in a burst of song? How totally we have forgotten this! Sacrifice is giving—giving something to God. But our "sacrifices" disregard the first laws of giving among men and women. A whole coil of contradiction lies in the thoughtlessness of our popular notion of sacrifice. In the first place, that the pain which accompanies it is its most important feature; secondly, that it is God who so esteems it, taking pleasure in man's self-inflicted misery; thirdly, that we are first to devalorize what we offer to God.... But if this thing is vile and dangerous, how dare I offer to God what is, so to speak, too bad for me? Here, too, a more "natural" way of thinking and feeling is necessary, if we are to grasp aright the supernatural quality of Christian sacrifice, instead of turning it into something unnatural, both ignoble and senseless.

If a man makes a gift, we take it that he knows its value. A man who is incapable of happiness himself can rarely give it to others. To give to others he must, of course, deprive himself of his gift, must renounce instead of keeping, and just because he is aware of its value, the renunciation must often be felt as painful. But this is merely a concomitant, the most unimportant feature in his eyes; he does not give in order to hurt himself, he gives to please the receiver: the pain accompanying the gift is at most the price of his precious right to give, and he does not haggle or complain about it, nor is he proud of it. But do we not often mistake this mere by-product, due to our narrowness and niggardliness, for the essential factor, make it an end in itself? When we speak of "sacrifice," do we not think primarily of the shadow, this negative element, this pain inflicted on ourselves, rather than of the light, the joy it gives the recipient? Just think of the absurdity of a man who only wanted to give so as to feel the loss of his gift, and knew, moreover, that the receiver's only pleasure in receiving it was his knowledge of the pain it gave! And we think of God like that, or act as if we did and are not ashamed.

Of course there are things which we must renounce because they really are worthless, although the renunciation is painful to our baser nature which would fain cling to them. But dare we degrade the noble word "sacrifice" to describe a loss of this type? Scarcely. If I allow my appendix or some other part of me to be removed (excuse the banality of the example), well, my life may be imperiled, and the operation may be exceedingly painful, but a sacrifice in the strict sense, such a "renunciation" it is not. The precious meaning of sacred words should be preserved, and they ought not to be indiscriminately cheapened.

A: In your eagerness to prove your point, you contradict yourself. In the first place a sacrifice and a gift have a price after all, what costs nothing is worth nothing. That is a truism. Secondly, how can one give anything at all to God? He who owns everything, even all that I hold! Both these—giving and keeping alike—seem to me childish and meaningless notions. Particularly as regards material objects! That surely is sheer paganism. Can we still believe that God esteems the firstling more than the rest of the flock which He also made, or that gold is more precious in His sight than any other mineral, or that blood has a "sweet savor" for Him? Did not every prophet thunder against the crude belief that the Lord took pleasure in burnt flesh? And is the more refined Christian conception, as you defend it, so very different? Is it not an offence to every healthy intelligence that even today the populace offers gold and silver hearts and marble tablets to the Mother of God? And it is precisely our religious feeling which rebels against it, our reverence for the Invisible, the Intangible, the Lord of Heaven. They, however, ascribe their own childish greed to God and His saints. That is where your comparison with gifts from man to man breaks down.

B: I believe I can justify myself all the same. To take your first point first: the value of a sacrifice depends on its cost, true. But that cost is not its unpleasantness, but the love it expresses. The worth of a human gift also does not primarily consist in its mere cash value, but in the love of the giver. If it were not so, we ought to show the account with every present. With God we are often vulgar enough to take pleasure in laying before Him the account for our sufferings. No doubt the "difficulty" of the sacrifice has its importance, but only as the indicator, the pointer on the scales which tells me what a strong balance of happiness in possession, or fear of loss, my love has overcome.... But it is to be hoped that the point will come when I no longer take interest in reckoning, weighing, and measuring the size of my love. And now: Whether one can give anything to God? There are gifts and gifts. One is the concrete expression of the wish to give the recipient something he has not yet had. We all know that kind, and there is nothing further to be said about it. But there is another way of giving. Perhaps among the many to whom I ought to give, there is one to whom long ago I have given something else: my heart, my soul, as far as God permits, myself. I want to give myself for his use, with all that I am or have. I want to give myself into his hands and say: there, take me, make use of me, use me up.... But one cannot, very well, say that in so many words. So I take a "thing"—something that one can literally take hold of, use, and use up—fill it brimful with my love and surrender, my longing to serve, to be of use—and give it to the friend. Do you not see? It is as though I said: this is myself. Be me, gift, take my place. You understand what has happened. The object has become transparent, of double meaning. It no longer means just itself. It means me, the giver; it has become a representative, a symbol. Such gifts are points where the invisible becomes visible and tangible, like a sunken world whose summits rise as islands out of the sea. The actual object all but completely vanishes, becomes a pleasant accompaniment, nothing more. Between lovers gifts are signs, the dumb but real message of the one thing they have to tell each other. And the outwardly most worthless thing which we could not give a stranger without offending him, given to a friend, may be a genuine gift which he delights to receive. A double consequence follows: an insatiable, inventive, tireless urge to heap up such tokens, for the message is never fully expressed, and again the consciousness that fundamentally it is not possible to express it, and no token can be other than a poor, utterly inadequate expression, indeed only a distant indication...that no gift is truly worth acceptance, and that "acceptance" is, in fact, the real, the supreme gift. Raise all this from the finite and narrow human sphere into the life with God, and that is what sacrifice means. The gift, though in itself a mere "thing," has become wholly transparent, perfectly representative. All the love of my heart, my prayer, my thanks, I put into my gift, and present it in my open hands to God, with but one trembling request—for one repayment, one return: that He will not spurn it, that He will accept it, that it may find favor in His sight. Here the difference between large and small sacrifices disappears—every gift is now only a window, whether of worthless glass or cut crystal, for the light of the far greater, the only true gift, the loving heart to shine through.

A: As if God could not see it apart from that!

B: Granted God needs no "window"; He can see even the dumb love deep hidden at the bottom of the soul. But *man* needs it to believe in his own love. Love is ever travailing for expression. And at the beginning when love is still anxious, still growing, new and strange to itself, it measures itself against other things, tries to fill ever larger vessels, is amazed at itself when it succeeds and demands ever new ways of proving itself to the beloved. It sets itself tests, acts of heroism, displays you might almost call defiant; yes, it is a kind of showing-off before oneself, tests that the beloved by no means demands. Do you not see that in the lives of all the saints? "But God really does not ask this" is the recurrent exclamation of the bourgeois, afraid such exaggeration might be set up as the normal standard. Of course God does not require some of these things. (He requires other things though.) The saint requires it of himself because he is a lover, a young lover who thinks he must continually draw his sweetheart's attention to himself and his love, so that she may have no doubts of it or him; the young and inexperienced lover who is himself not quite sure yet how far his love is equal to his words, how true it rings, and whether, in the excess of his desire it is not greater in intention than in fact. So he tests and proves himself again and again, each time more severely, more madly if you like, and recks nothing of the labor and bitter pains. With every test successfully passed and overcome he exults and leaps, for he can say to himself: "I've achieved that too, for your sake." But when the flood has reached the full, so that all vessels overflow or are swept away, then each is of equal capacity, because they are all equally small, too small. Then to be together in silence means as much as or more than the most exuberant declaration or gesture, and a hardly noticeable service equals the most splendid gift. Does this not help us to understand why believers under the Old Covenant or pious heathens could slaughter fifty thousand beasts to do homage to God—only to attain the painful realization that the most gorgeous hecatomb could not fill the gulf between man and Deity? The Christian on the other hand takes a little wafer and some drops of wine and water, prays: *suscipe sancte Pater*, and knows himself accepted in this sign, which is indeed only a sign, so accepted that the miracle which he craves for himself, to be changed into the living Christ, takes place representatively in the sign; he knows that his sign has been so fully accepted—that God replies to it by *His* gift, His Son.

So profoundly is the symbolism of human giving fulfilled in sacrifice. And I believe we ought not to take these votive offerings in places of pilgrimage, to which you objected, too literally but rather as symbols. Perhaps the simple worshiper who has given a silver or even a golden heart at Mariazell or Einsiedeln could not discourse to you on the symbolism of his gift, but that he understands and intends it primarily and in all seriousness is shown by his naif yet so surprisingly right choice of symbol—the heart that I have made of the most precious material I can afford. Or take the most simple and most beautiful of all symbols: the votive candle which stands in my stead in the holy place, watchful and burning before the Face of God. I am always strangely moved when I see the white beams of the votive candles in a church, modestly crowded together in some corner by the altar—as if they were living souls shining there, and consuming away in their own fire; the faithful candles which we put there. We have to go, but they remain in our place in the sacred building, until their service has wasted them to the last drop. You see, the sacrificial acts of the saints are candles before the Face of God. That at least is one thread in the web of their motives, whose whole secret texture God alone can know. We can only fumble and guess and get a faint inkling that it may be "thus or thus," employing the one standard of comparison at our disposal, our poor yet precious human love.

A: All this is, in theory, beautiful and good and illuminating. But the reports do not bear out your description. The picture of the saint, as I know it, is lacking in both these things: consciousness of the value of that which she sacrifices and especially the natural human pain accompanying it. That is what makes such a chilling impression on us; it is so remote from what we feel to be a noble and healthy humanity. On Ludwig's death, Elizabeth does react to her fate like a human being—but think of her *Te Deum* on the night of her banishment!

B: There were special circumstances about the banishment. But your objection, so far as it is fundamental, is beside the point. We all know how one love can be in opposition to another; and a bitter and grievous situation it is. Love of brothers and sisters for example against love of parents, love of family against love of husband. Love of friend against love of master, love of one's own kin against love of nation or Church; finally every human love against the love of God. Certainly these "loves" are reconcilable in "principle" with each other, all can be "harmoniously coordinated," but what does real life care for such "principles"? The immense web of circumstance arranges itself so that somehow there is no space for two, that a man's fate contracts as it were to a narrow gangway on which he can take only one with him and must drop the other: choice is imperative. It may be the loves are almost equally strong and have equal claims so that the man is wellnigh torn in two by the conflict. It may also be that when one love begins to grow in him its growth is so powerful, so forceful, so luxuriant, that it simply thrusts all others imperiously aside. In the latter case, when the choice has to be faced there is no long struggle, the power of this almost sole love is overwhelmingly victorious, winning the whole being to its side. He hardly sees or knows that he loses anything by it, he does not count what he leaves behind so long as he is assured of this one thing—that he may keep his great love. This has been happening since the world began: it is written in the *Song of Songs*, in the *Phaedrus* and the *Nibelungen Lied*—how the man leaves father and mother to cleave to the one woman; leaves wife and children to fight for country or leader; the exile renounces his home for the sake of a hope, an ideal; the martyr gives his life for his love. And we do not even find it surprising, what we term enthusiasm is one of the fundamental capacities of man.

There is a point in earthly love when everything outside it, be it the most enticing promise or the darkest threat, becomes equally unimportant, ludicrously irrelevant; parents, home, possessions, reputation, danger, health, life, death; all alike absurdly insignificant. Anything and everything is risked insanely and lost without regret, as though unworthy of a sigh or a thought; and this without any consciousness, pride or satisfaction in the sacrifice made, merely a passing incident, as one brushes away an encumbrance with a hasty flick of the hand.

That this point can be, and really is reached in man's love of God seems to us scarcely credible. The love of God seems so equal to, if not often so much less than, any other love that the choice between them really must be a doubtful issue, a severe tension. There must be a life-and-death struggle, and at best a hard-won victory, after which the conqueror comes stumbling, with bleeding heart, to God, and must rest for a long while after his "victory." And we find even this a great and beautiful thing.

So you see, when we look at the saints making their sacrifices with smiles and songs, we measure them by our measure and say: It can have been of no great value to them from the beginning, this thing they had to abandon.

Think then of Elizabeth when the Crusaders come back to Germany with Ludwig's bones, and the bier is set in the lofty choir of the Bamberg Minster, and the young widow, called by the Bishop, walks to the open coffin and sees the little heap of white bones—all that remains of the dearest being in the world. When she finds words, this is all she says: "Lord, I thank Thy goodness and mercy that Thou hast granted Thy poor handmaid's great desire and hast comforted me in my sorrow by the sight of these dear bones...of my dearest brother and friend. And although I loved him above all earthly things and with my whole heart, I do not grudge that he offered himself to Thy service and for Thy sake came to his end in a strange land. Thou knowest well that could he be restored by Thy Holy Will, his life, his happy and beloved presence and the sight of his countenance were dearer to me than all the joy and honor of this world...so that I would willingly go a-begging with him all my life.... *But against Thy Will, dearest Lord, I would not have him brought back to life, though I could do it at the cost of a single hair.*"

Did we know only of these last words, how quickly we should judge hers to have been no genuine "earthly" love. It is a good thing we know the other stories as well, of the happy married years, of the bitter leave-taking at his departure, of the "thousand kisses" on the mouth of this man, now dead, and of her measureless grief at the news of his death. How great is the love which does not extinguish this love—but outshines it in heavenly radiance!

But we prefer to twist the truth awry, to calumniate and abuse the love given to men and women for each other, and are ashamed of it because it so often makes God's victory difficult—instead of seeing that the evil does not consist in its strength, that may be the best thing about us in God's eyes, even now, but in the feebleness of our love to God, due to very different reasons. The man without the love of God has indeed good cause to worry about the threat to his salvation in "earthly" love: for it is a reality, and where it finds unclaimed territory it takes possession. Did we, however, love God, really love Him, then we should have no need to draw narrow boundaries round our love for His creatures, we could throw ourselves boldly into the sea and let the tide sweep us away, praying for the increase, not the death, of our love.

And I maintain that the way to Divine Love is not spiritual self-mutilation, however many weighty opinions declare it to be so, but that the gift of human love is a mirror, which though dim and broken, is still the plainest in which to see what our love to God might be; the alphabet from which, like children learning to read, we spell out the language we should speak to God.

There is, of course, disordered love, but there is not a "good" and a "bad" love. There is only good love. There are certainly relationships between human beings that are really base, furtive, and smirched, but to call such "love" is a shocking misuse of the word. We ought to be much more afraid of disparaging and aspersing love. When Plato represented Socrates as covering his head and expressing remorse because he has had the impiety to "speak of Eros as impure, and how can this be when he is a God?"—what ought we to say, we who know that everything human has been regenerated by water and the Holy Spirit? Anything, of course, can be misused, and the most beautiful is just the most endangered, but is it not against all reason for fear of this to break the mirror, and throw away the alphabet, refusing to learn anything? It is exactly like someone refusing to think for fear of getting "doubts." Even that has been taken for virtue. But coldness of heart is no more the way to God than any other cowardice.

I will go so far as to say that capacity for love is perhaps the only indispensable *natural* foundation for holiness. A man need not be wise, learned or even highly gifted to become holy, but he must be able to love. He must possess the power and the impetus, the "wings of the soul" to forget self for another's sake, to hold another more important than himself, to overcome fear and pain for another, to risk himself. Otherwise he can be upright, useful and virtuous and never raise a finger against the law, but if he is incapable of being any man's friend, whether the opportunity occurs is another matter, incapable because he could never put anyone before himself—he cannot possibly understand friendship with God.

The gift for loving, for it is a gift, a gracious gift, is no doubt, like every exceptional endowment, dangerous and often dancing on the edge of an abyss, can indeed prove a pitfall, can devastate a man like an avalanche, so that he is unable to rise again to the heights of God. This has happened countless times. But as I have already said: the danger lies not in its worthlessness, but in the dazzling splendor of its worth. The capacity for loving is a dangerous gift of God fraught with pain and calamity like Pandora's box in the myth: and perhaps its dark possibilities have been more often fulfilled than the bright. But, daring as it may sound, even he to whom this gift has brought destruction, who has been swept away from God on a tide of irregular love, and whose other powers were unequal to the glorious Daemon (for a man must be armored to meet him, or his end will be Phaeton's), was nearer to the possibility of being a saint, little as he may have known it, than the exemplary citizen who has no faintest inkling of the dangers to which the other has succumbed, but knows nothing of that stormy upward sweep of his soul.

This capacity we find in the nature of every saint. It assumes many colors and tones, different in men and women, and varying with age, race, and period; but it is never absent. The saints' biographies display every sort of psychological background and previous history, but as far as I know none was covetous or cold.

Now I can repeat the statement with which I started, with the utmost emphasis: the most human feature in Elizabeth was that she was a great lover, a heart endowed with extraordinary power of self-donation. And the formula of her sanctity is precisely the same. She was a great lover of God, a heart endowed with unequaled power of self-donation.

A: Your words recall Rilke's *Stundenbuch*:

I weigh and count and spare myself, my God,
But Thou hast the right to squander me.

But there remain unsolved problems like a dark undergrowth which still obscures the gradually clearing prospect of our saint. Again the facts go further than your theory allows for, and, forgive me, it is only a construction.

For instance, what room is there for the following consideration: In the last resort man has not the sole choice, what he will sacrifice. There are things that man *may* not offer—which to offer unasked would be ὕβρις. Many things, to be sure, may, and can, be offered freely, can, indeed, only be offered freely, losing value if withheld until asked for, however gently. But there are other things so precious or so entrusted to us by the pledge of our honor, that our sole duty is to guard them faithfully, a charge which can indeed be made impossible by sheer violence, but never deliberately surrendered. Is not this the case with the sanctity of life? Who may throw it lightly away? And above all the happiness and life of a dear one! Only in the inexorable grip of the highest claims may a man surrender that.

Even so, it is a "sacrifice," not merely a yielding of the spoil.

These, you see, are not sacrifices offered with smiles and songs, even fay the greatest and most generous love. They are offered with trembling and tears, and it is as though they were dragged out of our clutching hands, so that our torn flesh clings to them. But...can you understand this? I believe that these offerings are the freest, freer than all those "presents" you so poetically described. That in such agony to which no urge of the heart, no thrill of enthusiasm impels him a man may utter, amid all that pain the Yes of complete acceptance that presupposes a wellnigh terrifying freedom, is in truth a song of freedom, a *jubilate* of adoration, an *alleluia* of the creature before the Almighty, unheard by any human ear. We hear only the groans of the creature and even the offerer can hear nothing else, but it is a *Trisagion* hymned before the seraph-shadowed throne of God's darkness.

Such a sacrifice was Ludwig's death, such also the banishment from the Wartburg. But that she gave up her children, and, when expelled from the castle, took refuge in stables and the most ruined hovels, and had a *Te Deum* sung into the bargain, that in her relations with her maids she made herself cheap and ridiculous, forgetting even the dignity and strict decorum of her royal stock, and the way she allowed Meister Konrad to treat her—all this is rather childish, rather self-conscious and "original"...just because it was freely chosen and not laid upon her by a necessity willed by God.

B: Before I answer you, let me explain very briefly the story of the banishment from the Wartburg. Legend is responsible for a great deal here. It is so romantic a theme. The beautiful, tender, defenseless Princess driven out of the castle into the foggy night by her heartless kindred and the rough serving men.... But all that is a later invention. As so often, God's invention, the truth, was greater and more beautiful and even more fantastic than man's. Elizabeth left the Wartburg of her own free will because she could no longer satisfy her conscience there. She could no longer keep her rule of abstinence from food unjustly obtained. Her relatives did not give her her widow's portion, probably to check her known extravagance and thus oblige her to share the life of the Court—under constraint, no doubt, but with all the honor due to her rank. But Konrad's discipline, as expressed in this rule of abstinence, had sharpened her perception of just and unjust, and her life-long works of love had opened her eyes to her suffering of the masses. She shrinks from the "ill-gotten" goods tainted with the forced labor and misery of the exploited poor, and she draws the practical conclusion. To quote verbally the evidence of the maids: "she would not receive her support from the robbery and plunder of the poor, as is usual in princely houses, but *chose* rather exile and to earn her living with her own hands." We are so ready to believe that it has been reserved for our own agc to discover and act upon the social conscience, yet as Maria Maresch aptly expresses it, the banishment from the Wartburg was simply Elizabeth's decision to place her right to livelihood on a level with that of the poor. That was far nobler than the much admired action of Tolstoy's, for it plunged her immediately in bitter and real want, meant homelessness and hunger. Maria Maresch suggests this may have been her primary motive in parting with her children. For in such an uncertain and necessitous life the children could have no share; their future must be assured and this could only by separation. And Wenck also may be right in supposing that Elizabeth, who had herself come to a strange home at the age of four, might very well see nothing so terrible in such a fate for her children. The parents had dedicated the youngest child to the cloister before it was born; for the elder daughter there was the usual early betrothal, and the heir of the Wartburg could not grow up with a mother who was a beggar.

I am not trying to "excuse" Elizabeth, only to suggest that in this action, too, there was perhaps more compulsion from circumstances than at first sight appears. When indeed her relatives, the Abbess of Kitzingen and the Bishop of Bamberg had interfered on her behalf, and the Knights who brought Ludwig's remains back from the South had reinstated her in the Wartburg, and her rights of property had been settled, she could perhaps have fetched her two elder children back; the youngest remained in the convent at Altenburg. She may, however, really have been subject to an extraordinary inward call—that is, in fact, my personal conviction—not only to be ready for every sacrifice, even those man may not "offer," but actually and literally to accomplish them—sparing nothing—which brings us back to your question.

A: Let me put it clearer: Even with this reservation the fact remains that our saint, and the saint in general, knows not only the sacrifice of precious things because they are precious, but equally the search for painful, base, and ugly things because they are ugly, painful, humiliating. Only consider how prominently this characteristic stands out precisely in Elizabeth's care for the sick and poor.

B: The answer to that is not far to seek, but I hesitate to give it. For it is difficult and painful to speak of the most delicate secrets of another's inner life. First because it is only talk, and for the speaker perhaps only a "literary" construction, or at best a theoretical understanding; secondly, because there are certainly many living even among us whose lives, though they speak no word of it, are burnt and consumed by this secret to which I can only allude, a sacrifice, like Elizabeth's, offered in silence and measureless suffering. But as you ask....

The love of the saints, and Elizabeth's for God, is, if I may say so, incarnate in their love for Christ, just as God's love is visible in Christ's Incarnation. Can we at all conceive what it must be like really to love Christ "like a human being"—to enter into His life as into the life of our nearest and dearest: to share it? What to us is a pious and edifying phrase, a devotional metaphor, occasionally a powerful motive in face of a particular situation: to share the life of Our Lord, not to wish to be better off than He was—to them, to her, is a reality, obvious and constantly present, a destiny. And as we so often do, we turn what to the saints was a well-nigh intolerable burden into a pretty and attractive piece of phrase-making.

In our convent school we were reminded, at every disagreeable dish in the refectory, of Our Lord's sponge of hyssop and drink of myrrh. At every headache, of the crown of thorns? Possibly it is a "workable" method with very childlike children, that is, it may produce immediate results, for a normal child reacts to such an appeal with at least some feeling of shame. But is it not a very questionable method because of its superficiality and because it cheapens the deepest and most solemn things? Is it not yet another instance of the way in which we misread genuine features in the saints' lives like writing reflected in a mirror?

What those pious appeals to our childhood in the convent were struggling to say became suddenly clear to me much later on; and with an acute sense of shame I understood what kind of love it was that drove the saints to embrace suffering, because Christ had suffered. Perhaps you remember the story of the blind man's mother (it is told by Paul Keller or François Coppée). She was seen by a friend sitting for hours by her blind son with her eyes shut in the bright light of a summer day—shut that she might not be better off than he.

Or have you never stood longingly watching a suffering which seemed to enclose your friend like a wall, and feeling yourself shut out by it so that you begged to be admitted, to share "in it"?

This is actual experience, and has nothing to do with philosophical considerations of worth and worthlessness, acceptance or rejection, asceticism or training of character. It is the simplest thing in the world, and the most direct, not to be analyzed, defended, or refuted, simply the impulsive ardent gesture of love praying with outstretched hands: "Take me with you, let me be with you, let me go through what you are going through, live your life."

But the whole of Christ's life was a mystery of suffering. In that I see the essence of our saint's thirst for poverty. It was not the yearning of the philosopher for freedom from cares and independence of possessions, as we find it in the cynics. Nor was it the poverty inspired by the social conscience, nor yet the desire for an Edenic simplicity of life. On this point Lulu von Strauss-Torney's interpretation is altogether too modern and too complicated: "Elizabeth throws down all dividing barriers, rank, riches, power, brushes them aside as if they were cobwebs, that she may be nothing but a human being, sister to the poorest of her brothers, made one with them by her free and joyful sacrifice." How sentimental and self-important! Who thought, in those days, about "redeeming herself and others"? No, Elizabeth's poverty is nothing but love's instinctive plea "*nudus sequere Christum nudum*," "to follow naked a naked Christ."

That is why a rapture of delight possesses her that first night after her escape from the Wartburg, so that she must go at midnight to the Friars, they surely will understand, and beg them for a *Te Deum*. She has been admitted to share visibly and tangibly the poor life of Christ. So it goes on step by step; her homelessness, her gray Franciscan habit, her heart's loneliness when Meister Konrad ("in the knowledge that she desired perfection") sent away her faithful maids and replaced them by two repulsive termagants; her rigid obedience, the rough work, the miserable food, the bad lodging, the jeers of her former friends at "the fool." All is a sharing of Jesus' poor, hunted and wandering life, a blessed companionship, a penetration of His experience, as if every little bit of suffering which she learns like a child learning a new lesson, were a door opening on a new secret of His life, outside which she had hitherto stood as a stranger.

Here, to my mind, lies the secret of her boundless love for the sick and poor.

A: Once again I must disagree, gladly as I have followed you so far. You have spoken of a gift for loving. Is Elizabeth's love of her fellow men and women not primarily the uncontrollable impulse of a loving heart, not the product of religion; nature and not grace; independent of her piety, flowering apart from the root from which you would derive all her other characteristics? And more generally, is not the benevolence, the powerful love for men—usually claimed as the chief fruit of Christianity—rather a matter of disposition than motived by religion? Does it not strike deeper roots and flower more beautifully in the world of non-Christian ideals, among Socialists, the finest type of Jew, and similar groups, than among devout Christians? Does the official "love of your neighbor" of Christianity not have something altogether too painfully artificial, dry and external, about it? Something unreal and often insincere?

B: I was expecting this question, and not without considerable anxiety, for it is perhaps the most tangled knot we are attempting to loosen today, and we have attempted some knotty problems already! Is there a natural capacity for love of one's neighbor? First: I would call it, to avoid for the moment any valuation—for there is, in fact, a capacity of this kind—a capacity for sympathy; a social disposition. There is a special quality of heart, a clairvoyance, a sensitiveness of soul, almost as acutely aware of another's feelings and circumstances as of one's own. It is as though the walls of the self were somehow thinner, more transparent than with others who have to stick their heads out of the window before they can see what is going on around them.

This disposition, this peculiar sounding-board faculty has, I believe, nothing to do with the question Christian or non-Christian. Where it exists, it can, of course, be illumined, understood, deepened and directed by Christianity, be, in a word, baptized. I would say, further, that the consciousness of our essential human interdependence, which finds expression in this phenomenon, sleeps at the bottom of us all, and can be awakened and nourished by intellectual and volitional "radiation"; even by non-Christian "rays"—philosophy, for example. The teachings of the Stoa and Buddha can do it; the Enlightenment of the eighteenth century, Socialism can do it, or pacifism, even vegetarianism; indeed any humanitarian faith which, though making its appeal to sympathy, springs from the head rather than the heart and blood. No doubt the later in the Christian era such movements appear, the more difficult it is to say how far an unconscious Christian influence has been at work.

There is then an entirely natural disposition which is deceptively like "love of your neighbor." When a weak person, scarce capable of coping with his own destiny, is endowed with this additional burden—this intense psychological vulnerability—each of us is not born an Atlas to carry the world on his shoulders—you have the typical embittered man with his hopeless melancholy, nostalgia, and pessimism, at best a poet or philosopher—the mere "man of letters" is worse—but never a great man. But when this peculiar sensitivity is united with a strong active nature, able to fight for itself, such a man seizes, grips by the horns, other men's suffering as well as his own, and we get, according to circumstances, the revolutionary, the reformer, the philanthropist, the man who heads movements or builds schools, the Socialist politician, the Communist agent, the student of tropical medicine. There need be no Christianity in it. Of course Christian education has been working in this direction for centuries, but only to educate and purify—the material originates elsewhere. The love of man for God's sake is actually something altogether different from the love of man because he is man.

Indeed, I realize that the love of man for man's sake *must* necessarily be stronger and richer in other camps than ours. Are they not confined within a world from which heaven has been removed like a roof? On the level floor of a plain visible from end to end, objects stand out stark and bare, hopeless captives of the relentless light which has stripped them of every wonder, every blessed dream. And on such an earth, without cover or distance, where longing reaches into the void, these people are packed unendurably tight, treading on each other's feet, too close to escape.... These people, who have nothing but themselves, who are without God, how terribly important they must become to one another—important as we who live simultaneously and inseparably with God can never be important to each other!

For all the things we seek from God, they must seek from themselves and from each other. Until finally for everyone except the aristocratic hermit who in disdainful resignation withdraws into an interior or exterior cell—be it even a circle—only two possibilities remain: either a war of all against all, mutual destruction as we see it daily; or that almost desperate reaching out of hands to your neighbor, men clutching each other, one taking another's place, kindness as a refuge from a hate otherwise ineluctable. And for the weak it is at the same time a herding together of those who feel themselves wronged and are entirely dependent on their mutual support, crushing in its weight of mutual responsibility which puts forward those imperious and threatening claims termed "the rights of man": Be kind to me!

Such is the strange appearance presented by that socialist kindness and active philanthropy which is a continual surprise to me; it is so different from the brotherly love of Christianity. It is so much more energetic and enterprising, earnest and passionate; it breathes a bitter and keen vehemence, is inspired by a conviction of its immense, almost absolute, importance, a grim yet sublime sense of loneliness beneath the burden and a consciousness that save for themselves there is no one to help and no help given. There is no "sympathizing heart above the clouds." Our globe, like a drifting, rudderless ship over the ocean, is roaming solitary and purposeless through the endless void of space with none to guide and none to care. Its population, like that ship's crew, is welded together by a common doom, wholly abandoned to each other and dependent solely on each other. Woe to the weak, the defenseless, who stray into such a world! Their plight must arouse the giant's strength, the protective instinct of strong natures. Hence also the indictment, the denunciation, constant, and passionate like a dark fierce flame, at the heart of all this benevolence: the search for a scapegoat to be responsible for everything. For just as every benefit and improvement comes from humanity, so all misery and every obstacle to betterment must also come from our fellow *men*. They alone are responsible for everything. Mutual aid and mutual hurt alike are raised to the absolute.

Now contemplate those people of a naturally kind, alert and sympathetic disposition such as we have spoken of placed in such a world. No, I am not all surprised that rabid Communists who speak and write only in tones of blood and thunder are often at the same time the "kindest people," almost unhealthily sensitive to every shade of harshness and hardship to all that is defenseless and ill-used; almost effeminate in their tenderness for tormented children, animals, flowers, the oppressed proletariat, slave-driven women: people who cherish a standing grievance in the name of the whole world, take as a personal injury every wrong to another however remote, who resent as an insolent mockery of human woe the mere existence of people who are not miserable, but well-fed and comfortable; men who bear in their hearts a measureless and frenzied compassion for the whole world which they suffer beyond reason or cure.

Such an attitude must no doubt also produce an intoxicating sense of power and importance which the man who has realized the truth of the "unprofitable servant" can hardly even comprehend. Humanly speaking, the invasion of the supernatural, of faith in God, involves at first a weakening of this iron bond between man and man. We are so constituted that the immediate effect of belief in Providence is rather to relieve and calm our sense of other people's suffering than to summon us to the active service of Providence. No doubt in adopting this attitude we often make our faith a cloak for our selfishness. There is nevertheless a truth behind it, rightly understood. It is a most powerful guarantee that the compassionate shall not be tormented to death by their feelings; that beyond all their anxious and harrowing sympathy and sense of responsibility there is actually the supreme relief: *Sub umbra alarum tuarum*, "beneath the shadow of thy wings."

There is no question that Christianity has not multiplied this "natural gift" for kindness, any more than it has multiplied the talent for painting or music. But it is not the function of Christianity to multiply natural talent. That it has, as we know, brought out, deepened, and elevated every kind of pre-existing talent, is only a very secondary concomitant, a byproduct, not its task. We cannot, therefore, measure its significance by the number of talents, artistic or ethical, to which it has given a home—that depends on a thousand other circumstances. The novelty in the relation between Christianity and benevolence lies rather in the fact that it does not leave kindness as a natural gift, but makes love of our fellow-man a general, inescapable *duty*. It has made it possible for those countless numbers, to whom natural benevolence is denied, to provide themselves by the effort of conscience and obedience with a kind of substitute or analogy of it, which, if with great labor, performs the function of benevolence in the world which it actually makes far more endurable.

It is, of course, self-evident that what is constructed of duty and stern control is not as fragrant or attractive as the natural growth—but what a gap there would be if everything were removed which sprang solely from this dutiful "love of our neighbor"!

All the secondary and more remote offshoots of benevolence: politeness, consideration, helpfulness; or, on another level: social responsibility, welfare work of all kinds—how much of these spring from the conviction formed in the first place by Christian doctrine of universal brotherhood—the conviction that love of mankind is the duty of all, so that he who has not got it at least must do his best to conceal the deficiency? That is by no means to be branded as insincerity, for it is an excellent training in self-discipline and submission to what is recognized as the greatest of all commandments. And it is equally a fact that Christianity has by its direct operation filled untold numbers of "untalented" souls with a genuine and true love and kindness.

But we must not mistake arrested developments, failures, caricatures of brotherly love, for Christian types, however numerous they may be, for brotherly love is indeed so difficult, and so little to be taken for granted, that many do not get beyond miserable attempts at it.

A: When we inspect it closer, your gift for love—for love of an individual which you hymned so lyrically and for which you claimed the exalted function of the alphabet of holiness, proves an obstacle to the universal love of mankind. In its widest and simplest sense Eros—Spranger has put it best—is love of living Beauty. Eros, who binds one human being to another, is love of a value, of an ideal, which is *above* myself; is a looking upward, a reverence, a desire to rejoice and enrich myself in the worth of the beloved: Eros is the child of Poverty. Eros is not perhaps "love" in the fullest sense, for that is directed towards a person, and no person is wholly ideal or wholly venerable. This Eros, therefore, is directed towards qualities of the beloved rather than the person, more strictly to the beauty in these qualities. Nevertheless, the way to *that* love, which, touching the inmost core of the other, finally and fatefully welds two lives into one, lies usually through Eros. Do not call it selfishness; it involves ready and wholehearted obedience to the ideal of perfection set up before me and the humility which knows that I cannot attain it by myself. Do not call it mere pleasure-seeking: the generous, blissful admiration of another's beauty and perfection is far more than that in its reverence and gratitude; it has also its religious expression which we call adoration, and its Christian expression is the jubilant cry of the Gloria—*gratias agimus Tibi propter magnam gloriam Tuam.* This natural way of love is familiar to folk-song simplicity as well as to the high flights of Platonism:

> This hath thy beauty done,
> Hath me to loving won,
> With great desire.[2]

Here, however, the danger lies. On him alone shall Eros descend who with all the might of his desire, will renounce all incomplete and limited satisfactions and wing his flight to the "eternal Beauty." Love of this kind can only be towards few, and many will be able to give it only to *one* person—and that only in virtue of countless illusions. Such love a man saves up and guards for a long time, until he meets someone whom he finds "worthy." But where is the link with that love which goes out to all without respect of persons, without question of worth or nobility? Can one man achieve both kinds of love? Does not the command of "universal brotherly love" demand of its very nature that a man should blunt the edge of that fine sense of values by which the generous soul discriminates the noble from the base?

Further, this gift for Eros, this sensitive eager response, to worth, nobility and beauty, has its necessary complement in an equally keen repulsion from the unworthy, the ugly, the ignoble. That is not the dark reverse of a glorious gift, but its indispensable protection, its necessary presupposition—what Nietzsche called inner purity. Who loses this power of discrimination loses his dignity. One must be able to feel disgust—yes, one must be capable of contempt. But your brotherly love demands an indiscriminate, universal embrace.

B: Nietzsche is in your mind; but he also says: "Love of man is only *permissible* for God's sake—otherwise it is merely bad taste." In my opinion it is rather the non-Christian humanitarian attitudes which involve that vulgar and leveling "love of man," blind to distinctions of worth, which to the noble soul is a ridiculous and detestable thing—command us to accept man *as he is*, and not primarily in the name of a Higher Power. In the Eros-endowed saints you will find disgust too, think of St. Francis and his unspeakable horror of lepers, and of Stanislaus and St. Philip Neri and others, who in the presence of a corrupt soul became physically ill and even fainted. They did not root out their disgust, but overcame it by the charity of Christ; out of flight from ugliness grew the battle against it and out of contempt the redemption of the evil man from his evil.

How many things are covered by that one word, love, a term so easy to misunderstand: social disposition, natural, capacity for Eros, supernatural love!

A: I see myself forced out of my position. Elizabeth *was* Eros-endowed; she was capable of lavishing body, soul, and spirit on *one* person who seemed to her more worthy of love than anyone else in the world, more lovable, more beautiful. And yet...

B: It seems to me highly doubtful whether "love of man" in the humanitarian sense ever really existed in the Middle Ages. I believe indeed that all the great friends of man during that period were only so because and in so far as they were great Christians, that is to say, saints. I have many reasons for this belief. Think of a world in which a weapon is the most necessary, important and obvious implement of daily life; an indispensable article of clothing; so deeply incorporated into a man's personal life that it received a name like a man; the weapon which is the horrible token and tool of an ever-watchful readiness for battle and wounds, killing and being killed. In such times there is not much room for humane feelings. So few are the ways to escape, everything was fated, pestilence was inevitable when it came, the doctor's art slight and accessible only to the few; the harvest so casual, and famine as little to be checked as a flood. Only he who succumbed in these conditions raised protests against them, the strong fought their way through and made little fuss about it, whether about their own or others' troubles. Only to the love of great Christians, like Elizabeth, did it occur that these destructive forces were controllable and could be mastered by the spirit, that is to say *by love, with God's help*. Perhaps this discovery of theirs has a deeper significance than we are apt to think; is the profound and hidden source of that mighty current of "progress" usually ascribed to very different causes.

They were stronger than all others through their compassionate love, these saints, and this proves their love free from resentment, as the pity of weak persons too often is not. But the driving impulse of this love is purely religious; Elizabeth really loved her fellow men, loved them "from the outset." To do good was not for her a tormented reaction to a wound, not a conscientious application of acquired principles, but streamed from the overflowing fount of her love of Christ: "What ye do to the least...." To her this was the literal truth—you know the story of the leper in the Landgraf's bed....

A: But that is not love of man any more—it is solely love of God. The neighbor has become only a casual medium, is no longer a person, hardly an object; love "practices" on him, sees him no longer, stays with him no more, goes straight through him like a glass—to God. In this there is a sinister devalorization of the human person, treated thus as a mere thing, and degraded to the status of a chance concomitant of God's service. Against that we are instinctively on the defensive, our natural pride and self-respect react on the mere suspicion, that we are an "object of Christian charity."

B: Perhaps this objection can also be solved by looking into our mirror, the analogy of human friendship.

Your friend sends you someone he loves, to be your friend and ward. You are to take the place of that distant friend, lend him your hands, your eyes, voice, time, strength, so that through you, as if in you, he can care for this other. Tell me, would not such a request, placing such trust in you, be a gift, an honor, a pleasure? Would it be an "impersonal" task to you? Would the stranger remain a stranger, would not he be welcomed familiarly for the friend's sake and seem a natural part of your life? Our saint feels like that towards all men; they seem sent to her care by God, for her to stand in God's stead to them: Love one another as I have loved you. Just as you receive that common friend with open heart and entire trust for the other's sake, with eager delight at receiving a message from him, so our saint receives *everyone*—"in the name of God." How the cold words come to life!

She does not see people any more from outside as we do. What to us is the rare gift of our happiest friendships is hers always: to see a person as God sees him, hear the name by which God calls him—that is her marvelous secret. She really sees with the eyes of God, or if you prefer, God looks through her eyes, and there are no more strangers or distances—for to God none is distant or a stranger. There is now only the "neighbor" and he is really nigh, and the first-comer truly the first and foremost.

Now she no longer asks who is "worthy" or "unworthy" before she loves. With her whole heart she mourns over the poverty or malformation of a child of God, bending in motherly concern over the sick and crippled—without disgust and without fear—for this one too was "worth" God's choice, to create him and no other in his place. She believes with childlike faith in this choice of God, even where all its grounds are hidden; and the glory of His choice outshines all "unworthiness." The natural man is *dead*; the significance of this hallowed phrase is now evident; the narrow "self," who saves his love, chooses its recipient, and gives it only to a few. But the resurrection has taken place: this same human love and no other streams from the new and God-born "self," extravagant, burning and alive, now for the first time awake to keenest sensibility; unfettered for the first time, boundlessly free from every barrier of selfish caution, from every parsimonious withholding, bold enough now to dare an overflowing tenderness, sowing now with both hands, conscious of inexhaustible riches. That is what makes this Christian love so humble, so pure and sweet and reverent towards the recipient, without the least shadow of wounding condescension. For God is giving through His saint what He could have given through a thousand other channels, and is willing to accept from her in her neighbor's person what He could have demanded from a thousand others.

This is the love of the saints who give themselves to all but belong to none but God. To us, indeed, such love is an enigma, for it has never yet "entered into the heart of man," and to "the world" a scandal, a folly, a contradiction, an illusion. Yet it is the full, genuine human love of a human heart; such a love as we too give to one or a few. The saints also give it only to *One*. That is why it is truly love. But this One calls every man His friend, and so the miracle happens that they can love every man with the same love which can be given only to one.... That is why St. Elizabeth fell ill when Konrad ordered her to give up her tender nursing of the sick, as anyone might collapse if he saw his beloved in pain and was not allowed to tend and comfort him. That is why her "work among the poor," that chilly expression, is so amazingly, so passionately warm and devoted; that is why she cannot help kissing the wounds as she binds them, why for her poor she most often breaks her obedience to the stern and prudent Magister who understands the wise and approved "path of Perfection" which she must be taught, but not the wild, undisciplined heart that only knows one thing: its boundless love. This, indeed, is the strange feature in the relationship between these two, at once their tragedy and its reconciliation. Konrad is perpetually "found guilty," as it were held responsible for the holiness of his penitent, yet in all those years he could hardly hold back this soul, which, far stronger than his dreaded severity, rushed on "its way with an indomitable simplicity and assurance. He guides her conscientiously and according to a definite plan with laws and prohibitions; a vigilant guardian of sound reason, he gives her rules of life, sanctioned by long experience, imposes penances, inflicts severe punishments; and she does all he wishes, obediently and gladly. But we are conscious how far he lags behind, how childishly trifling these orders are, even at the moment she obeys them, how unnecessary, pedantries of a theoretical asceticism, which her heart has outsoared long since. This is evident in the depositions of the maids, and it is pathetic to hear her women and friends, they too, no doubt, perceiving that the roles were reversed, repeat again and again, after telling of the harshness of his discipline in words through which their almost indignant amazement still burns under the dry old legal Latin, "he meant well, so well," "*Magister Cuonradus tamquam, bono zelo...*" "But he feared," they continue, "that the sight of the two faithful women who followed her from the Wartburg and shared her penury might fill her with pain and longing for her former life, so he took them away because of the temptation."

Does not that speak volumes? He "feared," it says further, she might slip from her good resolutions and therefore he beat her so hard "*bono zelo.*" Elizabeth obeyed, but such a fear was strange to her. What danger for her, the lover! With endless tears she dismisses her faithful friends: "me, Isentrudis, who was dearest to her, and Guda, my companion, whom she heartily loved." Such endless tears she would certainly not have wept were she giving up a "temptation."

Is not this the recurrent tragedy in the lives of so many saints, that such a timid direction in accordance with the letter, and even that often not understood, instead of the spirit, has restricted them, at least outwardly, to small, narrow, and oblique paths...they who were secretly pledged long ago by God to hidden laws of whose mysterious inexorability these teachers of methods of perfection have no inkling? But we have now been brought back to the starting point of our long journey. You also were right: not everything in a saint's life need have been as it was. None escaped minor twists and distortions in his development. How many, alas, suffer terrible mutilations as well! And you are right; this foreign or false element arises from adaptation to an abstract system, a pedantic scheme of "perfection." But surely these inconsistencies are the least and most insignificant factor in this great life? The guiding force of the Holy Spirit is marvelously sure in the souls of His choice, its Reality entwines and covers the law which it adorns like a luxuriant, flowering creeper covering the hard fence which supports it. We shall have some system or other for the attainment of holiness, as long as there are men and women not having sanctity in themselves but only seeking it, who delve and reckon and write and ransack the lives of saints for their "systems," But where the Holy Spirit is the teacher, the soul, of whom He has taken hold, knows that there is only one "form," unconditionally valid: the life of Christ Jesus. And he lives it, as he understands it with the clear vision of love, and we others must recognize once again how far from the living original are our artificial and abstract constructions.... For we see it in the picture of the "real saint," in whose countenance are visible the features of Him who was at once the Son of God and the Son of Man.

A: From the beginning God ordained men to walk before His face in holiness. But we could not know what holiness is, because the law gave birth to sin and not to holiness. So He lived among us that whoever saw Him might see the Father also. But even His likeness is continually darkened by human interpretation, painted over, until His features are scarcely recognizable. Then the saint comes and lives before the eyes of his contemporaries the very life of Christ, and from his picture we glean and guess with longing what Christ was like. That, maybe, is the greatest gift of the saints to us; not the stream of good deeds which they shower on the earth, not the great works of their hands, not the books of their wisdom, nor the triumph of the Church: but that the living likeness of our Lord Jesus Christ never quite disappears from the earth, can never die; that "He is with us, even, in human form, to the end of the world."

We will bid farewell to St. Elizabeth. We have wandered a long way from her during the evening, but her friendly star has been guiding us all the time. She is still *Saint* Elizabeth for me; no longer because of the "embroidered cloak of legend" that hangs around her, but because in her childlike heart, burning and overflowing with a love, that gave itself like bread to all in need, the Lord Himself journeyed, a living presence, through the fields of Thuringia.

Epilogue

This dialogue does not suppose a detailed knowledge of Saint Elizabeth's life; all the more important events come to be mentioned it its course.

For the saint's biographers the principal materials come from rather scanty sources: mainly the process of Canonization, of which the most important part is the *Libellus de dictis quator ancillarum*, the collected sayings of the four serving-women—two of whom were Elizabeth's most intimate friends and companions from her childhood onwards—and the letter from Konrad of Marburg to Pope Gregory IX. Soon after her death appeared the first "biographies." The Romantic Age "discovered" the saint again as it discovered the Middle Ages—that is to say, from its own point of view; but still her best and clearest portrait is to be seen in the frescoes of the Wartburg. Historical research takes possession of the materials at the end of the nineteenth and beginning of the twentieth centuries and, in our own time, psychology and even psycho-analysis have been brought to bear on them. So that the inquiring reader will find theories enough.

In this connection one is brought up against the question of the significance and value of biography in general. The scantier the existing sources, the greater the scope for the interpretative imagination and the more freely it is used. Leaving out of account those tendential writings where a person is used for the illustration of some special thesis, and taking only the writer who, as far as he knows, approaches his material with the honest intention of presenting as far as possible what he has himself observed in it, does not such a writer's problem consist precisely in this—that actually he is dealing not with "material" but with a person?

Who can ever discover the riddle of a life, let alone solve it? How like a world under water, from which only a peak here and there rises up to show the way, is the secret of a human life! And when life has gone, when the one person who had the right or the power to speak is silenced, when others come to fish the flotsam into the net of their "research," how are the fragments faded, shrunken, or swollen—changed—and the salvage of them is called biography.

Even when the material is plentiful—letters, notes—the questionableness of the attempt is not less. We know in our own experience the tragic inability of most people to express what is deepest in them (incidentally this has its good side, inarticulateness is often the powerful though unwished-for guardian of what really needs hiding; how much some people would expose themselves if only they could!): we know how the important is suppressed and the unimportant said, how much is left in conversation to be guessed from the tone of voice, gesture, look—which may leave no impression on us; and what differences there are in silences—how different the very sound of one silence from another!

And is not even the word spoken by intention a *mask*, consciously and "unconsciously chosen with care—chosen out of defiance or sadness, out of shame or pride, out of tenderness of helplessness—yes, the most impenetrable mask? It moves at least as much in "sign" and symbol, in imitation and disguise, as it would in a dream. And is this not especially true of any intimate colloquy? Who would dare to claim to restore from dead "material" and "documents" alone anything resembling the "true" picture of a relationship between two people? How, above all, when it is a question of the most intimate of all relationships, the most secret, the most "inarticulate"—the relationship to God, which of its very nature remains an absolute riddle to the creature—impenetrable and hidden to the point of terror, of darkness—a true mystery of God, living only in His light and standing only to a very slight degree within the comprehension of human consciousness.... And where there have been but a few meager witnesses of this most mysterious thing—who have gathered a few sayings, from a whole lifetime, and preserved them in the leveling framework of conventional literary formula; there we come to the kind of Saint's life that has been handed down to us from the Middle Ages.

These few reflections are sufficient to make confidence in the value of a biography somewhat threadbare. Who can throw light upon the mystery of a human life?

Perhaps the mediaeval historian, in whom we have so little confidence, felt something of this and the reserve of his biographies seems, indeed, to be due to it. The chronicler simply gives the raw materials of a life, only "events," experiences and actions, and these sparingly and rigorously selected in order to illustrate a single point of view—the sanctity of his hero. And in this often very rigid scheme most of the reports about the other circumstances and events of life are omitted with a complete lack of interest which is incomprehensible to us and which our inquisitive psychology can hardly forgive. "His life was thus; through these things he attracted the attention of his contemporaries." Seldom is a motive sought for his actions and when it is, it strikes us as "conventional," not as having been performed once by a particular person, but as belonging to the typical "saint." But, in spite of everything, it does succeed to some extent in making clear the paradox of the "saintly life"—that what was most openly striking about him, what brought him before the world and attracted universal attention, was at the same time the inexpressible mystery hidden beneath the veil of silence: the impenetrable is at the same time the best known; it is precisely this relationship of his to God which constitutes his sanctity. An outward happening can be related and described, and the splendor of an inner life which no word can unveil blazes forth figuratively.

Such are the lives of the chroniclers. Close by them stands the legend, explaining and poetizing. It is an almost essential complement; it is the only form of "explanation," and a very sparing, very reserved yet extraordinarily bold one. Can our "psychological" interpretation of the soul, which distills and constructs thick volumes from a few pages, add much that is essential to such a portrait?

Who can say: "It was thus"? It is for this reason that the dialogue form was chosen in the foregoing. It makes no claim to final validity; it does not seek to lift the veil which lies over the mystery of every life, and of every real saint's life. It attempts an explanation, well knowing that it is but one of many such. A dialogue is the reciprocated form of a discourse, passing in its course from clarity to clarity, from depth to depth, open on all sides alike, open to correction and another's consciousness, enlivened by friendly contradiction, enriched by contrast and hindered by the uncertainty of the first attempt at formulation.

Not: "It was thus," but "Perhaps the figure of the Saint means this too." Perhaps—yes a "perhaps" at once full of reserve and confidence. This and no more will be what underlies this work.

Chronological Table

1207	Elizabeth born at Pressburg (?) in Hungary.
1211	Journey of the four-year-old daughter of the King to the Palatinate of Thuringia for the fiançailles (1212 Children's Crusade).
1221	Marriage to Count Ludwig of Thuringia and Hesse.
1218	Murder of her mother, Gertrud von Meranien, in Hungary.
1223	The first Franciscans come to Germany and settle at Eisenach.
1225	Konrad of Marburg takes over the spiritual direction of Elizabeth. (1226: death of St. Francis of Assisi.)
1227	Fifth Crusade. Departure and death of Ludwig.
1227–1228	Elizabeth flies (or is driven out?) of the Wartburg.
1228	Good Friday. Elizabeth becomes a tertiary of the Franciscan Order.
1228–1231	In hospital at Marburg.
1231	Death of the Saint (November 17).
1235	Canonization.

Notes for The Nature of Sanctity: A Dialogue

1. This essay first appeared serially in his review *Die Schildgenossen*.
2. *Das hat Deitie Schönheit gemacht,*
   hat mich zum Lieben gebracht
   mit grossem Verlangen.

CHRISTIANITY AND THE NEW AGE

by CHRISTOPHER DAWSON

I. *Humanism and the New Order*[1]

For centuries a civilization will follow the same path, worshiping the same gods, cherishing the same ideals, acknowledging the same moral and intellectual standards. And then all at once a change will come, the springs of the old life run dry, and men suddenly awake to a new world, in which the ruling principles of the former age seem to lose their validity and to become inapplicable or meaningless. This is what occurred in the time of the Roman Empire, when the ancient world, which had lived for centuries on the inherited capital of the Hellenistic culture, seemed suddenly to come to the end of its resources and to realize its need of something entirely new. For four hundred years the civilized world had been reading the same books, admiring the same works of art, and cultivating the same types of social and personal expression. Then came the change of the third and fourth centuries, A.D., when the forms of the Hellenistic culture suddenly lost their vitality and men turned to a new art, a new thought and a new way of life—from philosophy to theology, from the Greek statue to the Byzantine mosaic, from the gymnasium to the monastery.

This species of cultural discontinuity is not unknown in other civilizations—for example in China in the third and fourth centuries A.D.—but it seems specially characteristic of the West. It took place once more in the fifteenth and sixteenth centuries at the close of the Middle Ages, and we seem to be experiencing something of the kind in Europe today. During the last period of the nineteenth century and the first years of the twentieth century a further phase of Western civilization came to an end. The old capital was exhausted and there was nothing to take its place. Liberalism and Nationalism had won their long fight with the old order, but they had lost their own ideals. In Italy the Risorgimento had given place to the age of Crispi and the Triple Alliance, and in France the centenary of the Republic was being celebrated by the Panama scandals. It was a dark age—dark not as in the early Middle Ages with the honest night of barbarism, but with the close uneasy gloom that comes before a storm. In the past, the periods of climax, as a rule, have been ages of material distress and economic decline, but the terrifying thing about that age was its prosperity, its confidence, its material success. "There has never," wrote Péguy, "been an age in which money was to such a degree the only master and god. And never have the rich been so protected against the poor and the poor so unprotected against the rich.... And never has the temporal been so protected against the spiritual; and never has the spiritual been so unprotected against the temporal."[2]

The goal of the Liberal Enlightenment and Revolution had been reached, and Europe at last possessed a completely secularized culture. The old religion had not been destroyed; in fact throughout Protestant Europe the churches still possessed a position of established privilege. But they held this position only on the condition that they did not interfere with the reign of Mammon. In reality they had been pushed aside into a backwater where they were free to stagnate in peace and to brood over the memory of dead controversies which had moved the mind of Europe three centuries before.

On the other hand the intellectuals who had contributed so much to the victory of the new order of things were in a somewhat similar plight. They found themselves powerless to influence the movement of civilization, which had cut itself free, not only from tradition, but also from art and thought. The spiritual leadership that was possessed by Voltaire and Rousseau, by Goethe and Fichte, was now a thing of the past. The men of letters were expected to follow society, not to lead it. And this is what many of them did, whether with the professional servility of the journalist or with the disinterested fanaticism of the realist, who affirmed his artistic integrity by the creation of an imaginary world no less devoid of spiritual significance than was the social world in which he lived. But a large number, probably the majority, found neither of these alternatives satisfactory. They turned to literature and art as a means of escape from reality. That was the meaning to many of the catchword, "Art for Art's sake."[3] Symbolism and aestheticism, the Ivory Tower and the Celtic Twilight, Satanism and the cult of "Evil," hashish and absinthe; all of them were ways by which the last survivors of Romanticism made their escape, leaving the enemy in possession of the field.

There was, however, one exception, one man who refused to surrender. Whatever his weakness Friedrich Nietzsche was neither a time-server nor a coward. He at least stood for the supremacy of spirit, when so many of those whose office it was to defend it had fallen asleep or had gone over to the enemy. He remained faithful to the old ideals of the Renaissance culture, the ideals of creative genius and of the self-affirmation of the free personality, and he revolted against the blasphemies of an age which degraded the personality and denied the power of the spirit in the name of humanity and liberty.

Nevertheless, Nietzsche himself was far from being a humanist. Humanism is essentially a *via media*, and in the nineteenth century the *via media* had become identical with mediocrity. In Nietzsche's eyes humanity had become something either ridiculous or shameful, and the attempt to pass beyond humanity led him to the negation of humanism and the destruction of his own personality; as he said, the way of the creator is to burn himself in his own fire. Yet the tragedy of Nietzsche is the tragedy of the end of humanism, since it only reveals with exceptional clearness the ultimate consequences of the antinomy that was inherent in the humanist tradition from the beginning.

The essentially transitory character of the humanist culture has been obscured by the dominance of the belief in Progress and by the shallow and dogmatic optimism which characterized nineteenth-century Liberalism. It was only an exceptionally original mind, like that of the late T. E. Hulme, that could free itself from the influence of Liberal dogma and could recognize *the signs of the times*—the passing of the ideals that had dominated European civilization for four centuries, and the dawn of a new order.

In the years that followed the war this consciousness has become general, at least on the Continent, owing largely to the popularity of Spengler's well-known book, *The Decline of the West*. But Spengler's arbitrary and subjective theorizing threw no light upon the inner meaning of the change. A much more profound analysis of the modern situation is to be found in the works of the modern Russian thinkers of the school of Solovyov, above all Nicholas Berdyaev. In his book *Der Sinn det Geschichte* and in his later essays on "The New Middle Ages," Berdyaev has dealt with the passing of humanism not as an instance of historical fatality, but in its ultimate significance for the spiritual life of humanity, and has shown how the disintegration of the Renaissance culture was the result of a spiritual disunity and conflict which it was never able to overcome.

In spite of its ideal of a purely human perfection and its cult of classical form, there was in humanism something excessive, a kind of *hubris* which led it to destruction. We see this already in the brilliant culture of fifteenth-century Italy, where the unbridled individualism of princes and cities led to the loss of national independence. But that is only a superficial instance of the instability of the new order. It is not in any obvious material failure, but in its very triumphs and successes, that the real weakness of the movement is to be found. For each fresh victory of the humanistic spirit undermined the foundations of its own vitality.

The Renaissance has its beginning in the self-discovery, the self-realization and the self-exaltation of Man. Medieval mad had attempted to base his life on the supernatural. His ideal of knowledge was not the adventurous quest of the human mind exploring its own kingdom; it was an intuition of the eternal verities which is itself an emanation from the Divine Intellect—*irradiatio et participatio primae lucis.* The men of the Renaissance, on the other hand, turned away from the eternal and the absolute to the world of nature and human experience. They rejected their dependence on the supernatural, and vindicated their independence and supremacy in the temporal order. But thereby they were gradually led by an internal process of logic to criticize the principles of their own knowledge and to lose confidence in their own freedom. The self-affirmation of man gradually led to the denial of the spiritual foundations of his freedom and knowledge. This tendency shows itself in every department of modern thought. In philosophy, it leads from the dogmatic rationalism of Descartes and the dogmatic empiricism of Locke to the radical skepticism of Hume and the subjectivism of later German thought. Reason is gradually stripped of its prerogatives until nothing is left to it but the bare "as if" of Vaihinger.

In science, the growth of man's knowledge and his control over nature is accompanied by a growing sense of man's dependence on material forces. He gradually loses his position of exception and superiority and sinks back into nature. He becomes a subordinate part of the great mechanical system that his scientific genius has created.

In the same way, the economic process, which led to the exploitation of the world by man and the vast increase of his material resources, ends in the subjection of man to the rule of the machine and the mechanization of human life. Finally, in the political and social sphere, the revolt against the mediaeval principle of hierarchy and the reassertion of the rights of the secular power led to the absolutism of the modern national state. This again was followed by a second revolt—the assertion of the rights of man against secular authority which culminated in the French Revolution. But this second revolt also led to disillusion. It led, on the one hand, to the disintegration of the organic principle in society into an individualistic atomism, which leaves the individual isolated and helpless before the new economic forces, and, on the other, to the growth of the new bureaucratic state, that "coldest of cold monsters," which exerts a more irresistible and far-reaching control over the individual life than was ever possessed by the absolute monarchies of the old regime.

So we have the paradox that at the beginning of the Renaissance, when the conquest of nature and the creation of modern science are still unrealized, man appears in godlike freedom with a sense of unbounded power and greatness; while at the end of the nineteenth century, when nature has been conquered and there seem no limits to the powers of science, man is once more conscious of his misery and weakness as the slave of material circumstance and physical appetite and death. Instead of the heroic exaltation of humanity which was characteristic of the naturalism of the Renaissance, we see the humiliation of humanity in the anti-human naturalism of Zola. Man is stripped of his glory and freedom and left as a naked human animal shivering in an inhuman universe.

Thus humanism by its own inner development is eventually brought to deny itself and to pass away into its opposite. For Nietzsche, who refused to surrender the spiritual element in the Renaissance tradition, humanism is transcended in an effort to attain to the superhuman without abandoning the self-assertion and the rebellious freedom of the individual will—an attempt which inevitably ends in self-destruction. But modern civilization as a whole could not follow this path. It naturally chose to live as best it could, rather than to commit a spectacular suicide. And so, in order to adapt itself to the new conditions, it was forced to throw over the humanist tradition.

Hence the increasing acceptance of the mechanization of life that has characterized the last thirty years. Above all, in the period since the war there has been a growing tendency towards the de-intellectualization and exteriorization of European life. The old fixed canons of social and moral conduct have been abandoned, and society has given itself up to the current of external change without any attempt towards self-direction or the preservation of spiritual continuity. But this acceptance of new conditions is in itself negative, and possesses no creative quality. It points to the dying-down and stagnation of culture rather than its renewal. Nor is this surprising. For centuries, Western civilization has received its impetus from the humanist tradition, and the dying-away of that tradition naturally involves the temporary cessation of cultural creativeness.

From this point of view it is very significant that almost the only original element in the thought of the new age should be the work of Jews. In physical science the dominant figure is Einstein, in psychology it is Freud, in economics and sociology it is Marx—and each of them has exerted an influence on the thought of the age that far transcends the limits of his particular subject. And it is easy to understand the reasons of this. The Jewish mind alone in the West has its own sources of life which are independent of the Hellenic and the Renaissance traditions. It has seen too many civilizations rise and fall to be discouraged by the failure of humanism. On the contrary it thrives in an atmosphere of determinism and historical destiny, which seems fatal to the humanist spirit. This holds good especially of the Marxian attitude, which is characteristic of the new conditions, although it originated at a time when liberalism and romanticism were still flourishing. But Marx addressed himself to those elements in the modern world which were already deprived of any share in the heritage of humanist culture. He found the proletariat enslaved to the machine, and he sought, not to destroy this servitude, but to equalize and rationalize it by extending it to the whole social organism.

Thus, in Marx, the cult of equality and social justice led to the sacrifice of human freedom and spiritual creativeness to an inhuman economic whole. He condemned the whole humanistic morality and culture as bourgeois, and accepted the machine, not only as the basis of economic activity, but as the explanation of the mystery of life itself. The mechanical processes of economic life are the ultimate realities of history and human life. All other things—religion, art, philosophy, spiritual life—stand on a lower plane of reality; they are a dream world of shadows cast on the sleeping mind by the physical processes of the real world of matter and mechanism. Hence Marxism may be seen as the culminating point of the modern tendency to explain that which is specifically human in terms of something else. For the Marxian interpretation of history is in fact nothing but an explaining away of history. It professes to guide us to the heart of the problem, and it merely unveils a void. And thus, according to Berdyaev, the essential importance of Marxism is to be found not in its constructive proposals, but in its negations, its sweeping away of the semi-ideological constructions of nineteenth-century thought. For the optimistic rationalism of the nineteenth century tended to hide the true significance of the conflict between materialism and spiritualism. Just as behind all religion and all spiritual philosophy there is a metaphysical assent—the affirmation of Being—so behind materialism and the materialist explaining away of history there is a metaphysical negation—the denial of Being—which is the ultimate and quasi-mystical ground of the materialistic position. In Berdyaev's words, "Man must either incorporate himself in this mystery of Not-being, and sink in the abyss of Not-being, or he must return to the inner mystery of human destiny and unite himself once again with the sacred traditions" that are the true basis of the historical process.[4]

The Western observer will probably question the metaphysical importance which Berdyaev attributes to the Marxian doctrine. It is, however, impossible to deny the connection between Communism and historical materialism, and the former actually derives much of its moral driving force from a quasi-religious devotion to the materialistic theory. There is no mistaking the note of somber religious enthusiasm that characterizes, for example, Lenin's attitude to the metaphysical side of the Marxian creed. When he attacks Mach for having "betrayed materialism with a kiss," he is not speaking in jest. He is condemning what he regards as an act of spiritual apostasy.

But this attitude finds a much more congenial atmosphere in Russia, where the religious impulse has always had a tendency towards Nihilism, than in the West. In Western Europe the decadence of the humanist tradition has left the European mind so weak that it is no longer capable of any metaphysical conviction. The greatest danger here is not that we should actively adopt the Bolshevik cult of Marxian materialism, but rather that we should yield ourselves passively to a practical materialization of culture after the American pattern. The Communists may have deified mechanism in theory, but it is the Americans who have realized it in practice. They have adapted themselves to the conditions of the new age earlier and more completely than the peoples of the Old World, partly because the external circumstances of American life were more favorable, but most of all because they were spiritually more independent of the humanist tradition. The Renaissance culture that had its center in the courts and capitals of Europe left America almost untouched. The American tradition is founded on Calvinism, which governed the social life of the Northern States down to the nineteenth century, and which possessed an almost complete monopoly of higher education; while in the new lands outside the old colonial territory, the churches, whether Calvinist or Baptist or Methodist, were still all-important, and humanist education, which was still so powerful in Europe, was practically non-existent.

Now the social effect of Calvinism and of American Protestantism in general is to create an immensely strong moral motive for action without any corresponding intellectual ideal. It is a culture of the will rather than of the understanding—a purely ethical discipline which neglects intellectual and aesthetic values. This attitude remains characteristic of American civilization even in its secular development. Thus the ideals of humanist democracy, which were received from France in the revolutionary period, were stripped of their intellectual element and moralized as a justification for the unregulated activity of the ordinary man. This led, on the one hand, to the individualistic cult of material success and, on the other, to a humanitarian idealism that is in reality nothing else but the same ideal in a socialized form. No doubt these ideals still preserved some of the moral inspiration that derives from the Puritan tradition, just as European liberalism retained something of the humanist tradition. But when this religious inspiration has evaporated, American civilization without Calvinism, like modern European civilization without humanism, becomes a body without a soul. And it is this dead civilization which is apotheosized in the mythology of Hollywood and which is invading the Old World with all the prestige of its vast material achievement. It possesses a kind of pseudo-humanist appeal since it offers the ordinary man and woman the vision of a wider and richer life. The new machine-made civilization may be destructive of the finer pleasures in life, but under the old conditions these were only accessible to a small number. The ordinary man gets more satisfaction from his cinema and his daily paper than from grand opera or classical literature. If modern civilization is able to pay its way, if it is not upset by some unexpected economic or military catastrophe, we have no reason to suppose that it will be undermined by any movement of popular dissatisfaction. On the contrary, the whole tendency of democratic politics and social reform and economic progress is to extend the sway of this standardized industrial mass-civilization. Nor can education improve matters, since if the teacher himself is without a humanist tradition or a spiritual discipline he cannot impart them to others. And science is equally unhelpful, since, when it is once separated from the humanist tradition, it becomes as utilitarian and materialistic as industrialism. The ordinary man knows and cares nothing for it, and the leader of industry and the politician value it only as the servant of the machine. The only remedy is to be found in man himself—in the renewal of the human image which was once impressed so clearly on our Western civilization, but which has now become disfigured and effaced.

II. *Humanism and Religious Experience*

The realization of the decline of the humanist tradition and the prospect of the complete mechanization of our civilization have produced a striking change in the modern intellectual attitude towards religion. The last generation—the generation of H. G. Wells and Bernard Shaw—was still prepared to idealize the machine and to place its hopes in a mechanized Utopia. The present generation has lost this confidence and is beginning to feel the need for a return to religion and a recovery of the religious attitude to life which the European mind has lost during the last two or three centuries.

And this feeling is no longer confined to the Conservatives and the supporters of the traditional intellectual order, as was largely the case in the last century. On the contrary, it is especially characteristic of the most modern of the moderns and of those who are in revolt against the existing order of things—of men like the late D. H. Lawrence and Middleton Murry and T. S. Eliot in this country, of Hugo Ball and Stefan Georg in Germany, and of Jacques Rivière, Charles du Bos and François Mauriac in France.

In the latter country alone it has taken the form of a complete acceptance of orthodox Catholicism. Elsewhere, and especially in

England, it still retains to a great extent the ideals of humanism and of the Enlightenment, for it is found most of all among those who have remained faithful to the humanist tradition, while at the same time they feel the necessity of finding a new spiritual basis which may protect it against the standardized mass-civilization of the new age. Consequently they retain the old rationalist hostility to the idea of the supernatural and the transcendent. They have come to realize the dangers that a thoroughgoing scientific materialism or even a rationalism of the eighteenth-century type involves from the point of view of humanism. They are prepared to admit spiritual values and even the validity of mystical experience, but they still hold fast to the fundamental dogmas of naturalism—the denial of the transcendent and the conception of the universe as a closed order ruled by uniform scientific law. They seek a *natural* religion in the sense of a religion without metaphysic or dogma or revelation—a religion without God.

Now a religion of this kind would certainly possess the advantage of being easily reconcilable on the one hand with the ethical tradition of humanism and on the other with the world-view of scientific naturalism, but it does not follow that it would solve our religious problems or provide modern civilization with the spiritual dynamic of which it stands in need. For there are two factors to be considered. Just as it is possible to conceive of a religion which will satisfy man's religious needs without being applicable to the social situation of modern Europe—as, for example, in Buddhism—so we can construct, at least in theory, a religion which would be adapted to the social needs of modern civilization, but which would be incapable of satisfying the purely religious demands of the human spirit. Such a religion was constructed with admirable ingenuity and sociological knowledge by Comte in the nineteenth century, and it proved utterly lacking in religious vitality, and consequently also in human appeal. And a similar experiment which is being carried out with far less knowledge and greater passion by the modern Communists in Russia threatens to be even more sterile and inimical to man's spiritual personality.

It is useless to judge a religion from the point of view of the politician or the social reformer. We shall never create a living religion merely as a means to an end, a way out of our practical difficulties. For the religious view of life is the opposite to the utilitarian. It regards the world and human life *sub specie aeternitatis*. It is only by accepting the religious point of view, by regarding religion as an end in itself and not as a means to something else, that we can discuss religious problems profitably. It may be said that this point of view belongs to the past, and that we cannot return to it. But neither can we escape from it. The past is simply the record of the experience of humanity, and if that experience testifies to the existence of a permanent human need, that need must manifest itself in the future no less than in the past.

What, then, is man's essential religious need, judging by the experience of the past? There is an extraordinary degree of unanimity in the response, although, of course, it is not complete. One answer is God, the supernatural, the transcendent; the other answer is deliverance, salvation, eternal life. And both these two elements are represented in some form or other in any given religion. The religion of ancient Israel, for example, may seem to concentrate entirely on the first of these two elements—the reality of God—and to have nothing to say about the immortality of the soul and the idea of eternal life. Yet the teaching of the prophets is essentially a doctrine of salvation—a social and earthly salvation, it is true, but nevertheless a salvation which is essentially religious and related to the eternal life of God. Again, Buddhism seems to leave no room for God and to put the whole emphasis of its teaching on the second element—deliverance. Nevertheless, it is based, as much as any religion can be, on the idea of Transcendence. Indeed, it was an exaggerated sense of Transcendence that led to its negative attitude towards the ideas of God and the Soul. "We affirm something of God, in order not to affirm nothing," says the Catholic theologian. The Buddhist went a step further on the *via negativa* and preferred to say nothing.

Now, a concentration on these two specifically religious needs produces an attitude to life totally opposed to the practical utilitarian outlook of the ordinary man. The latter regards the world of man—the world of sensible experience and social activity—as the one reality, and is skeptical of anything that lies beyond, whether in the region of pure thought or of spiritual experience, not to speak of religious faith. The religious man, on the contrary, turns his skepticism against the world of man. He is conscious of the existence of another and greater world of spiritual reality in which we live and move and have our being, though it is hidden from us by the veil of sensible things. He may even think, like Newman, that the knowledge of the senses has a merely symbolic value; that "the whole series of impressions made on us by the senses may be but a Divine economy suited to our need, and the token of realities distinct from them, and such as might be revealed to us, nay, more perfectly, by other senses as different from our existing ones as they are from one another."[5]

The one ultimate reality is the Being of God, and the world of man and nature itself are only real in so far as they have their ground and principle of being in that supreme reality. In the words of a French writer of the seventeenth century: "It is the presence of God that, without cessation, draws the creation from the abyss of its own nothingness above which His omnipotence holds it suspended, lest of its own weight it should fall back therein; and serves as the mortar and bond of connection which holds it together in order that all that it has of its Creator should not waste and flow away like water that is not kept in its channel."

Thus, although God is not myself, nor a part of my being,

> yet the relation of dependence that my life, my powers, and my operations bear to His Presence is more absolute, more essential, and more intimate than any relation I can have to the natural principles without which I could not exist... I draw my life from His Living Life...; I am, I understand, I will, I act, I imagine, I smell, I taste, I touch, I see, I walk and I love in the Infinite Being of God, within the Divine Essence and substance....
>
> God in the heavens is more my heaven than the heavens themselves; in the sun He is more my light than the sun; in the air He is more my air than the air that I breathe sensibly.... He works in me all that I am, all that I see, all that I do or can do, as most intimate, most present, and most immanent in me, as the super-essential Author and Principle of my works, without whom we should melt away and disappear from ourselves and from our own activities.[6]

Or again, to quote Cardinal Bona, God is "the Ocean of all essence and existence, the very Being itself which contains all being. From Him all things depend; they flow out from Him and flow back to Him and *are* in so far as they participate in His Being."[7]

Thus the whole universe is, as it were, the shadow of God, and has its being in the contemplation or reflection of the Being of God. The spiritual nature reflects the Divine consciously, while the animal nature is a passive and unconscious mirror. Nevertheless, even the life of the animal is a living manifestation of the Divine, and the flight of the hawk or the power of the bull is an unconscious prayer. Man alone stands between these two kingdoms in the strange twilight world of rational consciousness. He possesses a kind of knowledge which transcends the sensible without reaching the intuition of the Divine.

It is only the mystic who can escape from this twilight world; who, in Sterry's words, can "descry a glorious eternity in a winged moment of Time—a bright Infinite in the narrow point of an object, who knows what Spirit means—that spire-top whither all things ascend harmoniously, where they meet and sit connected in an unfathomed Depth of Life." But the mystic is not the normal man; he is one who has transcended, at least momentarily, the natural limits of human knowledge. The ordinary man is by his nature immersed in the world of sense, and uses his reason in order to subjugate the material world to his own ends, to satisfy his appetites and to assert his will. He lives on the animal plane with a more than animal consciousness and purpose, and in so far, he is less religious than the animal. The life of pure spirit is religious, and the life of the animal is also religious, since it is wholly united with the life-force that is its highest capacity of being. Only man is capable of separating himself alike from God and from nature, of making himself his last end and living a purely self-regarding and irreligious existence.

And yet the man who deliberately regards self-assertion and sensual enjoyment as his sole ends, and finds complete satisfaction in them—the pure materialist—is not typical; he is almost as rare as the mystic. The normal man has an obscure sense of the existence of a spiritual reality and a consciousness of the evil and misery of an existence which is the slave of sensual impulse and self-interest and which must inevitably end in physical suffering and death. But how is he to escape from this wheel to which he is bound by the accumulated weight of his own acts and desires? How is he to bring his life into vital relation with that spiritual reality of which he is but dimly conscious and which transcends all the categories of his thought and the conditions of human experience? This is the fundamental religious problem which has perplexed and baffled the mind of man from the beginning and is, in a sense, inherent in his nature.

I have intentionally stated the problem in its fullest and most classical form, as it has been formulated by the great minds of our own civilization, since the highest expression of an idea is usually also the most explicit and the most intelligible. But, as the writers whom I have quoted would themselves maintain, there is nothing specifically Christian about it. It is common to Christianity and to Platonism, and to the religious traditions of the ancient East. It is the universal attitude of the *anima naturaliter Christiana,* of that nature which the mediaeval mystics term "noble," because it is incapable of resting satisfied with a finite or sensible good. It is "natural religion" not, indeed, after the manner of the religion of naturalism that we have already mentioned, but in the true sense of the word.

It is, of course, obvious that such conceptions of spiritual reality presuppose a high level of intellectual development and that we cannot expect to find them in a pre-philosophic stage of civilization. Nevertheless, however far back we go in history, and however primitive is *the type* of culture, we do find evidence for the existence of specifically religious needs and ideas of the supernatural which are the primitive prototypes or analogues of the conceptions which we have just described.

Primitive man believes no less firmly than the religious man of the higher civilizations in the existence of a spiritual world upon which the visible world and the life of man are dependent. Indeed, this spiritual world is often more intensely realized and more constantly present to his mind than is the case with civilized man. He has not attained to the conception of an autonomous natural order, and consequently supernatural forces are liable to interpose themselves at every moment of his existence. At first sight the natural and the supernatural, the material and the spiritual, seem inextricably confused. Nevertheless, even in primitive nature-worship, the object of religious emotion and worship is never the natural phenomenon as such, but always the supernatural power which is obscurely felt to be present in and working through the natural object. The essential difference between the religion of the primitive and that of civilized man is that for the latter the spiritual world has become a cosmos, rendered intelligible by philosophy and ethical by the tradition of the world religions, whereas to the primitive it is a spiritual chaos in which good and evil, high and low, rational and irrational elements are confusedly mingled. Writers on primitive religion have continually gone astray through their attempts to reduce the spiritual world of the primitive to a single principle, to find a single cause from which the whole development may be explained and rendered intelligible. Thus Tylor finds the key in the belief in ghosts, Durkheim in the theory of an impersonal *mana* which is the exteriorization of the collective mind, and Brazer in the technique of magic. But in reality there is no single aspect of primitive religion that can be isolated and regarded as the origin of all the rest. The spiritual world of the primitive is far less unified than that of civilized man. High gods, nature spirits, the ghosts of the dead, malevolent demons, and impersonal supernatural forces and substances may all co-exist in it without forming any kind of spiritual system or hierarchy. Every primitive culture will tend to lay the religious emphasis on some particular point. In Central Africa witchcraft and the cult of ghosts may overshadow everything else; among the hunters of North America the emphasis may be laid on the visionary experience of the individual, and the cult of animal guardians; and among the Hamitic peoples the sky-god takes the foremost place. But it is dangerous to conclude that the point on which attention is focused is the whole field of consciousness. The high gods are often conceived as too far from man to pay much attention to his doings, and it is lesser powers—the spirits of the field and the forest, or the ghosts of the dead—who come into closest relation with human life, and whose malevolence is most to be feared. Consequently primitive religion is apt to appear wholly utilitarian and concerned with purely material ends. But here also the confusion of primitive thought is apt to mislead us. The ethical aspect of religion is not consciously recognized and cultivated as it is by civilized man, but it is none the less present in an obscure way. Primitive religion is essentially an attempt to bring man's life into relation with, and under the sanctions of, that other world of mysterious and sacred powers, whose action is always conceived as the ultimate and fundamental law of life. Moreover, the sense of sin and of the need for purification or catharsis is very real to primitive man. No doubt sin appears to him as a kind of physical contagion that seems to us of little moral value. Nevertheless, as we can see from the history of Greek religion, the sense of ritual defilement and that of moral guilt are very closely linked with one another, and the idea of an essential connection between moral and physical evil—between sin and death, for example—is found in the higher religions no less than among the primitives. *Libera nos a malo* is a universal prayer which answers to one of the oldest needs of human nature.

But the existence of this specifically religious need in primitive man—in other words, the naturalness of the religious altitude—is widely denied at the present day. It is maintained that primitive man is a materialist and that the attempt to find in primitive religion an obscure sense of the reality of spirit, or, indeed, anything remotely analogous to the religious experience of civilized man, is sheer metaphysical theorizing. This criticism is partly due to a tendency to identify any recognition of the religious element in primitive thought and culture with the particular theories of religious origins which have been put forward by Tylor and Durkheim. In reality, however, the theories of the latter have much more in common with those of the modern writers whom I have mentioned than any of them have with the point of view of writers who recognize the objective and autonomous character of religion. All of them show that anti-metaphysical prejudice which has been so general during the last generation or two, and which rejects on *a priori* grounds any objective interpretation of religious experience. On the Continent there is already a reaction against the idea of a "science of religion" which, unlike the other sciences, destroys its own object and leaves us with a residuum of facts that belong to a totally different order. In fact, recent German writers such as Otto, Heiler, and Karl Beth tend rather to exaggerate the mystical and intuitive character of religious experience, whether in its primitive or advanced manifestations. But in this country the anti-metaphysical prejudice is still dominant. A theory is not regarded as "scientific" unless it explains religion in terms of something else—as an artificial construction from non-religious elements.

Thus Professor Perry writes: "The idea of deity has grown up with civilization itself, and in its beginnings it was constructed out of the most homely materials." He holds that religion was derived not from primitive speculation or symbolism nor from spiritual experience, but from a practical observation of the phenomena of life. Its origins are to be found in the association of certain substances, such as red earth, shells, crystals, etc., with the ideas of life and fertility and their use as amulets or fetishes in order to prolong life or to increase the sexual powers. From these beginnings religion was developed as a purely empirical system of ensuring material prosperity by the archaic culture in Egypt and was thence gradually diffused throughout the world by Egyptian treasure-seekers and megalith-builders. The leaders of these expeditions became the first gods, while the Egyptian practices of mummification and tomb-building were the source of all those ideas concerning the nature of the soul and the existence of a spiritual world that are found among primitive peoples.

It is needless for us to discuss the archaeological aspects of this pan-Egyptian hypothesis of cultural origins. From our present point of view the main objection to the theory lies in the naive Euhemerism of its attitude to religion. For even if we grant that the whole development of higher civilization has proceeded from a single center, that is a very different thing from admitting that a fundamental type of human experience could ever find its origin in a process of cultural diffusion. It is not as though Professor Perry maintained that primitive man lived a completely animal existence before the coming of the higher culture. On the contrary, the whole tendency of his thought has been to vindicate the essential *humanity* of the primitive. It is the claim of "the new anthropology" that it rehabilitates human nature itself and "disentangles the original nature of man from the systems, tradition, and machinery of civilization which have modified it."[8] If, then, primitive man is non-religious, the conclusion follows that human nature itself is non-religious, and religion, like war, is an artificial product of later development.

But this conclusion has been reached only by the forced construction that has been arbitrarily put upon the evidence. Because the primitive fetish has no more religious value for us than the mascot that we put on our motor-cars, we assume that it can have meant nothing more to primitive man. This, however, is to fall into the same error for which Massingham rightly condemns the older anthropology—the neglect of the factor of degeneration. Our mascot is a kind of fetish, but it is a degenerate fetish, and it is degenerate precisely because it has lost its religious meaning. The religious man no longer uses mascots, though if he is a Catholic he may use the image of a saint. To the primitive man his fetish is more than the one and less than the other. It has the sanctity of a relic and the irrationality of a mascot. Professor Lowie has described how an Indian offered to show him "the greatest thing in the world";

how he reverently uncovered one cloth wrapper after another; and how at length there lay exposed a simple bunch of feathers—a mere nothing to the alien onlooker, but to the owner a badge of his covenant with the supernatural world. "It is easy," he says, "to speak of the veneration extended to such badges…as fetishism, but that label with its popular meaning is monstrously inadequate to express the psychology of the situation. For to the Indian the material object is nothing apart from its sacred associations."[9]

So, too, when Massingham speaks of primitive religion as "a purely supernatural machinery, controlled by man, for insuring the material welfare of the community," he is right in his description of facts, but wrong in his appreciation of values. To us, agriculture is merely a depressed industry which provides the raw material of our dinners, and so we assume that a religion that is largely concerned with agriculture must have been a sordid materialistic business. But this is entirely to misconceive primitive man's attitude to nature. To him, agriculture was not a sordid occupation; it was one of the supreme mysteries of life, and he surrounded it with religious rites because he believed that the fertility of the soil and the mystery of generation could only be ensured through the cooperation of higher powers. Primitive agriculture was in fact a kind of liturgy.

For us nature has lost this religious atmosphere because the latter has been transferred elsewhere. Civilization did not create the religious attitude or the essential nature of the religious experience, but it gave them new modes of expression and a new intellectual interpretation. This was the achievement of the great religions or religious philosophies that arose in all the main centers of ancient civilization about the middle of the first millennium B.C.[10] They attained to the two fundamental concepts of metaphysical being and ethical order, which have been the foundation of religious thought and the framework of religious experience ever since. Some of these movements of thought, such as Brahmanism, Taoism, and the Eleatic philosophy, concentrated their attention on the idea of Being, while others, such as Buddhism, Confucianism, Zoroastrianism, and the philosophy of Heraclitus, emphasized the idea of moral order; but all of them agreed in identifying the cosmic principle, the power behind the world, with a spiritual principle, conceived either as the source of being or as the source of ethical order.[11] Primitive man had already found the Transcendent immanent in and working through nature as the supernatural. The new religions found it in thought as the supreme Reality and in ethics as the Eternal Law. And consequently, while the former still saw the spiritual world diffused and confused with the world of matter, the latter isolated it and set it over against the world of human experience, as Eternity against Time, as the Absolute against the Contingent, as Reality against Appearance, and as the Spiritual against the Sensible.

This was indeed the discovery of a new world for the religious consciousness. It was thereby liberated from the power of the nature daimons and the dark forces of magic and translated to a higher sphere—to the Brahma-world—"where there is not darkness nor day nor night, not being nor not-being, but the Eternal alone, the source of the ancient wisdom," to the Kingdom of Ahura and the Six Immortal Holy Ones, to the world of the Eternal Forms, the true home of the soul. And this involved a corresponding change in the religious attitude. The religious life was no longer bound up with irrational myths and non-moral taboos; it was a process of spiritual discipline directed towards the purification of the mind and the will—a conversion of the soul from the life of the senses to spiritual reality. The religious experience of primitive man had become obscured by magic and diabolism, and the visions and trances of the Shaman belong rather to the phenomena of Spiritualism than of mysticism. The new type of religious experience, on the other hand, had reached a higher plane. It consisted in an intuition that was essentially spiritual and found its highest realization in the vision of the mystic.

Thus each of the new religio-philosophic traditions—Brahmanism, Buddhism, Taoism, and Platonism—ultimately transcends philosophy and culminates in mysticism. They are not satisfied with the demonstration of the Absolute; they demand the experience of the Absolute also, whether it be the vision of the Essential Good and the Essential Beauty, through which the soul is made deiform, or that intuition of the nothingness and illusion inherent in all contingent being which renders a man *jivana mukti*, "delivered alive." But how is such an experience conceivable? It seems to be a contradiction in terms—to know the Unknowable, to grasp the Incomprehensible, to receive the Infinite. Certainly it transcends the categories of human thought and the normal conditions of human experience. Yet it has remained for thousands of years as the goal—whether attainable or unattainable—of the religious life; and no religion which ignores this aspiration can prove permanently satisfying to man's spiritual needs. The whole religious experience of mankind—indeed, the very existence of religion itself—testifies, not only to a sense of the Transcendent, but to an appetite for the Transcendent that can only be satisfied by immediate contact—by a vision of the supreme Reality. It is the goal of the intellect as well as of the will, for, as a Belgian philosopher has said, "The human mind is a *faculty in quest of its intuitions*, that is to say, of assimilation with Being," and it is "perpetually chased from the movable, manifold and deficient towards the Absolute, the One and the Infinite, that is, towards *Being pure and simple*."[12] A religion that remains on the rational level and denies the possibility of any real relation with a higher order of spiritual reality, fails in its most essential function, and ultimately, like Deism, ceases to be a religion at all. It may perhaps be objected that this view involves the identification of religion with mysticism, and that it would place a philosophy of intuition like that of the Vedanta higher than a religion of faith and supernatural revelation, like Christianity. In reality, however, the Christian insistence on the necessity of faith and revelation implies an even higher conception of transcendence than that of the oriental religions. Faith transcends the sphere of rational knowledge even more than metaphysical intuition, and brings the mind into close contact with super-intelligible reality. Yet faith also, at least when it is joined with spiritual intelligence, is itself a kind of obscure intuition—a foretaste of the unseen[13]—and it also has its culmination in the mystical experience by which these obscure spiritual realities are realized experimentally and intuitively.

Thus Christianity is in agreement with the great oriental religions and with Platonism in its goal of spiritual intuition, though it places the full realization of that goal at a further and higher stage of spiritual development than the rest. For all of them religion is not an affair of the emotions, but of the intelligence. Religious knowledge is the highest kind of knowledge, the end and coronation of the whole process of man's intellectual development.

Herein they all differ profoundly from the conceptions of religion and religious experience that have been developed by modern European thinkers. For the modern mind no longer admits the possibility or the objective value of spiritual knowledge. The whole tendency of Western thought since the Renaissance, and still more since the eighteenth century, has been to deny the existence of any real knowledge except that of rational demonstration founded upon" sensible experience. Intuition, whether metaphysical or mystical, is regarded as an irrational emotional conviction, and religion is reduced to subjective feeling and moral activity. Such a religion, however, can have no intellectual authority, and in consequence it also loses its social authority and even its moral influence. Civilization becomes completely rationalized and secularized, as may be seen from the last two centuries of European history.

Nevertheless, man cannot live by reason alone. His spiritual life, and even his physical instincts, are starved in the narrow and arid territory of purely rational consciousness. He is driven to take refuge in the non-rational, whether it be the irrational blend of spirituality and emotionalism that is termed romanticism, or, as is increasingly the case today, in the frankly sub-rational sphere of pure sensationalism and sexual impulse.

Today we are faced with the bankruptcy of rationalism and with the necessity of finding some principle of the religious order which can rescue us from the resultant confusion. One alternative is that of the late D. H. Lawrence, who accepts the failure of reason, and who seeks to find a basis for the religious consciousness not in spiritual intuition, but in "that lower intuition of the senses and the physical life, the reality of which cannot be denied even by the rationalist." He writes:

> Come down from your pre-eminence, O mind, O lofty spirit!
> Your hour has struck,
> Your unique day is over,
> Absolutism is finished in the human consciousness too.
>
> A man is many things: he is not only a mind.
> But in his consciousness he is twofold at least:
> He is cerebral, intellectual, mental, spiritual,
> But also he is instinctive, intuitive, and in touch.
>
> The blood knows in darkness, and forever dark,
> In touch, by intuition, instinctively.
> The blood also knows religiously,
> And of this the mind is incapable.
> The mind is non-religious.

> To my dark heart gods *are.*
> In my dark heart love is and is not.
> But to my white mind
> Gods and love alike are but an idea,
> A kind of fiction.[14]

This is, so it seems to me, the inevitable conclusion of the religious mind that no longer conceives the possibility of spiritual intuition or supernatural revelation. It is driven back upon the lower type of religious experience, which primitive man possessed when he worshiped the daimonic powers that seemed to rule his life. And yet, even so, Lawrence's position is not wholly consistent, for even the lower type of religious experience is in a real sense spiritual. It is the result of a spiritual intuition, even though that intuition is, as St. Paul says, in bondage to "the weak and beggarly elements" of nature. The religion of the blood of which Lawrence writes, the religion of pure sense and animal instinct, can only be attained by the unreflecting animal soul. If we were conscious of it, we should not have it. It is a true spiritual instinct which prompted Lawrence to revolt against the tyranny of "the white mind" and to seek a deeper wisdom than that of the rational consciousness; but, owing to the denial and repression of true spiritual intuition, it has been deflected into a false cult of the primitive and the physical which can afford no true solution of his problem.

This is fully realized by another writer, who has considerable sympathy with his point of view and who also seeks escape from the present *impasse* in a religious experience. J. Middleton Murry not only admits the possibility of a spiritual intuition, but makes it the center of his whole theory of life.

He recognizes the insufficiency of the modern scientific point of view that identifies reality with the physical and biological world. The human mind can only achieve unity with itself and harmony with the universe on the higher "metabiological" plane, in an experience which transcends both sensible and rational knowledge. This experience finds its highest expression in the life of Jesus, and thereby Jesus was the creator of a new series of values and the starting-point of a new phase in the evolution of humanity. Nevertheless, Murry holds that the reality that is apprehended in this way is not metaphysical or transcendent; it is simply the organic unity of nature, the unity of biological being. There is no eternal and transcendent being which we can think of as divine, but only the natural organism which is the product of the evolutionary process. For Murry is an adherent of the dogma of "emergence," a worshiper of the God that we create as we go along.[15] God is a useful fiction, a creature of the human mind, not the ultimate ground of reality. This relativism, however, ill accords with the absolutism of his theory of knowledge. It is difficult to see how we can attain to a metabiological plane of consciousness and activity if there is no corresponding metabiological stage of being. For metabiological activity implies metaphysical being, no less than biological activity involves physical being. We must either accept the reality and autonomy of spiritual being or abandon the possibility of spiritual knowledge. It is true that the intuition of unity of which Murry speaks does not necessarily involve the belief in the transcendent personal God of Christian doctrine. It has more affinity with the monism of the Vedanta, or still more with that of Taoism. But it does necessitate, no less than Taoism, the idea of an eternal transcendental principle which is the source and not the product of the cosmic process.

It may be objected that Murry's philosophy has in fact arisen directly from his spiritual experience, and, consequently, that it cannot be inconsistent with it. But this is not exactly the case. Certainly Murry's theory of the existence of metabiological values and of a higher form of knowledge than the purely rational springs directly from his experience. But this is not so with regard to his denial of the transcendent and the supernatural. That was due not to his mysticism, but to his adherence to the dogmas of scientific naturalism, and he has interpreted his experience to accord with these preconceived ideas.

He himself points out that his first reaction to his experience was purely religious—a conviction of spiritual reality and spiritual regeneration—and that his mature philosophy is not so much a logical consequence of his mystical experience as the means by which he succeeded in "disintoxicating" himself from it. It is conditioned throughout by his fundamental hostility to any form of supernaturalism—by his conviction that the introduction of the category of the supernatural involves "mental" and spiritual suicide."[16]

This prejudice has been firmly implanted in the modern mind by two centuries of dogmatic naturalism, but it is difficult to understand its rational justification in the present instance. From the point of view of scientific mechanism there is certainly no room for the supernatural, but on that assumption Murry's category of the metabiological must also be excluded. The anti-supernaturalist view rests fundamentally on the hypothesis of a universe in which quality and value have no meaning and where everything is reducible to matter and energy. If we once admit the possibility of a mode of spiritual consciousness or being which transcends the biological, there seems no reason to regard the human mind as its only field of manifestation.

It is no less reasonable to suppose that the metabiological plane is the point at which a higher order of being has inserted itself into the life of humanity than to suppose that it is a completely new order which has "emerged" from below. Even in the sensible world we have an example of the way in which a higher order of being can intervene to modify the natural development of a lower order. From the animals' standpoint, man himself is a supernatural being whose action governs their life in a mysterious way and who even creates, as it were, new creatures like the setter and the racehorse, and admits them to a certain participation in his own life. And why, then, is it irrational to believe that, as Plato says, mankind is "the flock of the Gods," that human life is susceptible to the influence of a higher power which fosters in it those new capacities and modes of being which we call spiritual and metabiological? Such a belief may seem to us incredible, but it is not really irrational. It would indeed be strange if reality did not transcend man's comprehension qualitatively as well as quantitatively. The refusal to admit this possibility rests not so much on reason as on the humanist prejudice which insists that the human mind is the highest of all possible forms of existence and the only standard of reality. It is this prejudice which prevents Murry from developing the full implications of his religious experience. He has recognized one truth that is vital for religion—that the path of human development must lie in the spiritual, not the physical, world, and that his nature is not wholly earthbound—that it has a window that is open to the infinite. But, on the other hand, he rejects the other truth that is equally vital—the transcendence and absoluteness of spiritual reality. The religious attitude is only possible in the presence of the eternal and the transcendent. Any object that falls short of this fails to inspire the sense of awe and self-surrender, which is essential to true religion. Man cannot worship himself, nor can he adore a Time God that is the creation of his own mind. As soon as he recognizes its fictitious character such an idea loses all its religious power. And for the same reason every attempt to create a new religion on purely rational and human foundations is inevitably doomed to failure.

III. *The Claim of Christianity*

If we accept the necessity of an absolute and metaphysical foundation for religion and religious experience, we still have to face the other aspect of the problem—namely, how this spiritual experience is to be brought into living relation with human life and with the social order. The ecstasy of the solitary mind in the presence of absolute reality seems to offer no solution to the actual sufferings and perplexities of humanity. And yet the religious mind cannot dissociate itself from this need, for it can never rest content with a purely individual and self-regarding ideal of deliverance. The more religious a man is, the more is he sensitive to the common need of humanity. All the founders of the world religions—even those, like Buddha, who were the most uncompromising in their religious absolutism—were concerned not merely with their private religious experience, but with the common need of humanity. They aspired to be the saviors and pathfinders—ford-makers, as the Indians termed them—who should rescue their people from the darkness and suffering of human life.

Nowhere is this social preoccupation more insistent than in the religious tradition of the West, and it is to be found even in the most abstract and intellectualist type of religious thought. It is to be seen above all in Plato, the perfect example of the pure metaphysician, who, nevertheless, made his metaphysics the basis of a program of political and social reform. Indeed, according to his own description in the Seventh Epistle it was his political interests and his realization of the injustice and moral confusion of the existing state which were the starting point of his metaphysical quest. But though Plato realized as fully as any purely religious teacher the need for bringing social life into contact with spiritual reality and for relating man's rational activity to the higher intuitive knowledge, he failed to show how this could be accomplished by means of a purely intellectual discipline. He saw that it was necessary on the one hand to drag humanity out of the shadow world of appearances and false moral standards into the pure white light of spiritual reality, and, on the other hand, that the contemplative must be forced to leave his mountain of vision and "to descend again to these prisoners and to partake in their toils and honors."[17] But, as he says, the spiritual man is at a disadvantage in the world of politics and business. The eyes that have looked upon the sun can no longer distinguish the shadows of the cave. The man who cares only for eternal things, who seeks to fly hence and to become assimilated to God by holiness and justice and wisdom, is unable to strive for political power with the mean cunning of the ordinary "man of affairs."[18] In fact nothing could show the impossibility of curing the ills of humanity by pure intelligence more completely than Plato's own attempt to reform the state of Sicily by giving a young tyrant lessons in mathematics. The political problems of the Greek world were solved not by the philosopher-king, but by condottieri and Macedonian generals, and the gulf between the spiritual world and human life grew steadily wider until the coming of Christianity.

In the East, however, the religious conception of life was victorious and dominated the whole field of culture. In India, above all, the ideal of spiritual intuition was not confined to a few philosophers and mystics, but became the goal of the whole religious "development." It was, as Professor de la Vallée Poussin has said, "the great discovery that has remained for at least twenty-five centuries the capital and most cherished truth of the Indian people." The man who cannot understand this cannot understand the religion of India or the civilization with which it is so intimately connected. It is, however, only too easy for the Western mind to misconceive the whole tendency of Indian thought. It is apt to interpret the teaching of the Upanishads on the lines of Western idealist philosophy, and to see in the Indian doctrine of contemplation a philosophic pantheism that is intellectualist rather than religious. In reality it is in Western mystics such as Eckart or Angelus Silesius rather than in philosophers such as Hegel or even Spinoza that the true parallel to the thought of the Vendanta is to be found. It leads not to pantheism in our sense of the word, but to an extreme theory of transcendence which may be termed super-theism. Western pantheism is a kind of spiritual democracy in which all things are equally God; but the "non-dualism" of the Vedanta is a spiritual absolutism in which God is the only reality. At first sight there may seem to be little practical difference between the statement that everything that exists is divine and the statement that nothing but the divine exists. But from the religious point of view there is all the difference in the world. For "if this transitory world be the Real," says a mediaeval Vedantist, "then there is no liberation through the Atman, the holy scriptures are without authority and the Lord speaks untruth.... The Lord who knows the reality of things has declared 'I am not contained in these things, nor do beings dwell in Me.'"[19]

God is the one Reality. Apart from Him, nothing exists. In comparison with Him, nothing is real. The universe only exists in so fat as it is rooted and grounded in His Being. He is the Self of ourselves and the Soul of our souls. So far the Vedanta does not differ essentially from the teaching of Christian theology. The one vital distinction consists in the fact that Indian religion ignores the idea of creation and that in consequence it is faced with the dilemma that either the whole universe is an illusion—Maya—a dream that vanishes when the soul awakens to the intuition of spiritual reality, or else that the world is the self-manifestation of the Divine Mind, a conditional embodiment of the absolute Being.

Hence there is no room for a real intervention of the spiritual principle in human life. The Indian ethic is, above all, an ethic of flight—of deliverance from conditional existence and from the chain of re-birth. Human life is an object of compassion to the wise man, but it is also an object of scorn. "As the hog to the trough, goes the fool to the womb," says the Buddhist verse; and the Hindu attitude, if less harsh, is not essentially different "Men are held by the manifold snares of the desires in the world of sense, and they fall away without winning to their end like dykes of sand in water. Like sesame-grains for their oil, all things are ground out in the mill-wheel of creation by the oil-grinders, to wit, the taints arising from ignorance that fasten upon them. The husband gathers to himself evil works on account of his wife; but he alone is therefore afflicted with taints, which cling to man alike in the world beyond and in this. All men are attached to children, wives, and kin; they sink down in the slimy sea of sorrow, like age-worn forest-elephants."[20]

It is true that orthodox Hinduism inculcates the fulfillment of social duties, and the need for outward activity, but this principle does not lead to the transformation of life by moral action, but simply to the fatalistic acceptance of the established order of things. This is the theme of the greatest work of Indian literature, the *Bhagavad-Gita*, and it involves a moral attitude diametrically opposed to that of the Western mind. When Arjuna shrinks from the evils of war and declares that he would rather die than shed the blood of his kinsfolk, the god does not commend him. He uses the doctrine of the transcendence and impassibility of true being to justify the ruthlessness of the warrior.

> Know that that which pervades this universe is imperishable; there is none can make to perish that changeless being.
>
> This Body's Tenant for all time may not be wounded, O Thou of Bharata's stock, in the bodies of any beings. Therefore thou dost not well to sorrow for any born beings. Looking likewise in thine own Law, thou shouldst not be dismayed; for to a knight there is no thing more blest than a lawful strife.[21]

The sacred order that is the basis of Indian culture is no true spiritualization of human life; it is merely the natural order seen through a veil of metaphysical idealism. It can incorporate the most barbaric and non-ethical elements equally with the most profound metaphysical truths; since in the presence of the absolute and the unconditioned all distinctions and degrees of value lose their validity.

The experience of India is sufficient to show that it is impossible to construct a dynamic religion on metaphysical principles alone, since pure intuition affords no real basis for social action. On the other hand, if we abandon the metaphysical element and content ourselves with purely ethical and social ideals, we are still further from a solution, since there is no longer any basis for a spiritual order. The unity of the inner world dissolves in subjectivism and skepticism, and society is threatened with anarchy and dissolution. And since social life is impossible without order, it is necessary to resort to some external principle of compulsion, whether political or economic. In the ancient world this principle was found in the military despotism of the Roman Empire, and in the modern world we have the even more complete and far-reaching organization of the economic machine. Here indeed we have an order, but it is an order that is far more inhuman and indifferent to moral values than the static theocratic order of the Oriental religion-cultures.

But is there no alternative between Americanism and Orientalism, between a spiritual order that takes no account of human needs and a material order that has no regard for spiritual values? There still remains the traditional religion of our own civilization: Christianity, a religion that is neither wholly metaphysical nor merely ethical, but one that brings the spiritual world into vital and fruitful communion with the life of man.

The whole spiritual inheritance of European civilization is based upon Christianity, and even today whatever there is of religious life and spiritual aspiration in the West still draws its vitality from Christian sources.

Nevertheless it must be admitted that for centuries Christianity has been progressively losing its hold on Western culture, and both its doctrines and its moral ideals have fallen into discredit. The causes of this state of things lie deep in that process of the humanization and rationalizing of Western culture which I described in the earlier part of this essay. Ever since the Renaissance the centrifugal tendencies in our civilization have destroyed its spiritual unity and divided its spiritual forces. The Western mind has turned away from the contemplation of the absolute and the eternal to the knowledge of the particular and the contingent. It has made man the measure of all things and has sought to emancipate human life from its dependence on the supernatural. Instead of the whole intellectual and social order being subordinated to spiritual principles, every activity has declared its independence, and we see politics, economics, science, and art organizing themselves as autonomous kingdoms which owe no allegiance to any higher power.

And these tendencies were not confined to the secular side of life; they made themselves felt in religion also. Religion came to be regarded as one among a number of competing interests—a limited department of life, which had no jurisdiction over the rest. And as it lost its universal authority, it lost its universal vision; it became sectionalized and rationalized with the rest of European life. The ancient unity of Christendom fell asunder into a mass of warring sects, which were so absorbed in their internecine feuds that they were hardly conscious of their loss of spiritual vision and social authority. In Catholic Europe, it is true, the Church maintained its universal claims and its absolute metaphysical principles, but there also it was gradually extruded from the control of social and intellectual life, and forced to concentrate itself on the inner defenses of the altar and the cloister. By the nineteenth century the forces of secularism and "anti-clericalism" were everywhere triumphant, and the new Latin democracies seemed bent on the creation of a purely "lay" culture, which should eliminate the last traces of religious influence from the national life.

But it is in Northern Europe that we can most clearly trace the disintegrating effects of modern culture within Christianity itself. Here Catholicism was replaced by a new conception of Christianity that gave free scope to the centrifugal tendencies of the Western mind. Protestantism eliminated the metaphysical element in the Christian tradition. It abolished asceticism and monasticism; it subordinated contemplation to action and the intelligence to the will. God was no longer conceived as the Super-essential Being, from Whom the created universe receives all that it has of reality and intelligibility, but as a "magnified non-natural man, who likes and dislikes, knows and decrees, just as a man, only on a scale immensely transcending anything of which we have experience."[22]

It is true that Luther's own religious experience was both genuine and profound, but it was not the positive intuition of the contemplative; it was a dark and tormented sense of man's utter helplessness and of the otherness of the Divine Power. For his discarding of the intellectual element in religion had brought his mind back, as it were, to the religious attitude of primitive man who sees the Divine as an unknown and hostile power from which he recoils in terror. "Yea," he writes, "God is more terrible and frightful than the Devil, for He dealeth with us and bringeth us to ruin with power, smiteth and hammereth us and payeth no heed to us. In His majesty He is a consuming fire. For therefrom can no man refrain; if he thinketh on God aright his heart in his body is stricken with terror.... Yea, as soon as he heareth God named he is filled with trepidation and fear." "For He assaileth a man and has such a delight therein that He is of His jealousy and wrath impelled to consume the wicked."[23]

But Luther's personal attitude is decidedly abnormal and non-representative; the normal Protestant religious experience is of the milder and more emotional type represented by pietism and revivalism. Here faith is no longer conceived as a super-rational knowledge founded on the Divine Reason, but as a subjective conviction of one's own conversion and justification, and in place of the spiritual ecstasy of the "mystic, who realizes his own nothingness, we have the self-conscious attitude of the pietist, who is intensely preoccupied with his own feelings and with the moral state of his neighbor. And this substitution of the ideal of pietism for those of asceticism and mysticism eventually led to the weakening and discrediting of the ethical ideals of Christianity, just as sectarianism undermined its social authority. However unjust may be the popular caricature of the pietist as a snuffling hypocrite of the type of Tribulation Wholesome or Zeal-of-the-Land Busy or Mr. Chadband, there can be no doubt that Puritan and Evangelical pietism succeeded in making religion supremely unattractive in a way that mediaeval asceticism had never done.

And, at the same time, the divorce of dogma at once from ecclesiastical tradition and from philosophy eventually left it helpless before rationalist criticism. It is true that nothing could have been further from the intention of the Reformers. In fact, it was the very vehemence of their conviction of the absolute transcendence and incomprehensibility of the Divine action that led them to reject alike the supernatural authority of the Church and the natural rights of human intelligence, and to fall back on the testimony of personal experience and the infallible authority of Scripture. But, though they succeeded in erecting on these foundations a system of dogma more rigid and more exclusive than that which it replaced, the whole dogmatic edifice rested on an arbitrary subjective basis and had no internal coherence or consistency. It incorporated a great part of the traditional patristic and scholastic theology, which really formed an organic element of the Catholic tradition that it professed to reject. Hence, as Harnack has shown, the work of the Reformation was confused and incomplete, and produced at first merely an impoverished version of traditional Catholicism. It required a long process of criticism and historical inquiry before the kernel of Protestant doctrine could be freed from its husk of traditional dogma.

With the advance of historical scholarship in the nineteenth century, it finally became clear that the dogmatic tradition of Christianity could not be separated from its ecclesiastical and sacramental elements. Catholicism was not, as the Reformers believed, the result of the apostasy of the mediaeval Papacy; it was a continuous process of organic development which is as old as Christianity itself. And so the modern Protestant scholar, who admitted that Christianity and Catholicism were identical down to the age of the Reformation, that "the Christianity of the apostolic age is itself incipient Catholicism, and that the Catholicizing of Christianity begins immediately after the death of Jesus," was forced to reject the Reformation compromise. He was left with the choice of two alternatives—either to deny the organic unity of the whole development and to view Christianity as mere syncretism—"a varying compound of some of the best and some of the worst elements of Paganism and Judaism, molded in practice by the innate character of certain peoples of the Western world,"[24] as Huxley puts it—or else to go back behind the early Church, behind even the New Testament, to the original purity of the gospel of Jesus.

This second alternative is the Liberal Protestant solution, and it is the logical conclusion of the appeal of the Reformers from the Church to the Bible and of their attempt to set up an abstract ideal of primitive Christianity against the historic reality of the Catholic Church. In the moral teaching of the Gospel and in the personality of "the historical Jesus" the Liberal Protestants believed that they had at last found a firm basis for a faith that should be purely ethical and religious without any contamination of metaphysics or theological speculation. This is what Harnack means when he says that the work of the Reformation is only completed when *faith cancels dogma*, and that the Reformation is the end of dogma as the Gospel was the end of the Law. The divorce of dogma from intelligence that was inaugurated by the Reformers consummates itself in the dissolution of dogma itself in the interests of that moral pragmatism which is the essence of modern Protestantism. Christianity, it is said, is not a creed but a life; its sole criterion is the moral and social activity that it generates. And thus religion loses all contact with absolute truth and becomes merely an emotional justification for a certain standard of behavior.

But this intensely subjective attitude to religion is no less inconsistent with a genuinely historical understanding of the Gospels than it is with theology or metaphysics. Liberal Protestantism selects those elements in the Gospel which appeal to the modern liberal mind, and disregards or rejects the uncompromising supernaturalism on which the ethical teaching of Jesus rests. It condemned the Catholic tradition for replacing the historical Jesus by a metaphysical abstraction—the incarnation of a Divine hypostasis—while its own interpretation was nothing but an ethical abstraction—the incarnation of the ideals of liberal humanitarianism.[25]

It was inevitable that the one-sidedness of the Liberal Protestant solution should produce a corresponding reaction, and at the beginning of this century advanced criticism turned abruptly to the opposite extreme. The eschatological school was inspired by a justifiable distrust of the Liberal tendency to interpret the life of Jesus in terms of modern thought and sentiment, and they were consequently led to depreciate the ethical element in the Gospel and to accentuate its catastrophic and apocalyptic character. In Dean Inge's words, "They stripped the figure of Jesus of all the attributes with which the devotion of centuries had invested it and have left us with a mild specimen of the Mahdi type, an apocalyptic dreamer whose message consisted essentially of predictions about the approaching catastrophic 'end of the age,' predictions which of course came to nothing."

Thus we are left with two contradictory solutions, neither of which affords any basis for an explanation of the emergence of Christianity in the form in which it is known to history. Hence it is not surprising that those, like Loisy, who have followed the path of criticism to its extreme conclusion, should have ended in the despairing skepticism of a completely negative theory of religious syncretism. But even in this final stage there is no finality. All the resources of comparative religion are at the disposal of the critic, and the figure of the historical Jesus disappears in an ever-changing mist of Oriental myths and Hellenistic mystery religions. Neo-Pythagoreanism, Orphism, Iranian soteriology, the mystery religions, Mandaeanism; in each of them some scholar has found the key to the origins of Christianity, and each successive solution is equally convincing or unconvincing, for in this phantom world all things are shadows, and the shadows change their shape as the spectator changes his position.

We may well ask how it is that the relatively simple story of the birth of Christianity, concerning which, moreover, we possess fuller and more authentic documents than in the case of any other of the world religions, should have become involved in such a web of sophistication and misplaced ingenuity. And it would be incomprehensible were it not that the whole development has been conditioned from the outset by a series of *a priori* prejudices. The most obvious of them is the anti-metaphysical prejudice to which I referred in the last chapter—the refusal to admit the objective and autonomous character of religion and of spiritual reality, and the affirmation that everything in the world is *of the same color*, as Renan puts it, and that there is no free spiritual principle in the universe apart from the will of man. Hence it becomes necessary not only to eliminate every supernatural element in the Gospel and in the history of the Church, but, furthermore, to deny the essential originality and spontaneity of Christianity and to explain it away as a composite development derived from elements that were already in existence.

This prejudice has had an incalculable influence on the modern mind, since it could invoke the prestige of "science," that is to say, the dogmatic conception of scientific materialism. But its influence might have been limited to rationalist circles had it not been reinforced by a second prejudice, which was based on religious preconceptions. This was the Protestant conviction that a vital breach had intervened between the Gospel of Jesus and the Faith of the Church. The Reformers, it is true, placed this breach as late as the Middle Ages, but, as we have seen, the growth of historical knowledge gradually increased the antiquity of the Catholic development until its origins became actually coterminous with the foundation of Christianity as an organized religion. Thus the way is laid open for the acceptance of the rationalist explanation of Christian origins, excluding only the person of Jesus and an ethical abstraction of His teaching, which are preserved as an isolated and unrelated ideal of spiritual religion that is to inspire the religious life of modern men.

The moral earnestness and erudition of the advocates of this view have caused its fundamental illogicality and its unhistorical character to be overlooked, and even at the present day it enjoys enormous prestige, for it offers a *via media* between traditional Christianity and pure rationalism that appeals both to the Christian who has lost his faith in the dogmatic teaching of the Church and to the rationalist who has preserved a sense of religious values. It has recently found a distinguished adherent in Middleton Murry, who bases his own theory of religious naturalism on the personality and the religious ideal of Jesus. But Murry, at least, is more logical or more honest than his predecessors in that he does not claim the name of Christianity for his new religious ideal. On the contrary, he explicitly recognizes the inseparable connection between the Christian religion and the Christian Church. "There is not," he writes, "and never will be any reconciliation between Christianity and the experimental method. Christianity is the great Church and nothing else is Christianity. To call anything else Christianity is to plunge into confusion and chaos; and it is an insult to Christianity. Christianity is a great tiling, not a little one; one thing not many things; a rich thing not a poor thing; a majestic thing not a thing of shreds and patches. Christianity is Christianity at its noblest, truest and most comprehensive, and that is the Catholic Church. If you desire to be a Christian, join it. It will make no demands upon you that are more fearful than the demands made upon you by any peddling form of Christianity. It asks no greater sacrifice than Little Bethel or the Church of England; and it does not insult your intelligence by inviting you to become a member of a contradiction in terms."[26]

But when we have reached this point there is no longer any reason for one who is not under the influence of rationalist or Protestant prejudices to refuse to admit that the historic faith and life of the Church were founded on the life and gospel of the historic Jesus. It is, in fact, only so that we can account for the creative originality of the Christian religion. A great spiritual unity like Christianity cannot be the accidental product of a series of misunderstandings. It must have had its origin in some great spiritual force; and where is this to be found if not in the life of that Person whom even the rationalist admits to have been the greatest and most original religious genius in the history of humanity?

And as soon as we set aside these *a priori* conceptions and approach the study of Christian origins with an open mind, the vital relation between the Church and the teaching of Jesus at once becomes manifest. Christianity did not arise *in vacuo* as an abstract theory of salvation, like Buddhism or the Gnostic sects; it was organically and consciously linked with a pre-existing historic religion; and this religion alone among the great faiths of the world was essentially based on the belief in a Holy Society. The One God had chosen for Himself one people and had bound it to Him by an eternal covenant. Israel was a theophoric community; not only a witness to the Divine unity but the bearer of the Divine purpose of mankind; for this little people "despised by man, the servant of rulers," was to be the source of a universal Kingdom of God, which should embrace all nations, and in which the creative purpose of God should find its ultimate fulfillment. Thus Israel was not a nation in the ordinary sense so much as a church, and the loss of political independence under the Roman Empire tended still further to accentuate its religious aspect. Faced by the universalism of the Roman world-power, the spiritual universalism of Israel acquired yet clearer consciousness, and the mind of the people was pre-occupied, as never before, by the hope of the coming of a Messianic deliverer who would break the power of the nations and set up the eternal kingdom of prophecy.

It was to those who lived in the expectation of this hope and "waited for the consolation of Israel" that the preaching of Jesus was addressed. His gospel consisted essentially in the announcement of the coming of the Kingdom; and this was not, as so many moderns hold, merely a figurative expression for an abstract ethical ideal; it was an absolutely realist conception of the coming of a new supernatural order—the culminating event in the history of Israel and of the world. So far the eschatological school is right; their error consists in their tendency to interpret this teaching in the spirit of the apocryphal apocalypses rather than in that of the prophets, and in their depredation of its spiritual and universal character. For the Kingdom of the gospels is not a national triumph of Israel over his foes; it is the mystical and spiritual reign of God in humanity. It is already immanent in the present order, which it is destined to transform and supersede—it is a leaven and a seed and a hidden treasure. It is open not to the Jews as such—the children of Abraham—nor to the Scribes and Pharisees, who observe meticulously all the outward prescriptions of the Mosaic law, but to the poor and the meek, the seekers after justice and those who follow the Son of Man in his sufferings and humiliation.

Nevertheless, the spirituality of the Kingdom does not imply that it was purely internal and individual. It retained the objective social character that *it* possessed in the prophetic tradition. It was to find its realization in and through a community. But this community was no longer the national church-state of Jewish history; it was a new Messianic society—the "little flock" of which the gospels speak (Luke 12:32). The mission of Jesus consisted essentially in the foundation of this society, not by doctrine alone, but by an act of creative power. Nothing can be further from the colorless Liberal picture of Jesus as a great moral idealist than the figure of the Son of Man in the Gospels, filled with the consciousness of his Messianic office and inaugurating a new supernatural dispensation by the New Covenant of his voluntary sacrifice. All the mythological parallels invoked by rationalist critics from the vegetation cults of primitive peoples and the mystery religions of the Hellenistic world sink into insignificance by the side of the profound spiritual reality of the words of Jesus, "I have a baptism wherewith I am to be baptized and how am I straitened until it be accomplished?", or of that great scene in the Upper Chamber, which only the most arbitrary preconceptions can remove from its place in the most ancient and authenticated documents of primitive Christianity.

Nor is it possible to deny that the actual beginnings of the historic Christian Church were rooted in this doctrine of a new order inaugurated by the Death and Resurrection of Jesus and incorporated in a spiritual society. The outpouring of the Spirit on the disciples at Pentecost was regarded as the fulfillment of prophecy and of the promises of Jesus to His apostles. For the possession of the Holy Spirit was the essential characteristic of the new society. It was, even more than Israel, a *theophoric* community, since it was the external organ of the Holy Spirit and enjoyed supernatural powers and authority. And at the same time the early Christians preserved the historical associations and the social self-consciousness of the Jewish tradition; they felt themselves to be a true people, "a chosen race, a royal priesthood, a holy nation." Such a conception is almost incomprehensible to the modern mind, which has become accustomed to treat religion as a matter for the individual conscience, and it is not surprising that Protestant thinkers, such as Dean Inge, should repudiate the very idea of the existence of an objective supernatural society.[27] But there is not the shadow of a doubt that the early Christians believed in it with an intense conviction and devotion as the very center and ground of their faith. To Hermas, the Roman prophet, the Church is the first-born of creatures, and it is for her sake that the world itself was made.[28] As Christ is the New Adam the Church is the New Eve, the mother of the new humanity. And this mystical conception of the Church was in no way inconsistent with a strict insistence on its corporate authority and discipline. Although the eyes of the Christian were fixed on the future glory of the Kingdom of Christ rather than on the present order of things, this future kingdom was organically connected with the visible hierarchical Church, in the same way that the Messianic kingdom of prophecy was associated with the historic Israel. Indeed the Church was itself the future kingdom in embryo. In the vision of Hermas it is a tower, which is being built of living stones brought from every quarter of the earth and thus the process of its construction is, in Newman's phrase, *the measure of the duration of the world.*

This faith in a holy society and in a historical process of redemption distinguished Christianity from all its religious rivals in the ancient world, and gave it the militant and unyielding quality that enabled it to triumph in its struggle with secular civilization. But this is not sufficient to explain its religious appeal. If it had been nothing more than this, it would have merely a Jewish heresy or an apocalyptic sect of the type that we actually find in Ebionism or Montanism. But in addition to the social and historical side of its teaching, Christianity also brought a new doctrine of God and a new relation of the human soul to Him. Judaism had been the least mystical and the least metaphysical of religions. It revealed God as the Creator, the Lawgiver, and the Judge, and it was by obedience to His Law and by the ritual observances of sacrifice and ceremonial purity that man entered into relations with Him. But the transformation by Jesus of the national community into a new universal spiritual society brought with it a corresponding change in the doctrine of God. God was no longer the national deity of the Jewish people, localized, so to speak, at Sinai and Jerusalem. He was the Father of the human race, the Universal Ground of existence "in Whom we live and move and are." And when St. Paul appealed to the testimony of the Stoic poet, he recognized that Christianity was prepared to accept the metaphysical inheritance of Hellenic thought as well as the historic revelation of Jewish prophecy.

This is shown still more clearly in St. John's identification of the Logos and the Messiah in the prologue to the Fourth Gospel. Jesus of Nazareth was not only the Christ, the Son of the Living God; He was also the Divine Intelligence, the Principle of the order and intelligibility of the created world. Thus the opposition between the Greek ideal of spiritual intuition and the Living God of Jewish revelation—an opposition that Philo had vainly attempted to surmount by an artificial philosophical synthesis—finally disappeared before the new revelation of the Incarnate Word. As St. Augustine has said, the Fourth Gospel is essentially the Gospel of contemplation, for while the first three evangelists are concerned with the external mission of Jesus as Messianic King and Savior and teach the active virtues of Christian life, St. John is, above all, "the theologian" who declares the mysteries of the Divine Nature and teaches the way of contemplation.[29] Jesus is the bridge between Humanity and Divinity. In Him God is not only manifested to man, but vitally participated. He is the Divine Light, which illuminates men's minds, and the Divine Life, which transforms human nature and makes it the partaker of Its own supernatural activity.

Hence the insistence of the Fourth Gospel on the sacramental element in Christ's teaching,[30] since it is through the sacraments that the Incarnation of the Divine Word is no longer merely a historical fact, but is brought into vital and sensible contact with the life of the believer. So far from being an alien magical conception superimposed from without upon the religion of the Gospel, it forms the very heart of Christianity, since it is only through the sacramental principle that the Jewish ideal of an external ritual cult becomes transformed into a worship of spiritual communion. The modern idea that sacramentalism is inconsistent with the "spiritual" or mystical element in religion, is as lacking in foundation as the allied belief in an opposition between religion and theology. It is only when we reduce theology to religious rationalism and spiritual religion to a blend of ethics and emotion that there is no place left for sacramentalism; but under these conditions genuine mysticism and metaphysical truth equally disappear. Each of them forms an essential element in the historical development of Christianity. In the great age of creative theological thought, the development of dogma was organically linked with sacramentalism and mysticism. They were three aspects of a single reality—the great mystery of the restoration, illumination and deification of humanity by the Incarnation of the Divine Word. This is clearly recognized by Ritschl and his followers such as Harnack, although they involve mysticism, sacramentalism and scientific theology in a common condemnation.

Nevertheless, their criticism of the development of Greek Christianity is not entirely unjustified, for the historical and social elements, on which Ritschl laid so exclusive an emphasis, form an integral part of the Christian tradition, and apart from them the mystical or metaphysical side of religion becomes sterile or distorted. The tendency of the Byzantine mind to concentrate itself on this aspect of Christianity did actually lead to a decline in moral energy and in the spiritual freedom and initiative of the Church, and Eastern Christianity has tended to become an absolute static religion of the Oriental type.

It is true that this ideal, since it is a purely religious one, has much more in common with Catholic Christianity than have the secularized ideals of modern European culture. Catholicism and

Orientalism stand together against the denial of metaphysical reality and of the primacy of the spiritual, which is the fundamental Western error. As Sir Charles Eliot has truly said, "The opposition is not so much between Indian thought and the New Testament... the fundamental contrast is rather between both India and the New Testament, on the one hand, and, on the other, the rooted conviction of European races, however much orthodox Christianity may disguise their expression of it, that this world is all-important. The conviction finds expression not only in the avowed pursuit of pleasure and ambition, but in such sayings as that the best religion is the one that does most good, and in such ideals as self-realization or the full development of one's motive and powers. Though monasteries and monks still exist, the great majority of Europeans instinctively disbelieve in asceticism, the contemplative life and contempt of the world."[31]

And yet, for all this, there is no getting over the profound differences that separate Christianity from the purely metaphysical and intuitive type of religion.

Against the Oriental religions of pure spirit, which denied the value and even the reality of the material universe, the Church has undeviatingly maintained its faith in a historical revelation that involved the consecration not only of humanity but even of the body itself. This was the great stumbling-block to the Oriental mind, which readily accepted the idea of an Avatar or of the theophany of a divine Aeon, but could not face the consequences of the Catholic doctrine of the Two Natures and the full humanity of the Logos made flesh. This conception of the Incarnation as the bridge between God and Man, the marriage of Heaven and Earth, the channel through which the material world is spiritualized and brought back to unity, distinguishes Christianity from all the other Oriental religions, and involves a completely new attitude to life. Deliverance is to be obtained not by a sheer disregard of physical existence and a concentration of the higher intellect on the contemplation of pure Being, but by a creative activity that affects every part of the composite nature of man. And this activity is embodied in a definite society, which shares in the divine life of the Spirit, while at the same time it belongs to the visible order of social and historical reality.

Thus Catholic Christianity occupies an intermediate position between the two spiritual ideals and the two conceptions of reality which have divided the civilized world and the experience of humanity. To the West its ideals appear mystical and other-worldly, while in comparison with the Oriental religions it stands for historical reality and moral activity. It is a stranger in both camps and its home is everywhere and nowhere, like man himself, whose nature maintains a perilous balance between the worlds of spiritual and sensible reality, to neither of which it altogether belongs. Yet by reason of this ambiguous position the Catholic Church stands as the one mediator between East and West, between the ideal of spiritual intuition and that of moral and social activity. She alone possesses a tradition that is capable of satisfying the whole of human nature and that brings the transcendent reality of spiritual Being into relation with human experience and the realities of social life.

IV. *Christianity and the New Order*

It is clear from what has gone before that Christianity is not to be identified either with ethical idealism or with metaphysical intuition. It is a creative spiritual force, which has for its end nothing less than the recreation of humanity. The Church is no sect or human organization, but a new creation—the seed of the new order which is ultimately destined to transform the world. Such, at least, is the Catholic belief, and though the non-Catholic may deny the reality of this faith and the supernatural character of this life, he cannot shut his eyes to the fact that they have actually had a profound influence on the course of history and have been one of the main sources of the spiritual achievement of European civilization. For, notwithstanding the materialism and secularism that have always been present in our culture, and which today seem everywhere triumphant, that achievement has been perhaps the most remarkable that the world has ever known. Europe is not a true racial or geographical unity; it is, in its essence, a spiritual community, and even its vast material expansion in modern times would have been impossible without the moral force and spiritual inspiration that it owes ultimately to the Christian faith.

However secularized a civilization may become, it can never entirely escape from the burden of its spiritual inheritance. Péguy has said of the Jews that they are a people which has no natural love of spiritual adventures. They ask only to be left alone, like other peoples, to dwell in their own land, to grow rich, and to enjoy the good things of life. But the prophetic destiny with which their religion has charged them has forced them time after time against their will to leave their comfortable security and to go out into exile and the wilderness. And the same thing is true of Christendom: it cannot escape from the contagion of the divine fire that has been kindled in its midst.

Why is it that Europe alone among the civilizations of the world has been continually shaken and transformed by an energy of spiritual unrest that refuses to be content with the unchanging law of social tradition which rules the Oriental cultures? It is because its religious ideal has not been the worship of timeless and changeless perfection, but a spirit that strives to incorporate itself in humanity and to change the world. In the West the spiritual power has not been immobilized in a sacred social order like the Confucian state in China or the Indian caste system. It has acquired social freedom and autonomy, and consequently its activity has not been limited to the religious sphere but has had far-reaching effects on every aspect of social and intellectual life.

These secondary results are not necessarily of religious or moral value from the Christian point of view, for they may be deflected and distorted by the social medium through which they pass or contaminated by materialism and selfishness. But the fact remains that they are secondary and dependent on the existence of a spiritual force, without which they either would not have been or would have been utterly different.

For example, the Industrial Revolution, which appears at first sight one of the most materialistic aspects of Western civilization, would have been impossible without the moral earnestness and sense of duty that were generated by the Puritan ideal—an ideal far removed from that of Catholic Christianity, but one that owed its existence to a one-sided and sectarian interpretation of the Christian tradition.

And this is true also of the Renaissance and the humanist culture, in spite of the secularism and naturalism which seem so characteristic of them. The more one studies the origin of humanism the more one is brought to recognize the importance of an element which is not only spiritual, but definitely Christian. The old conception of the Renaissance as a revival of paganism—an idea which was popularized by nineteenth-century writers such as Burckhardt and J. A. Symonds—is today rejected not only by philosophers like Berdyaev, but by historians and critics, such as Karl Burdach and Giuseppe Toffanin. The Renaissance had its origin not only in the recovery of classical antiquity, but in the mystical humanism of St. Francis and Dante. The element survives in the later Renaissance in such representative figures as Francesco Pico and Marsilio Ficino, Botticelli and Michelangelo, Sadoleto and Tasso; and it finds a clear expression in the poems of Campanella, above all in his great canzone "Delia possanza deli' uomo," in which the purely humanist ideal of man's power and glory is united with the Christian conception of the Divine Humanity.

It may be said that this is only one aspect and that not the most important, of the humanist movement. But even the purely naturalistic achievements of the Renaissance were dependent on its Christian antecedents. Humanism was, it is true, a return to nature, the rediscovery of man and the natural world. But the author of the discovery, the active principle in the change, was not the natural man; it was Christian man, the human type that had been produced by ten centuries of ascetic discipline and intensive cultivation of the inner life. The great men of the Renaissance were spiritual men, even when they were most deeply immersed in the temporal order. It was from the accumulated resources of their Christian past that they acquired the spiritual energy to conquer the material world and to create the new secular culture. It is true that the disparity between the source and the object of their activity tended to produce a sense of strain and spiritual tension, which is perceptible in the work of typical Renaissance geniuses such as Shakespeare and Cervantes, as well as in definitely religious characters like Michelangelo or Campanella. But, at least in Catholic Europe, the two elements had attained to a relatively stable equilibrium by the end of the sixteenth century, and had an equal share in the development of the later Renaissance culture. The spirit of Christian humanism dominated the whole of the seventeenth century and manifested itself alike in the Baroque art of Spain and Italy and Central Europe, in the Jacobean and Caroline literature of England and in the classical culture of France. This religious current which runs through seventeenth-century culture cannot be set aside as a reactionary or negative phenomenon, for it lies at the heart of the higher civilization of the time and is responsible for some of its greatest achievements. Indeed, when in the eighteenth century this equilibrium was destroyed by the final victory of the naturalistic and rationalist tendencies, it involved the fall of the Renaissance couture itself. The new humanism of the Enlightenment was lacking in the vitality and spiritual depth of the earlier type. The one-sided rationalism of the Encyclopaedists provoked the one-sided subjective emotionalism of Rousseau and the Romantics. And though both rationalism and romanticism were in a sense the heirs of the Renaissance tradition, neither of them was the true representative of the earlier humanism. Rationalism had lost its spiritual inspiration and romanticism lacked its intellectual order and its sense of form.

Thus the disappearance of the Christian element in humanism has involved the loss of its vital quality. If we attempt to resuscitate it on a purely naturalistic foundation, we may get something like the humanism of Anatole France, but we shall certainly not recover the creative humanism of the Renaissance period. This is admitted by the protagonist of the new humanism, Professor Babbitt, who fully realizes that every culture is a spiritual order and that humanism is only possible if we throw over naturalism and return to spiritual principles. But, while he recognizes that the very survival of Western civilization depends "on the appearance of leaders who have rediscovered in some form the truths of the inner life and repudiated the errors of naturalism," he is unwilling to make a complete return to the metaphysical and religious foundations. He prefers a kind of spiritual positivism based on the accumulated moral wisdom of the great historic traditions—Greek, Buddhist, and Confucian. His desire to be "modern and individualistic and critical" causes him to shrink from committing himself absolutely to that which is eternal and universal.

Yet without such an affirmation, no true spiritual order is possible. Each of the great spiritual traditions to which he appeals rested on a metaphysical foundation, and if this is removed their moral order falls with it. Even Epicurus himself had to pass beyond the "flammantia moenia mundi" before he could bring peace to the minds of his disciples. By his insistence on the critical and individualistic attitude, Professor Babbitt is taking his stand on the weakest point in his position. The tradition of critical individualism still survives; indeed, the modern intellectual has carried it to its extreme limits. But this excess is a last desperate reaction against the all-pervading pressure of a collectivist civilization. In the days of Voltaire the critic was leading a victorious advance against the routed forces of the old order; today be is fighting for his very existence against the ruling tendencies of the age. It is easier to restore a spiritual purpose to civilization than to reverse its tendency towards collectivism and solidarity. To a critic like Babbitt,

Christianity is unacceptable on account of its weakness during the last two centuries against the dissolvent forces of rationalist criticism; but this type of criticism is already losing its power. The modern criticism of organized religion is in part the survival on a lower cultural plane of the rationalist thought of a past age, and in part a reaction against the romantic and individualist forms of religion that were characteristic of the nineteenth century or at least of the post-Reformation period. But Christianity in itself is in no way bound up with the individualist culture that is passing away. It was in origin a religion of order and solidarity which throve in an atmosphere of anonymity and collectivism. It was not itself responsible for the dying down of classical culture, the loss of civic liberty and the inauguration of the regime of compulsion and state socialism, which were, on the contrary, the necessary consequences of the inherent inconsistencies and weakness of the later classical culture itself. But it was able to accommodate itself to conditions in which a purely secular type of individual culture must inevitably perish.

And it seems possible that Christianity may survive modern humanism in the same way that it survived ancient Hellenism. However seriously Christianity is threatened by the materialism and mechanicism of modern civilization, it is in a much stronger position than the tradition of critical intellectualism, which can find neither a material nor a spiritual basis in the new conditions of life. The latter belongs essentially to the culture of a leisured class—not the new plutocracy of millionaires and leaders of industry, but the privileged classes of the old Europe, whether bourgeois or aristocratic, who stood outside the economic arena. This class has already practically disappeared, and its civilization and ideals of life are bound to disappear in like manner. The choice that is actually before us is not between an individualistic humanism and some form of collectivism, but between a collectivism that is purely mechanistic and one that is spiritual. Spiritual individualism is incapable of standing out against the collectivism and standardization of modern life: it is only by a return to spiritual solidarity that modern civilization can recover the spiritual principle of which it stands so greatly in need.

It will no doubt be objected, by the modernist and the medievalist alike, that there is a fundamental and insurmountable contradiction between the Christian ideal of spiritual freedom and the scientific determinism and materialism that are inherent in the new order. But we must make a distinction between the metaphysical determinism of the dogmatic materialist or naturalist and the physical laws within their proper limits. And what is this but the Hellenic belief in the existence of a universal cosmic order, which was accepted by the Christian Fathers as a necessary consequence of the creative activity of the Divine Word, which orders and disposes all things in number and weight and measure?

Consequently the material organization of the world by science and invention is in no sense to be refused or despised by the Catholic tradition, for to the Catholic philosopher no less than to the scientist the progressive *rationalization* of matter by the work of scientific intelligence is the natural vocation of the human mind. This must seem a hard saying when we consider that science and discovery, like a second eating of the forbidden fruit of knowledge, have proved a curse rather than a blessing to humanity. But the disease of modern civilization lies neither in science nor in machinery, but in the false philosophy with which they have been associated. At the very moment that man was at last acquiring control over his material environment, he was abandoning the ideal of spiritual order and leaving the new economic forces to develop uncontrolled without any higher social direction. Economic activity was no longer regarded as a function of society as a whole, but as an independent world in which the only laws were the purely economic ones of supply and demand, and of the relations between population and capital. Money and commodities were not considered in relation to social life, but became hypostatized into abstract principles on which social life was dependent. But though these ideas accompanied the rise of the machine order, they are in reality profoundly inconsistent with that order and with the scientific genius, and today they are either dead or in the process of dissolution. It is now generally recognized—even by those who attach no importance to spiritual values—that the machine order involves social direction and that it is absurd to build up an elaborate artificial mechanism of production and to leave society itself at the mercy of private acquisitiveness. This was first clearly realized by the Socialists, and today Communism claims to be the only social theory that is consistent with the new scientific order. But Communism is itself a result of the same pseudo-scientific rationalism which produced the doctrine of Ricardo, and it gained consistency only by carrying the false principles of the older theory to their extreme conclusion. The old economists had excluded human values from economic life, but they had not attempted to deny them, entirely. Outside business hours "the economic man" was free to behave as a human being. But to the Communist no such dualism is possible. The economic life absorbs the whole man and the whole society. The political, intellectual and spiritual aspects of life are all subordinated to the economic end, which alone is absolute and consequently is the only ethical criterion. Thus man becomes the servant and not the master of the machine, since society exists for economic production and man exists for society.

But the history of Communism is itself sufficient to disprove this materialistic conception of history. For Communism was not the spontaneous product of impersonal economic forces. It had its origin in the mind of that atrabilious arch-individualist, Karl Marx, and the forces that inspired him were neither of the economic nor the material order. It was the instinct of spiritual self-assertion, the revolutionary ideal of abstract justice, and perhaps more than all the ineradicable Jewish faith in an apocalyptic deliverance that drove him from his own country and the interests of his bourgeois career to a life of exile and privation. Thus Communism, like every other living power in the world of men, owes its existence to spiritual forces. If it were possible to eliminate these, as the Communist theory demands, and to reduce human life to a purely economic activity, mankind would sink back into barbarism and animality. For the creative element in human culture is spiritual, and it triumphs only by mortifying and conquering the natural conservatism of man's animal instincts. This is true above all of science, for the path of the scientist leads him further from the animal than the rest of men. He lives not in the concrete reality of sensible experience, like the animal or the savage, but in a rarefied atmosphere of mathematical abstraction in which the ordinary man cannot breathe. If the materialist interpretation of history were true, the scientific intellectualization of nature could no more have arisen than could the metaphysical intuition of reality, and without science there could be no machine order. The true Marxian Communism is not that of a machine order which is the work of the creative scientific spirit, but rather that of the Eskimo, which is the direct product of economic necessity. For the machine is a proof not of the subordination of mind to matter, but of the subordination of matter to mind. So far from necessitating the substitution of material for spiritual order, it is itself a vindication of spiritual order, since it frees man from his age-long animal condition of dependence on nature and material circumstance.

But if the scientific order is to realize this ideal, it must be related to spiritual ends and must form part of a wider spiritual order. Material organization alone is incapable of saving civilization. Left to itself it may easily become a destructive force which is hostile alike to spiritual values and to human freedom. True civilization is essentially a spiritual order, and its criterion is not material wealth, but spiritual vision. It seeks a *Theoria*—an intuition of reality which is expressed in metaphysical thought and bears fruit in artistic creation and moral action. Thus Chinese civilization culminates in the metaphysical vision of cosmic law and in the ethical ideal of the Confucian just man; Indian civilization in the metaphysical vision of absolute being and in the moral ideal of the Sadhu; and Hellenic civilization in the vision of the intelligible world and in the ethical ideal of the philosopher.

In Christianity the idea of spiritual order acquires a yet wider and more profound significance. It is based upon the belief in a divine society which transcends all states and cultures and is the final goal of humanity. For as a modern Thomist has written, "The human personality is not entirely contained in political society; it belongs above all by its innermost and truest being, by its spiritual element, to another and more perfect society, to the universality of being, the World-Whole which includes the living Infinite, God Himself, as its Universal Good and Sovereign Head; and political society, however wide and numerous it may be, is but a minute section of this immense and innumerable Republic,"[32] this city of God of which St. Augustine and St. Thomas speak. This society exists in the nature of things as "the republic of all men under the law of God,"[33] although the actual disorder of human nature prevented its effective realization by man. It has therefore been reconstituted on a higher plane by the Incarnation, through which mankind is united in a direct and personal relation with the Divine Word. And this new unity is something more than a society; it is an organism, a living body whose head is Christ the Word and whose vital principle is the Divine Spirit.

> But this great society is not yet made; it is in the making—
> in process of becoming—it grows under the guidance of

> Christ, Whose mystical Body has not yet attained its full stature, to its immanent perfection, that is to say, to the perfect possession of God; it is a universal gravitation towards God "Who turns all things to the love of Himself."
>
> And it depends on us to push the universe with all our powers towards its sublime destiny, to contribute in our degree and for our part to the promotion and perfection of the kingdom of God.[34]

If this is the idea that should inspire Christian culture, it may well be asked whether a Christian civilization has ever existed. It is surely not to be found in the theocratic absolutism of the Byzantine East, nor in the feudal barbarism of the mediaeval West, nor in the humanism of the Renaissance. Yet through all their manifold imperfections each of them has aspired to it in their fashion, and if our own civilization is to recover a spiritual principle, it is here that we must seek it. The essential achievement of our culture—the conquest of material order—is not, as we have seen, inconsistent with this ideal. In fact it may be regarded as its natural complement, for the restoration of man to his true position as the master of nature and the organizer of the material world, which is the function of science, corresponds in the natural order to the spiritual restoration of human nature in itself, which is the work of Christianity in the supernatural order.

In a Christian civilization the scientific order would no longer offer, as it does at present, the tragic spectacle of vast resources of power and intelligence devoted to producing unsightly and unnecessary objects and to endowing mankind with new means of self-destruction; it would become an instrument for the realization of man's true destiny as the orderer of material things to spiritual ends. And so, too, with regard to the international aspects of our civilization. Without spiritual order the cosmopolitanism of modern culture does not make for peace; it merely increases the opportunities of strife. It destroys all that is best and most distinctive in the local and national cultures, while leaving the instincts of national and racial hostility to develop unchecked. It unites mankind in the common enjoyment of the cinema and the Ford car and the machine gun without creating any spiritual unity. The recovery of the Christian idea of order would give a spiritual expression to the universality of modern culture. Its material unification would become subservient to the ideal of the spiritual unity of mankind in justice and charity, an ideal that has a very real attraction for the modern mind, but which secular idealism is powerless to achieve.

We must make our choice between the material organization of the world—based either on economic exploitation or on an economic absolutism, which absorbs the whole of life and leaves no room for human values—and the Christian ideal of a spiritual order based on spiritual faith and animated by charity, which is the spiritual will. The triumph of such an ideal in a world that seems governed only by material forces and distracted by hatred and greed may seem a fantastic dream, but is it any more hopeless than the enterprise of that handful of unknown and uneducated men from a remote Oriental province who set out to conquer the imperial power of Rome and the intellectual culture of Hellenism? In history it is often the incredible that happens—*credo quia impossible* has been justified again and again. Sooner or later it is inevitable that men's minds should turn once more in search of spiritual reality, and when once the tide begins to flow all the sand-castles that we have built during the ebb disappear.

Every Christian mind is a seed of change so long as it is a living mind, not enervated by custom or ossified by prejudice. A Christian has only to be in order to change the world, for in that act of being there is contained all the mystery of supernatural life. It is the function of the Church to sow this divine seed, to produce not merely good men, but spiritual men—that is to say, supermen. In so far as the Church fulfills this function it transmits to the world a continuous stream of spiritual energy. If the salt itself loses its savor, then indeed the world sinks back into disorder and death, for a despiritualized Christianity is powerless to change anything; it is the most abject of failures, since it serves neither the natural nor the spiritual order. But the life of the Church never fails, since it possesses an infinite capacity for regeneration. It is the external organ through which the Spirit enters the social process and builds up a new humanity—*populus qui nasetur quem fecit Dominus.* The spirit breathes and they are created and the face of the earth is renewed.

Notes for Christianity and the New Age

1. The author desires to express his thanks to the editors and publishers of the *Criterion* and the *Dublin Review* for their kindness in allowing him to reprint, in the first two chapters of this essay, portions of articles which originally appeared in the pages of those reviews.
2. C. Péguy, *L'argent Suite*, pp. 170–171.
3. Its true meaning, however, is to be found rather in the dilettantism of Oscar Wilde.
4. Berdyaev, *Der Sinn der Geschichte*, pp. 34–35.
5. *University Sermons*, p. 350. In this remarkable passage he develops a parallelism between the symbolic character of sensible knowledge and that of mathematical calculi and musical notation.
6. Chardon, *La Croix de Jesus*, pp. 422, 423, in Bremond, *Histoire Littéraire du sentiment religieux en France*, VIII, pp. 21–22.
7. Bona, *Via Compendii ad Deum*.
8. H. J. Massingham, *The Heritage of Man*, p. 142.
9. R. H. Lowie, *Primitive Religion*, p. 19.
10. I have discussed this movement at greater length in *Progress and Religion*, ch. 6.
11. This may not appear obvious in the case of Buddhism. It is, however, implicit in the doctrine of Karma as the ground of the world process.
12. J. Maréchal, *Studies in the Psychology of the Mystics*, trans. Algar Thorold (1927), pp. 101, 133.
13. Cf. Rousselot, *Les Yeux de la Foi*.
14. *Pansies*, pp. 65–66.
15. It is true that he does not term this concept God. Unlike Professor Alexander, he reserves that title to the transcendent God of the old religions.
16. This dogmatic acceptance of naturalism has entered so deeply into Murry's mind that the very idea of the Supernatural is rejected with a kind of sacred horror as a blasphemous impiety. He writes: "To introduce, or to be prepared to introduce, the category of the supernatural into my thinking would be mental and spiritual suicide. A world which at a certain point...ceased to belong to the natural order is no world for me, a man of the twentieth century, to contemplate or live in; it would be a cheap and vulgar world from which it would be my duty as a man to escape immediately." *God*, p. 112.
17. *Republic*, 519.
18. *Theatetus*, 176.
19. *Vivekachudamani* (attributed to Sankara), trans. C. Johnston, p. 41.
20. *Mahabharata*, XII, ch. 174, trans. L. D. Barnett.
21. *Bhagavad-Gita*, II., pp. 17, 30–31, trans. L. D. Barnett.

22. Matthew Arnold, *St. Paul and Protestantism*, p. 14.
23. Quoted by R. Otto in *The Idea of the Holy*, pp. 102–103.
24. T. H. Huxley, *Essays*, V, p. 142.
25. The following passage from C. E. M, Joad's *The Present and Future of Religion* (p. 43) is a typical if somewhat extreme example of this attitude. "For many men of advanced ideas, today, Christ is primarily a great preacher and teacher of conduct, expounding doctrines of compelling force and originality. As such he despises ritual and ceremony, and lays stress upon what men do. He is a communist and an internationalist, advocating, the widening of the private family to include the whole family of mankind, He is humanitarian, denouncing punishment, crying for mercy instead of vengeance, and insisting, if only as a utilitarian measure, on counteracting evil, not with a contrary evil, but with good. Above all, he is a socialist, insisting on the organic conception of society, and affirming that we are members of one another in so intimate a sense that the misery and degradation of one are the misery and degradation of all." But "we realize regretfully that Christ's dream of a regenerated world is too lovely for the little minds that run the machine of instituted religion."
26. J. Middleton Murry, *God*, p. 229.
27. In *Christian Ethics and Modern Problems*, p. 138, he quotes a passage from Landor, which perfectly expresses this modern idea of religion as essentially a private matter. "Religion," says Landor, "is too pure for corporations. It is best meditated on in our privacy and best acted on in our ordinary intercourse with mankind." But Landor is a Deist rather than a Christian.
28. Hermas, *Vision* IV, p. 1; cf. II. *Clement*, XIV, 1, 2.
29. *de Consensu Evangelistarum* I, c. 3–5.
30. E.g., John 3:5; 6:32–58.
31. C. Eliot, *Hinduism and Buddhism*, vol. 1, p. ix.
32. T. Bésiade, *La Justice générale*, in *Mélanges thomistes* (1923), p. 334.
33. St. Thomas, *ST* I-II, q. 100, a. 5.
34. Bésiade, *La Justice générale*, p. 340.

CLUNY MEDIA

Designed by Fiona Cecile Clarke, the CLUNY MEDIA *logo*
depicts a monk at work in the scriptorium,
with a cat sitting at his feet.

The monk represents our mission to emulate
the invaluable contributions of the monks
of Cluny in preserving the libraries of the West,
our strivings to know and love the truth.

The cat at the monk's feet is Pangur Bán, from the
eponymous Irish poem of the 9th century.
The anonymous poet compares his scholarly
pursuit of truth with the cat's happy hunting of mice.
The depiction of Pangur Bán is an homage to the work
of the monks of Irish monasteries and a sign
of the joy we at Cluny take in our trade.

"Messe ocus Pangur Bán,
cechtar nathar fria saindan:
bíth a menmasam fri seilgg,
mu memna céin im saincheirdd."

Made in the USA
Las Vegas, NV
22 April 2021